Federal Contracting Made Easy

Fourth Edition

Federal Contracting Made Easy

Fourth Edition

Scott A. Stanberry

MANAGEMENTCONCEPTSPRESS

MANAGEMENTCONCEPTSPRESS
8230 Leesburg Pike, Suite 800
Tysons Corner, VA 22182
(703) 790-9595
Fax: (703) 790-1371
www.managementconcepts.com

Printed in the United States of America

Library of Congress Cataloging-in-Publication Data
ISBN: 978-1-56726-388-6

10 9 8 7 6 5 4 3 2 1

About the Author

Scott A. Stanberry has been working with government contractors for more than 20 years. He specializes in providing auditing and accounting services for commercial clients with federal government contracts and in assisting government agencies in the administration of federal contracts. Scott is a certified public accountant and is highly experienced in the application and interpretation of the Federal Acquisition Regulation.

I've missed more than 9,000 shots in my career. I've lost almost 300 games. Twenty-six times I've been trusted to take the game-winning shot and missed. I've failed over and over and over again in my life. And that is why I succeed.

—Michael Jordan

Author's Note

How times have changed . . .

Not long ago, many businesses considered selling to the federal government to be a dying industry. Old-school companies like IBM and Lockheed Martin would never be able to keep up with the new high-flying Internet enterprises, people said. Government contracting was fool's gold!

But I always knew that, like the weather in D.C., the contracting climate was sure to change . . . the naysayers would just have to wait a little while. Now, for the first time in my life I consider myself chic or the cool guy at the party for promoting the benefits of federal contracting all these years!

This new fourth edition continues to expand on the previous ones while concentrating on how the federal marketplace can help businesses, large and small, survive and prosper in this troubled (and troubling) economy.

Best wishes and happy contracting!

Scott Stanberry
June, 2012

Contents at a Glance

Contents

Preface

© 1999 Randy Glasbergen.
www.glasbergen.com
SUZY'S LEMONADE
INC.
GLASBERGEN
"I can offer you a great benefits package:
liberal use of the company bike, paid nap time,
free cootie insurance, and a pension at age 10."

Did you ever run a lemonade stand as a kid? Ever sit by the side of the road for hour after hour in the hot sun, waiting for someone—the mail carrier, the obnoxious neighbor kid, anyone—to walk by? Or maybe, as you got older, you decided to open a bicycle repair shop in your garage, dreaming of owning a bicycle empire, only to find that your business was still essentially sitting by the side of the road, waiting for customers?

That's the story of thousands of businesses that fail each year: their owners have a good idea or product, but no knowledge of how to run a business or attract customers.

This book was written to help you attract and make the most of working with the biggest customer of all: the U.S. government. The federal government spends more than $500 billion on just about anything and everything each year. That's a lot of lemonade!

What's more, every major federal agency and department is required by law to provide free assistance to businesses interested in bidding on federal work. So whether you're an entrepreneur interested in breaking into the federal market or a mid-size to large company seeking to maximize your use of (and financial return on) subcontractors, this book tells you what you need to know.

The downside to federal contracting? Marketing to the federal government is like trying to learn the rules to your kid's video games. The characters all have incomprehensible names, some players seem to have secret powers, and any second somebody can throw a bomb that completely knocks you off the screen. How can you win if you're not the 11-year-old king of the arcade with a never-ending roll of quarters and the insider knowledge that comes from devoting yourself to the game 16 hours a day?

That's why I've written this book: to help you decode all the confusing rules, get to know the other players, understand the obstacles thrown in your path, and maybe acquire some secret powers of your own. This book spells out everything you need to know to succeed in the federal arena—from the people who oversee the contracting process, to the regulations that govern contracting, to the types of contracts awarded. You'll get the inside scoop on government contracting, all from one source.

All you need to know is inside this book, and you can refer to these pages again and again as your business grows and you go after greater government opportunities. And while much of this book deals with small business programs and services, it also contains a significant amount of information that applies to all types of companies. Even if you or your staff are familiar with some pieces of the federal contracting puzzle, there may be areas where you could use some explanation or insight.

Of particular interest to current contractors, this book offers specific suggestions on how mid-size to large companies can take advantage of some of those small-business programs through subcontracting—something virtually every government contractor too big to qualify as a small business does on a regular basis. In short, if you're currently working for a business (large or small) or thinking of starting your own, this book is for you!

One word of caution: Government regulations and procedures do not make for keep-you-up-all-night, can't-put-it-down reading. Wading through some of this information may take patience and persistence but, just like that 11-year-old who suffers through hours of frustration to learn the video game, you'll find rewards at the end of the process. You can make good money—even big money—doing business with the federal government. Contracting with the government can make you king of the arcade *and* give you the biggest lemonade stand on the block!

What Is Federal Government Contracting?

Success is getting what you want;
happiness is wanting what you get.

—*Dave Gardner*

How Does Federal Government Contracting Work?

Berry's World
Up and down the City Road,
In and out the Eagle,
That's the way the money goes—
Pop goes the weasel!
11-26-96

What's in this chapter?

- The big picture
- Top buyers
- Future of federal contracting
- Can you sell to the federal government?
- Should you sell to the federal government?

Federal contracting is *big* business. By any measure, the U.S. government (a.k.a. Uncle Sam) is by far the largest consumer in the world. No other nation, or corporation for that matter, can begin to match its purchasing power.

Generally we hear only about government purchases for multimillion-dollar aircraft or those infamous $1,000 toilet seats and $500 hammers. But are you aware that there are currently over 350,000 government contractors receiving more than $500 billion worth of contracts each year—$100 billion of which goes to small businesses?

The federal government enters into contracts with American citizens like you to acquire the supplies and services needed to run its operations or fulfill its mission requirements. It uses a specific process designed to give business concerns the maximum practical opportunities to participate in federal contracting. Each year (actually, fiscal year, which begins on October 1 and ends on September 30), the federal government spends billions of dollars buying from nonfederal sources, or *commercial contractors*.

The government initiates or modifies more than 9 million contracts each year, two-thirds of which it grants to contractors outside the Washington, D.C., area. The key to getting a piece of the pie is to understand how the federal government does business and to position your company accordingly.

Ready? Set? Let's go win some government business! This chapter provides an overview of what federal contracting is all about.

THE BIG PICTURE

Look at it this way: Every 20 seconds of every working day, the federal government awards a contract, with an average value of $495,000. And Uncle Sam must tell us what, from where, and from whom it buys.

The government purchases a mind-boggling array of products and services, ranging from high-technology items like homeland security programs, missiles, ships, aircraft, and telecommunication systems to more mundane items like office furniture, maintenance services, shoes, computers, food, janitorial services, carpeting, accounting services, and real estate. You name it, and the government probably buys it!

Because the government's needs vary from those that individuals and small, singly owned enterprises can meet to those requiring the resources of large corporations, everyone has a potential share. In fact, it is no exaggeration to suggest that a small business can probably provide a service or create a product for nearly every federal agency.

Furthermore, a business can supply the government with its products or services from wherever it customarily operates. In other words, contractors are not restricted to selling to federal agencies in their own communities. A contractor in Memphis, Tennessee, can supply the Naval Surface Warfare Center in Dahlgren, Virginia, just as easily as a contractor operating from Dahlgren. Anyone looking for more customers or thinking about starting a new business should consider the federal government as a prospect.

To help small businesses participate in federal contracting, the government offers a variety of programs and services, including credit assistance, procurement opportunities, technical support, management assistance, and grants. (See Chapter 4 for what constitutes a small business in the eyes of the government.) These programs and services have created and sustained thousands of small firms, generating many millions of jobs in the process. As a result, many of these small businesses have grown into large businesses.

I have personally seen firms go from zero to $50 million or more in federal business in less than five years. No other industry provides more opportunities for small businesses than government contracting. Yet only 1 percent of the 22 million small businesses in the United States participates in federal contracting.

Why doesn't everyone contract with the government? Contracting with the government can be cumbersome, with its regulations, rules, laws, bureaucracy, and red tape. The primary purpose of these detailed rules and regulations is to ensure that the government spends public funds—our tax dollars—wisely. To be successful as a government contractor, you must understand these rules and regulations (see Chapter 2).

Although federal contractors use many of the same business practices as commercial vendors, a number of characteristics clearly differentiate the two. To begin with, the federal government operates in a market that is called *monopsonistic*—one with only one buyer and many sellers. As a result of this sovereignty, the government has certain unusual powers and immunities that differ significantly from those of more typical buyers, as detailed in the table below. Congressional mandate, rather than state laws, controls federal policy.

Significant differences include:

Government Contracting	Commercial Contracting
General	
Federal policy establishes formal competition criteria for purchases or procurements.	Company determines competition criteria.
Congress appropriates available funds.	Many sources provide funds.
Laws, directives, policies, and procedural regulations define procurement actions.	Company determines procurement actions within legal boundaries.
Profit Margins	
The government may negotiate a separate profit/fee.	Contractor builds profit into "total price."
The government may apply profit ceilings to certain contracts. (Profit/fee on federal contracts rarely exceeds 6%.)	Contractors rarely use profit ceilings. (Profit/fee on commercial contracts is often as high as 10%–20% of the total contract price.)
Contract Clauses	
Federal contracts contain extensive clauses, many of which are "take it or leave it."	Standard commercial code and those clauses agreed to by the parties regulate performance.

Contract Termination	
The government may terminate a contract for failure to make progress.	Termination is normally not available to commercial contractors.
The government may terminate a contract for its convenience.	Commercial regulations (such as the Uniform Commercial Code) ensure adequate performance.
Social and Economic Policies (such as a policy requiring contractors to maintain a drug-free workplace)	
Federal contracts must incorporate these policies.	Social pressures typically dictate company policies; however, some policies are required by law.
The government may use incentive contracts.	Commercial contractors rarely use incentive contracts.
Federal law prohibits gratuities.	Company policy determines gratuities.
The government may penalize contractors for noncompliance.	Penalties are illegal in commercial contracts.

Government business varies vastly, depending on the products or services being sold. Selling copiers has little in common with selling jet engines. Also, the contracting needs and guidelines of the Department of Defense (DoD) in many cases differ from those of civilian federal agencies.

You need to determine which federal agencies purchase your goods and services and what solicitation procedures those agencies use to acquire them. Part III of this book touches on a number of methods for soliciting and marketing to the various federal agencies.

It's not so much that doing business with the federal government is difficult; it's just different. Instead of selling directly to decisionmakers, as in the commercial world, government contractors must patiently wade through the government procurement process, which makes the sale more complex and longer to complete. If you learn the system and are patient and persistent, the federal government can be a great source of business revenue for both new and established businesses.

Not that simple . . .

Lisa Rein, Washington Post – April 8, 2012

Federal agencies must report their progress this week in complying with the Plain Writing Act, a new decree that government officials communicate more conversationally with the public.

Speaking plainly, they ain't there yet.

Which leaves, in the eyes of some, a basic and critical flaw in how the country runs. "Government is all about telling people what to do," said Annetta Cheek, a retired federal worker from Falls Church and longtime evangelist for plain writing. "If you don't write clearly, they're not going to do it."

But advocates such as Cheek estimate that federal officials have translated just 10 percent of their forms, letters, directives and other documents into "clear Government communication that the public can understand and use," as the law requires.

Official communications must now employ the active voice, avoid double negatives and use personal pronouns. "Addressees" must now become, simply, "you." Clunky coinages like "incentivizing" (first known usage 1970) are a no-no. The Code of Federal Regulations no longer goes by the abbreviation CFR.

But with no penalty for inaction on the agencies' part, advocates worry that plain writing has fallen to the bottom of the to-do list, like many another unfunded mandate imposed by Congress. They say many agencies have heeded the 2010 law merely by appointing officials, creating working groups and setting up Web sites.

What's more, the law's demand for clearer language seems like make-work to skeptics who say there is no money to pay for the promotion of clarity and that the status quo is the best path to accuracy.

"It's definitely an ongoing battle," said Glenn Ellmers, plain-writing coordinator for the Nuclear Regulatory Commission. "We're trying pretty hard. But when you're talking about something as complex as a nuclear power plant, you can't get around specialized language. The really technical people take a little pride in using it."

As a concession to them, the commission is simplifying only the cover letters of plant inspection reports, while leaving intact the highly technical and all-but-impenetrable text of the actual documents.

"Part of this is we have a change in culture," said Ed Burbol, the Defense Department's plain-language coordinator, who oversees two full-time staff members assigned to promoting clearer communication. "We're going to encounter resistance."

A retired lieutenant colonel in the Air Force, Burbol acknowledged that "some people here can write very well and some people can't write at all," a problem he attributes to the large number of service members who return to work as civilians.

Consider the next sentence: "This subpart identifies those products in which the Administrator has found an unsafe condition as described in Sec. 39.1 and, as appropriate, prescribes inspections and the conditions and limitations, if any, under which those products may continue to be operated."

And here's the revision of the sentence, a Federal Aviation Administration guideline, by the nonprofit Center for Plain Language: "Airworthiness directives specify inspections you must carry out, conditions and limitations you must comply with, and any actions you must take to resolve an unsafe condition."

Cheek, the retired federal worker, still devotes at least 20 hours a week to the tiny nonprofit plain-language center she founded for federal employees. To inspire healthy competition when the law passed two years ago, the group started giving out annual awards for the best and worst of government-speak, including a Turn-Around prize for most improved agency. The annual ClearMark awards banquet, scheduled this year for May 22, is held at the National Press Club.

In this era of shrinking government, advocates of plain writing say their cause can actually save money.

They cite Washington state's "Plain Talk" program: A revamped letter tripled the number of businesses paying a commonly ignored use tax, bringing $2 million in new revenue in a year, according to law professor Joseph Kimble, author of a forthcoming book on the benefits of plain language.

And after the Department of Veterans Affairs revised one of its letters, calls to a regional call center dropped from about 1,100 a year to about 200, Kimble said.

"People complain about government red tape and getting government out of your hair," said Rep. Bruce Braley (D-Iowa), House sponsor of the Plain Writing Act. "If every one of these forms was written in plain language, the number of contracts to federal agencies would plummet." He's started a "Stop B.S." (for "Bureaucrat Speak") campaign soliciting examples of badly written public documents.

The law exempts regulations from its mandate for clearer communication, although last fall the Obama administration ordered agencies to write a summary of their technical proposed or final regulations, and post it at the top of the text.

But Braley says that's not enough. He's introduced a bill to extend the law to the full text of regulations so ordinary people can understand them.

Americans have always loved plain talkers. But at some point, scholars point out, inscrutable language became associated with high status.

"A lot of people in government wield their jargon to make themselves seem very impressive," said Karen Schriver, a plain-language expert at Carnegie Mellon University.

There have been many attempts to turn this trend around, including at the presidential level. Richard Nixon required that the *Federal Register* be written in "layman's terms." Jimmy Carter issued executive orders to make government regulations "cost-effective" and easy to understand. (Ronald Reagan rescinded the orders.)

The Clinton White House revived plain language as a major initiative, and Vice President Al Gore presented monthly "No Gobbledygook" awards to federal workers who translated jargon into readable language.

None of these efforts stuck, although some agencies—including Veterans Affairs and the Internal Revenue Service—took the mission seriously. The IRS won the Center for Plain Language's top prize last year for "intelligible writing in public life."

And then there is the difficulty of promoting revision while preserving precision. At a January meeting of the Plain Language Information & Action Network, a group of federal employees devoted to the cause, members from 20 federal agencies listened as Meredith Weberg, an editor at the Veterans Affairs inspector general's office, described how she butted up against an "obstinate" boss.

In attempting to simplify a handbook for auditors, Weberg changed "concur" and "not concur" to "agree" and "disagree." The manager changed it back.

One of her allies in the cause of plain writing had to, well, concur with the boss's decision. "A concurring opinion says Justice so-and-so agrees with the conclusion of the court," said Ken Meardan, who writes regulations for the Agriculture Department. "He may not agree" with the reasoning.

Weberg said she let this one go.

The new law is hitting larger obstacles.

"They didn't really make it plain as to what my responsibilities are," said the newly appointed plain-language coordinator at the Department of Transportation, describing her assignment from management. She looked bewildered.

Her counterpart at the U.S. Agency for International Development had an even bigger problem: She could not get behind an electronic firewall for online training.

"We have a lot of classified information," Christine Brown told the group. "We're not getting very far with this. No one has the resources."

USAID has appointed a plain-language committee. But it is just starting to train its members to write plainly.

"A lot of people didn't think this was the kind of thing you should do a law about," Cheek said. "We'll see if it works."

TOP BUYERS

During FY 2011, the federal government purchased well over $500 billion worth of supplies and services. The following table shows the major federal agencies and categories in federal procurement:

Federal Agency Procurement, FY 2011

Federal Agency	Expenditures (in billions)
Department of Defense (DoD)	$ 374.03
Department of Energy (DOE)	$ 25.06
Department of Health and Human Services (HHS)	$ 19.46
Department of Veterans Affairs (VA)	$ 17.47
National Aeronautics and Space Administration (NASA)	$ 15.58
Department of Homeland Security (DHS)	$ 14.22
General Services Administration (GSA)	$ 12.42
Department of State (DOS)	$ 9.15
Department of Justice (DOJ)	$ 7.17
Department of Treasury (USTREAS)	$ 7.12
Top Product or Service Categories (by NAICS Code)	
Manufacturing: Metals, Machinery, Furniture (33)	$ 164.23
Professional and Scientific Services (54)	$ 147.26
Administration and Support (56)	$ 48.42
Construction (23)	$ 39.01
Wholesale Trade (42)	$ 25.78
Manufacturing: Printing, Petroleum, Rubber (32)	$ 18.63
Transportation (48)	$ 15.87

It's clear from this table that DoD is a major player in the federal contracting landscape, chipping in with over two-thirds of the government's annual purchases.

The following chart shows the value of federal contracts awarded by state (to the top nine states and Washington, D.C.) during FY 2011, in billions of dollars:

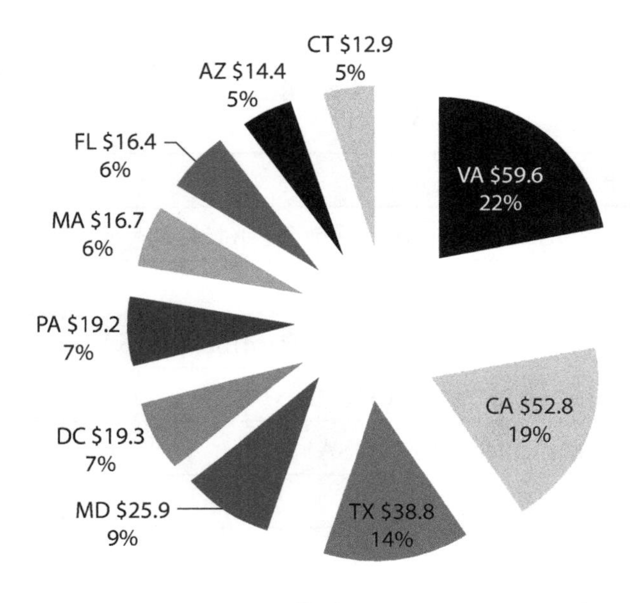

Federal Awards, by State, 2011

FUTURE OF FEDERAL CONTRACTING

During the decade immediately preceding the Obama administration, both the legislative and executive branches made a continuing effort to increase the number of services performed by private industry contractors and to reduce the number of government employees. This effort was based on the belief that the competitive forces of the commercial marketplace would produce better products and services at cheaper prices. As a consequence, the already significant contracting opportunities available in the services sector increased even more.

Under the Obama administration, there has been some backlash to this trend. Many government officials and federal employee unions have questioned the cost effectiveness of this "contracting out" philosophy. Additionally, government officials have expressed concern that contractors may be performing services that are inherently governmental in nature. They found support for this concern in the executive branch and among some members of Congress and elsewhere. A study report issued in September 2011 by the Project on Government Oversight, a nonprofit group, found that the government may sometimes pay more for contractor employees than for current government employees.

While the pace of growth in contracting out has slowed, the fact remains that contractors have far more flexibility in hiring, utilizing, and—when necessary—laying off employees. This considerable administrative advantage, coupled with the expanding use of task order contracts (see Chapter 16) and the limited public tolerance for an expanding government workforce, contributes to the continuation of a favorable environment for government service contracts going forward. For product and supply contracts, the government has relied, and will continue to rely, almost exclusively on private-sector vendors.

CAN YOU SELL TO THE FEDERAL GOVERNMENT?

To receive a contract, a contractor must agree to meet (be "responsive" to) the government's requirements. It must also be "responsible," which means that it must have or have provided for the resources needed to do the job and, if it is an established business, must have a satisfactory record of integrity and performance.

Depending upon the type of procurement and the circumstances involved, the contracting officer may do a very detailed examination for responsibility, such as conducting a physical pre-award survey of contractor facilities. In other occasions, such as for many commercial items, the contracting officer may assume that someone active in the marketplace is prima facie (at first sight) a responsible contractor.

Additionally, to receive a contract, a contractor may have to demonstrate or certify to specific criteria for a specific kind of contracting. For example, if the proposed contract is set aside for competition only among small businesses, the contractor may have to certify that it is a small business before being eligible for award.

In general, the government wants to know the following about a potential contractor:

- Is the contractor eligible, under existing laws, to do business with the government?
- Does the contractor have adequate financial resources to do the job?
- Does the contractor have a good performance record?
- Does the contractor's record demonstrate ethics and integrity?
- Does the contractor have the necessary skills to perform the job, or can it acquire them?
- Does the contractor offer prices that are fair and reasonable?
- Does the contractor have the necessary facilities and production capacity to deliver its products?
- Can the contractor meet the performance schedule (or delivery schedule), given other commitments?

The government then uses this information to determine whether a potential contractor is eligible for federal contracts.

SHOULD YOU SELL TO THE FEDERAL GOVERNMENT?

Once you understand the contracting process, the next step is to decide whether you should sell to the federal government.

Advantages

Working with the federal government offers tremendous advantages:

- The government purchases practically every type of supply and service. Plus, federal contracting work tends to be a more reliable source of income than private sector work because the government is open for business in both good economic times and bad.

- The government has more than 2,500 buying offices (or *contracting activities*) throughout the United States.
- Each major federal agency must provide free assistance to contractors.
- In some cases, the government provides financial assistance, such as guaranteed loans and progress payments (payments made to a contractor based on a percentage of costs incurred or work performed under the contract).
- The government has preference programs to encourage small business participation.
- For FY 2012, the federal discretionary spending budget was approximately $1.34 trillion.
- The government mandates "full and open competition." In other words, a contractor can compete for federal contracts without having to belong to an exclusive "club" of elite contractors.
- The government spends approximately 25 cents of every dollar spent in the United States.
- Generally, contractors do not need a massive product distribution system or a substantial advertising budget.
- Numerous regulations governing federal contracting ensure fair play by both the government and the contractor. (These regulations do, however, create a certain amount of red tape.)
- If you perform the work required by the contract, you will get paid—usually within 30 days. Checks cut by the federal government never bounce!
- Federal business programs often lead to business with other federal agencies, as well as with state and local governments.
- Many government contracts run for a base year with up to seven option years. So if you live up to expectations, you can expect to get your contract renewed.
- Average government orders/contracts tend to be larger than commercial orders—values of $10 million to $100 million are not uncommon.
- Government business tends to complement your commercial business. It's common for contractors to sell a product to the government and then sell additional versions of the product to government vendors that are compatible with the government's requirements.
- In spite of legal changes in recent years, the government awards about 45 percent to 50 percent of its contracts to sole-source providers. A

sole-source award is a contract that a federal agency awards after soliciting and negotiating with only one source. Therefore, contractors may be able to locate and bid on federal contracts that have limited competition.

- Contracting with the government is patriotic.

Disadvantages

With all these advantages, what businessperson wouldn't want to contract with the government? But as with any client, there are disadvantages to working with the federal government:

- Government red tape can produce volumes of paperwork. Contractors must fill out numerous federal forms, and even not knowing which one to do next, or to whom to send it, can be a major obstacle to your success. The best way to keep current with these forms is to use the General Services Administration's Web site at www.gsa.gov/forms. This book, of course, will also help you untangle the red tape.
- To be successful in government contracting, you must learn how the government operates. This includes learning the clauses, terms, conditions, proper terminology, and methodology.
- Recent estimates show it takes about 18 months to strike your first deal in the federal marketplace.
- Once you sign a federal contract, you are generally locked into performing according to the terms of that contract.
- Government contract specifications (*specs*) tend to be much more stringent than those for commercial contracts. For many contracts, for example, the government requires a company to establish a detailed quality assurance program.
- Government contracting can be very competitive—and seemingly unfair if competitors have established a personal relationship with a particular buying office.
- Certain common practices in commercial business, such as entertaining personnel, are illegal in government contracting. (See Allowable Costs in Chapter 15.)

These disadvantages are not intended to discourage you from seeking to do business with the government. On the contrary, if prospective contractors can become aware of and obtain the necessary information before embarking on government business, the chances of success—in terms of both profit and efficiency—are greatly enhanced. If you can avoid learning through trial and error, everyone comes out ahead.

■ ■ ■

Dr. Martin Luther King, Jr., said it best: "Give me an opportunity, not a handout." This book will help you learn how to do business with the federal government and take advantage of the many contracting opportunities the government offers. There is no better long-term customer than your federal government!

■ ■ ■

CHAPTER 2

The Rules of the Game

What's in this chapter?

- Constitutional authority
- Congressional responsibilities
- Central Contractor Registration
- Federal Acquisition Regulation
- Federal Acquisition Streamlining Act of 1994
- Cost Accounting Standards
- Defense Contract Audit Agency
- Government Accountability Office
- Federal Acquisition Reform Act of 1996
- Competition in Contracting Act of 1984
- Buy American Act
- Truth in Negotiations Act
- Service Contract Act of 1965
- Freedom of Information Act

Understanding the opportunities the federal government has to offer is one thing. It is quite another to understand the federal contracting rules and regulations. Let's face it: they are probably the biggest deterrent for businesses looking to enter the market. In fact, a contractor would find navigating through the government marketplace almost impossible without a reasonable level of knowledge about its requirements.

Although the government doesn't intend to put anyone out of business, it nevertheless expects a contractor to know and understand the technical and administrative requirements of a signed contract. In other words, the government will not rescue a company from the consequences of bad business decisions.

Far too many contractors have watched their profits on a government contract drastically shrink or totally disappear because they overlooked, misunderstood, or just plain ignored the applicable regulations. The bottom-line philosophy is the more you know the "rules of the game" or the more you understand about the federal contracting process, the greater the likelihood you'll succeed. I promise to make this chapter as painless as possible and smoothly navigate your way through the procurement maze!

CONSTITUTIONAL AUTHORITY

This part of the book reminds me of those Saturday morning "Schoolhouse Rock" cartoons from back in the day. Not sure what I'm talking about? Go to YouTube and have a look for yourself.

The U.S. Constitution gives the federal government the legal authority to enter into contracts with private citizens and commercial organizations. This is the case even though the Constitution does not contain any language that specifically authorizes such actions. The authority derives from a statement in the Preamble that says that the federal government shall "provide for the common defense, promote the general welfare, and secure the blessings of liberty."

For a contract to become the legal obligation of the federal government, it must be based on statutory authority. The federal government can actually avoid liability for a contract that is unsupported by a legally enacted provision.

CONGRESSIONAL RESPONSIBILITIES

The U.S. Congress derives its powers from article I, section 8, of the Constitution—General Powers of Congress—which states that Congress will:

> 1. . . . lay and collect taxes, duties, imports and excises, to pay the debts and provide for the common defense and general welfare of the United States;
>
> 12. . . . raise and support Armies;
>
> 13. . . . provide and maintain a Navy;
>
> 14. . . . make rules for the government and regulation of the land and naval forces;
>
> 18. . . . make all laws which shall be necessary and proper for carrying into execution the foregoing powers, and all other powers vested by the Constitution in the Government of the United States, or in any Department or Officer thereof.

Relevant to the topic of this book, Congress is responsible for drafting and passing the laws and statutes that establish the various federal agencies and the specific programs proposed by those federal agencies. These laws and statutes are called *authorization acts*. Congress is also responsible for passing the laws that regulate federal contracting. More than 4,000 of those laws are in effect. In addition, numerous bills pending in Congress could affect how the government exercises its contracting functions.

Suppose a senator includes a new code of contractor ethics in an appropriations bill. If Congress approves the bill and the president signs it, this code of ethics becomes applicable to all future agency pronouncements. Regulation writers, therefore, must prepare a new regulation that accurately reflects this change.

Similarly, if Congress passes a law that restricts the purchase of products from Iraq, regulation writers must write a regulation to reflect this law. The gradual pileup of these laws and restrictions over the years has created a contracting process that is convoluted, confusing, and inefficient.

Why are these regulations so confusing? Is the government trying to hide something from us? I keep thinking about a political advertisement I saw a while back that said, "There's got to be something in the water" in Washington,

D.C. The government is notorious for binding its affairs with red tape, and federal contracting regulations certainly entail their fair share.

Well, believe it or not, these regulations are convoluted for a good reason, and no, it's not because the government is hiding something. Although the Constitution gives the federal government the power to contract for supplies and services, it also mandates that "No Money shall be drawn from the Treasury, but in Consequence of Appropriations made by Law. . . ." This basically means that the government may purchase only those items that Congress votes to fund. Sounds simple enough.

In approving funds, Congress often places restrictions and conditions on the money for various programs and socioeconomic goals. It's those restrictions that create many of the contradictions, exceptions, and loopholes in the contracting regulations.

Funding Requirements

Congress supports each federal agency and its programs by putting into law an *appropriations act*. This act provides the funds with which that federal agency functions. Congress derives the authority to enact appropriations acts from article I, section 9 of the Constitution.

Each appropriations act specifies the period for which the funds are available for use by the agency. The appropriation can be for a single year, for multiple years, or unrestricted. Most appropriations are awarded for a single year. This approach requires federal agencies to return annually to Congress to justify the budgets for their operations and programs.

Multiple-year appropriations usually apply to major multiple-year programs and projects, such as research and development. Federal agencies prefer multiple-year appropriations because they tend to provide significant savings to both the government and contractors. For the savings to be realistic, however, the multiyear program requirements must remain stable and predictable, and the requesting agency must ask for enough money to carry out the contract. Once Congress approves the funds, they are available for use.

Budget Process

The budget process is long and tedious. Each fiscal year (October 1 to September 30), federal agencies are required to submit budgets to Congress detailing their operating costs for the upcoming year. Preparing these proposed budgets usually takes federal agencies several years.

Once a federal agency completes its budget, it submits that budget to the president through the Office of Management and Budget (OMB). OMB reviews the proposed budget and makes recommendations to the federal agency. Upon agreement between the parties, OMB assembles the agencies' budget requests and the president submits the budget to Congress.

Once Congress receives the proposed budget, the budget is forwarded to the Congressional Budget Office (CBO) and the individual budget committees for in-depth review. During this review process, the CBO and the committees within Congress set targets and ceilings for the various federal functions or programs.

The budget is then dissected by the CBO and sent to various House and Senate authorization and appropriation committees. These committees and their subcommittees hold hearings on the proposed programs and draft legislation.

This draft legislation then moves on to the House and Senate for debate and approval. Only after both legislative bodies approve the final budget is it returned to the president for signature. If this process is not completed by the start of the government's fiscal year (October 1), the agency is in jeopardy of being shut down because of inadequate funding.

CONTRACTOR REGISTRATION

What's the first thing a business should do to become eligible for a government contract? You guessed it: register online with the System for Award Management (SAM)—what used to be called Central Contractor Registration (CCR). As of August 2012, SAM has replaced the General Services Administration's (GSA's) outmoded acquisition systems to be a one-stop repository and application service. CCR, the Online Representations and Certifications Application

(ORCA), and the Excluded Parties Listing System (EPLS) have been migrated to SAM. More acquisition systems—including FedBizOpps, the Past Performance Information Retrieval System (PPIRS), and the electronic subcontracting reporting system (eSRS)—are expected to migrate to SAM in coming years.

SAM is now the primary repository for contractor information required for conducting business with the federal government. It basically helps federal buyers locate you. With very limited exceptions, prospective contractors must be registered in SAM or the CCR before they can be awarded a federal contract. There is no charge to register. If you had an account in CCR, you may or may not need to register in SAM and migrate your CCR account to SAM. If your business information has changed, you will need to log in to SAM to change it.

Once registered, contractors must update or renew their information at least once a year to maintain an active status. **SAM:**

- Provides contractors worldwide visibility to government buyers
- Increases efficiency and lowers costs by simplifying and streamlining the procurement process
- Allows contractors to avoid registering with multiple buying offices
- Reduces errors and saves time by creating an accurate record of data for each business
- Most importantly, provides banking information to the Defense Finance and Accounting Service (DFAS), which enables contractors to be paid electronically.

To register in the SAM, you must first contact Dun & Bradstreet to obtain a DUNS (Data Universal Numbering System) number, which is a unique, nine-character company identification number. For assistance, contact Dun & Bradstreet at (800) 234-3867, or visit www.dnb.com.

After getting your DUNS number, you'll need to provide the following information to register in SAM:

- Taxpayer identification number or Social Security number
- Legal business name and corporate status
- Business address

- Statistical information about your business (e.g., gross receipts and number of employees)
- Banking and electronic funds transfer information.

To register in SAM, go to www.sam.gov. Also check this site for up-to-date information and guidance. Once registered, you will be assigned a Commercial and Government Entity (CAGE) code. The CAGE code is a five-character (alphanumeric) identifier generated by the Defense Logistics Information Service (DLIS). If you already have a CAGE code, DLIS will validate it during this process. To get your current CAGE code, call (877) 352-2255.

What if a year has come and gone since you last updated SAM for your business? Many businesses overlook the fact that it is necessary not only to revise their information yearly, but also to update any company changes throughout the year. Changes can include anything from a new address to a change in business status as the company grows. It is also important to note that if the point of contact has changed or left the company, he or she needs to be removed from the registration and a successor (with the proper reference materials) added.

Failure to maintain your information could lead to missed opportunities. And if your CCR or SAM record has expired, electronic payments from DFAS will cease until the account is reactivated.

FEDERAL ACQUISITION REGULATION

In the beginning, there was the FAR . . .

If you plan to contract with the federal government, the Federal Acquisition Regulation (FAR) will serve as your "bible." The FAR is the body of regulations governing federal acquisitions. It contains uniform policies and procedures for all procurements of products (and services), whether the products are obtained through purchase or lease and regardless of whether the products already exist or must be developed. In layman's terms, the FAR contains the rules of the game. With very few exceptions, each executive branch agency is required to adhere to FAR rules when making purchases with congressionally appropriated funds.

The FAR is jointly issued and maintained by the GSA, the Department of Defense (DoD), and the National Aeronautics and Space Administration (NASA). Currently, the FAR includes more than 1,600 pages and is divided into 53 parts, each dealing with a separate aspect of the procurement process.

FAR Numbering System

Each of the 53 parts of the FAR addresses a separate aspect of federal procurement. Parts 1 through 4 cover general matters such as definitions, policies, and ethics. Parts 5 through 12 address competition and acquisition planning. Parts 13 through 18 address contracting methods (such as simplified acquisitions, sealed bidding, and negotiation—see Part IV of this book), and contract types. Parts 19 through 26 address socioeconomic matters, including preferential treatment for certain categories of businesses.

The remaining parts address such matters as labor laws, contract administration, and clauses to be inserted in contracts. Standard and optional forms can also be found in Part 53, along with cross references to the paragraphs in the FAR that require or authorize the use of a particular form.

Each part is further subdivided into sections and paragraphs according to the numbering system shown below.

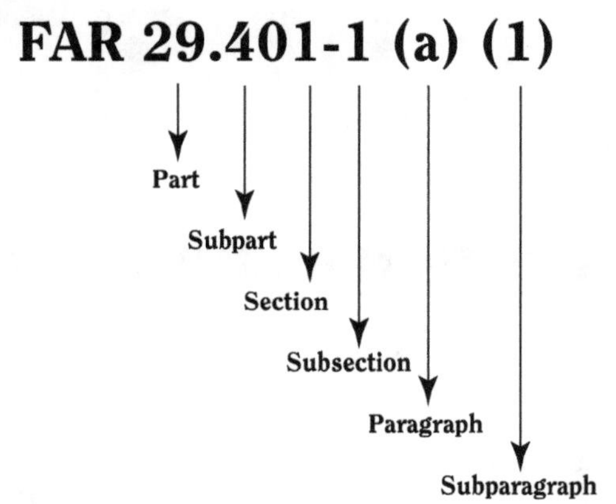

As an example, here's the current outline for the first item in Subpart 29.4:

PART 29	TAXES
. . .	
SUBPART 29.4	CONTRACT CLAUSES
29.401	DOMESTIC CONTRACTS
29.401-1	Indefinite-delivery contracts for leased equipment.
29.401-2	Construction contracts performed in North Carolina.
29.401-3	Federal, State, and local taxes.
29.401-4	New Mexico gross receipts and compensating tax.

1.000 Scope of part.

This part sets forth basic policies and general information about the Federal Acquisition Regulations System including purpose, authority, applicability, issuance, arrangement, numbering, dissemination, implementation, supplementation, maintenance, administration, and deviation. Subparts 1.2, 1.3, and 1.4 prescribe administrative procedures for maintaining the FAR System.

Subpart 1.1—Purpose, Authority, Issuance

1.101 Purpose.

The Federal Acquisition Regulations System is established for the codification and publication of uniform policies and procedures for acquisition by all executive agencies. The Federal Acquisition Regulations System consists of the Federal Acquisition Regulation (FAR), which is the primary document, and agency acquisition regulations that implement or supplement the FAR. The FAR System does not include internal agency guidance of the type described in 1.301(a)(2).

1.102 Statement of guiding principles for the Federal Acquisition System.

(a) The vision for the Federal Acquisition System is to deliver on a timely basis the best value product or service to the customer, while maintaining the public's trust and fulfilling public policy objectives. Participants in the acquisition process should work together as a team and should be empowered to make decisions within their area of responsibility.

(b) The Federal Acquisition System will—

(1) Satisfy the customer in terms of cost, quality, and timeliness of the delivered product or service by, for example—

(i) Maximizing the use of commercial products and services;

(ii) Using contractors who have a track record of successful past performance or who demonstrate a current superior ability to perform; and

(iii) Promoting competition;

(2) Minimize administrative operating costs;

(3) Conduct business with integrity, fairness, and openness; and

(4) Fulfill public policy objectives.

(c) The Acquisition Team consists of all participants in Government acquisition including not only representatives of the technical, supply, and procurement communities but also the customers they serve, and the contractors who provide the products and services.

(d) The role of each member of the Acquisition Team is to exercise personal initiative and sound business judgment in providing the best value product or service to meet the customer's needs. In exercising initiative, Government members of the Acquisition Team may assume if a specific strategy, practice, policy or procedure is in the best interests of the Government and is not addressed in the FAR, nor prohibited by law (statute or case law), Executive order or other regulation, that the strategy, practice, policy or procedure is a permissible exercise of authority.

1.102-1 Discussion.

(a) *Introduction.* The statement of Guiding Principles for the Federal Acquisition System (System) represents a concise statement designed to be user-friendly for all participants in Government acquisition. The following discussion of the principles is provided in order to illuminate the meaning of the terms and phrases used. The framework for the System includes the Guiding Principles for the System and the supporting policies and procedures in the FAR.

(b) *Vision.* All participants in the System are responsible for making acquisition decisions that deliver the best value product or service to the customer. Best value must be viewed from a broad perspective and is achieved by balancing the many competing interests in the System. The result is a system which works better and costs less.

1.102-2 Performance standards.

(a) *Satisfy the customer in terms of cost, quality, and timeliness of the delivered product or service.* (1) The principal customers for the product or service provided by the System are the users and line managers, acting on behalf of the American taxpayer.

(2) The System must be responsive and adaptive to customer needs, concerns, and feedback. Implementation of acquisition policies and procedures, as well as consideration of timeliness, quality, and cost throughout the process, must take into account the perspective of the user of the product or service.

(3) When selecting contractors to provide products or perform services, the Government will use contractors who have a track record of successful past performance or who demonstrate a current superior ability to perform.

(4) The Government must not hesitate to communicate with the commercial sector as early as possible in the acquisition cycle to help the Government determine the capabilities available in the commercial marketplace. The Government will maximize its use of commercial products and services in meeting Government requirements.

(5) It is the policy of the System to promote competition in the acquisition process.

(6) The System must perform in a timely, high quality, and cost-effective manner.

(7) All members of the Team are required to employ planning as an integral part of the overall process of acquiring products or services. Although advance planning is required, each member of the Team must be flexible in order to accommodate changing or unforeseen mission needs. Planning is a

Example Page of the Federal Acquisition Regulation

Suppose you want to locate information on time-and-materials (T&M) contracts. The first step is to determine which part of the FAR would likely contain this information. The list below is a handy reference.

Federal Acquisition Regulation by Part

Part 1 Federal Acquisition Regulation System
Part 2 Definitions of Words and Terms
Part 3 Improper Business Practices
Part 4 Administrative Matters
Part 5 Publicizing Contract Actions
Part 6 Competition Requirements
Part 7 Acquisition Planning
Part 8 Required Sources of Supplies and Services
Part 9 Contractor Qualifications
Part 10 Market Research
Part 11 Describing Agency Needs
Part 12 Acquisition of Commercial Items
Part 13 Simplified Acquisition Procedures
Part 14 Sealed Bidding
Part 15 Contracting by Negotiation
Part 16 Types of Contracts
Part 17 Special Contracting Methods
Part 18 Emergency Acquisitions
Part 19 Small Business Programs
Part 20 [Reserved]
Part 21 [Reserved]
Part 22 Application of Labor Laws to Acquisitions
Part 23 Occupational Safety
Part 24 Privacy Protection
Part 25 Foreign Acquisition
Part 26 Other Socioeconomic Programs
Part 27 Patents, Data, and Copyrights
Part 28 Bonds and Insurance
Part 29 Taxes
Part 30 Cost Accounting Standards Administration
Part 31 Contract Cost Principles and Procedures
Part 32 Contract Financing
Part 33 Protests, Disputes, and Appeals
Part 34 Major System Acquisition
Part 35 Research and Development Contracting
Part 36 Construction Contracts
Part 37 Service Contracting
Part 38 Federal Supply Schedule Contracting
Part 39 Acquisition of Information Technology
Part 40 [Reserved]
Part 41 Acquisition of Utility Services
Part 42 Contract Administration and Audit Services
Part 43 Contract Modifications
Part 44 Subcontracting Policies and Procedures
Part 45 Government Property
Part 46 Quality Assurance
Part 47 Transportation
Part 48 Value Engineering
Part 49 Termination of Contracts
Part 50 Extraordinary Contractual Actions
Part 51 Use of Government Sources by Contractors
Part 52 Solicitation Provisions and Contract Clauses
Part 53 Forms

After examining this list, the best place to start would be Part 16—Types of Contracts. The next step would be to examine the subparts within this part. Part 16 currently consists of the following subparts:

Subpart 16.1 Selecting Contract Types
Subpart 16.2 Fixed-Price Contracts
Subpart 16.3 Cost-Reimbursement Contracts
Subpart 16.4 Incentive Contracts
Subpart 16.5 Indefinite-Delivery Contracts
Subpart 16.6 Time-and-Materials, Labor-Hour, and Letter Contracts
Subpart 16.7 Agreements

In this example, the most obvious choice would be Subpart 16.6.

Finally, go to section 16.601 to find the required information. Once you get the hang of this numbering system, you will be able locate information in the FAR with ease.

Federal Acquisition Circulars

Amendments or changes to the FAR are issued in Federal Acquisition Circulars (FACs). Simply stated, FACs are updates to the FAR. Changes to the FAR are typically the result of congressional actions or presidential orders.

FACs are published daily in the *Federal Register*, the official publication used by the government to inform the public of congressional and federal enactments. Each FAC is issued sequentially, using the following numbering system:

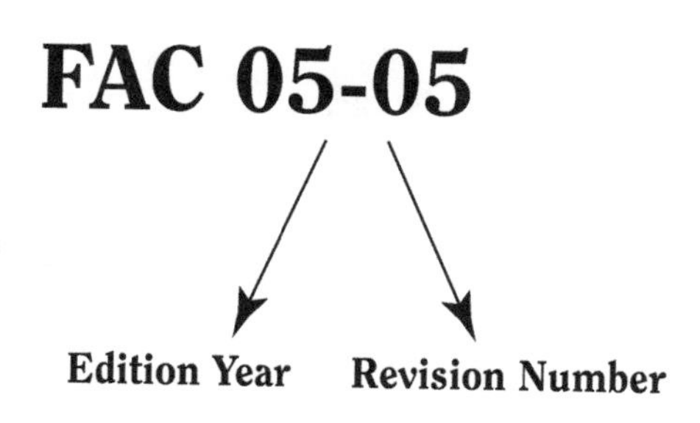

The first two digits in the FAC number identify the FAR edition. This particular FAC amends the 2005 edition of the FAR. The final two digits represent the revision number. This is the 51st revision to the 2005 FAR edition. (FAC 05-51 established the Women-Owned Small Business Program.)

The best way to keep current with FACs is to access the FAR using the Internet, because the online FAR reflects all FACs to date. The current FAR and other materials can be found at https://www.acquisition.gov/far.

Agency Supplements

Each federal agency is authorized by Congress to issue its own supplement to the FAR. These supplements contain policies and procedures that apply only to that particular agency. For example, the Department of Defense FAR Supplement (DFARS) provides contracting personnel detailed procedures for acquiring military-specific items.

The rules and regulations included in these supplements should not contradict the FAR; they just provide additional guidance for dealing with a particular agency. Only by congressional order may a federal agency deviate from the FAR. For instance, the Federal Aviation Administration was permitted to deviate from the FAR for the purpose of creating a simplified acquisition management system (AMS).

Currently more than 20 federal agencies issue supplements to the FAR. These supplements include:

- DFARS, Department of Defense
- HHSAR, Department of Health and Human Services
- AGAR, Department of Agriculture
- GSAR, General Services Administration
- AIDAR, Agency for International Development.

You can find a complete list of these supplements in Title 48 of the Code of Federal Regulations (CFR). The CFR is available at www.gpoaccess.gov/cfr/index.html.

Adhering to the FAR

Potential contractors must follow the rules of the FAR or risk being eliminated from consideration. Although some contractors feel that the FAR does not allow enough latitude, government officials also must adhere to the regulations protecting the expenditure of public funds.

Contractors should always have access to a current copy of the FAR. Because the FAR is updated throughout the year, however, you need to ensure that your copy remains current. Subscriptions with updates (including each agency's FAR supplements) are available from Commerce Clearing House, www.cch.com or (800) 248-3248. The latest version of the FAR is also available online at either www.acquisition.gov/far or http://farsite.hill.af.mil. The latter site also provides access to all the aforementioned agency supplements and an excellent FAR search tool.

FEDERAL ACQUISITION STREAMLINING ACT OF 1994

Congress enacted the Federal Acquisition Streamlining Act (FASA) of 1994 to help simplify and streamline the federal acquisition process. FASA was passed in response to calls for government downsizing and the recognition that red tape had caused the acquisition process to become convoluted and inefficient.

FASA directs federal agencies to maximize the use of commercial buying practices. For example, if a contracting activity in DoD wants to purchase an all-terrain boot, it must first seek commercial sources before issuing a solicitation for a military-specific boot.

Also, FASA requires the government to accept the terms and conditions offered by the private sector unless it can negotiate better terms and conditions through commitment guarantees or volume purchases. Other significant provisions of FASA, as amended, include:

- Purchases that fall within the micropurchase threshold of $3,000 are not subject to small business set-asides or the Buy American Act. The government can therefore make purchases without obtaining competitive quotes, assuming the prices are reasonable. Government buying offices are encouraged to make micropurchases using credit cards.

- Contracts for a dollar amount that is greater than the micropurchase threshold but does not exceed the simplified acquisition threshold of $150,000 must be set aside for small business when there is a reasonable expectation of offers from two or more responsible small businesses that are competitive in terms of price and quality. (More than 90 percent of annual federal purchase transactions are under $150,000.)

Government Purchasing Thresholds

$3,000 or less	Micropurchases (credit cards)
$3,001 to $150,000	Simplified acquisition procedures (SAP)
Over $150,000	Formal solicitation procedures

See Part IV for a detailed discussion of these thresholds and the associated procurement methods.

- A requirement for prompt notice of award. When a federal agency issues a solicitation, it must notify losing offerors in writing within three days of award.

COST ACCOUNTING STANDARDS

In the 1970s, primarily, some people in the federal government contended that generally accepted accounting principles (GAAP) did not go far enough for government contracts. They reasoned that GAAP applied to matters of financial accounting and not cost accounting. So the government created a Cost Accounting Standards Board to establish cost accounting principles applicable to government contracts.

Cost accounting standards (CAS) typically apply only to large businesses (i.e., businesses not considered "small businesses") and higher-dollar-value contracts (those in the millions). They provide uniformity and consistency in estimating, accumulating, and reporting costs in connection with the pricing and administration of negotiated procurements (see Part V). By following CAS, contractors are therefore able to track costs that apply to each government contract or major task they undertake.

Refer to the appendix of the FAR for a complete listing of the federal cost accounting standards.

> A detailed discussion of cost accounting standards (CAS) goes beyond the scope of this book, but the contract type examples and discussions in Part V follow many of the CAS principles.

DEFENSE CONTRACT AUDIT AGENCY

Dude, I'm kidding.
DCAA is not coming today.

Yikes! In this biz, the Defense Contract Audit Agency (DCAA) is the best known and most influential (or feared) of the government audit agencies because of its reputation for being an aggressive defender of taxpayers' money. DCAA is responsible for performing contract audit functions required by DoD and many civilian agencies. It currently has more than 300 field offices worldwide.

Audits typically include the examination of records, documents, and other financial data related to contract pricing, performance costs, and any cost, funding, or performance reports required under the specific contract.

Because audits require significant expenditures of time and money, they are generally conducted only for procurements (or modifications) beyond a threshold of $700,000 value and for which certified cost or pricing data have been submitted. Similarly, while many contracts may contain some sort of standard audit clause, postaward audits are routinely used only when needed to help determine final costs on cost-reimbursement contracts (see Chapter 15).

In addition to performing contract audits, DCAA assists federal agencies in reviewing and evaluating contractor:

- Efficiency
- Internal control systems
- Accounting system suitability (e.g., is the system capable of tracing and segregating costs on cost-reimbursement contracts?)
- Performance.

DCAA's Web site is at www.dcaa.mil.

GOVERNMENT ACCOUNTABILITY OFFICE

The Government Accountability Office (GAO) is the investigative arm of Congress. GAO has broad authority to oversee federal programs and operations and to review government contracts to ensure that appropriated funds are spent in accordance with the laws enacted by Congress. GAO also gets involved with:

- Contract award protests
- Investigations requested by a member of Congress
- Fraud allegations.

GAO's findings and recommendations are published as reports to congressional members or delivered as testimony to congressional committees. GAO's Web site is at www.gao.gov.

FEDERAL ACQUISITION REFORM ACT OF 1996

The Federal Acquisition Reform Act (FARA) of 1996, also called the Clinger-Cohen Act, expands on the Federal Acquisition Streamlining Act of 1994. FARA reinforces the commercial buying preference and limits the number of regulatory FAR clauses that apply to simplified acquisitions. Also, this act significantly changed protest and claim procedures by expanding the use of alternative dispute resolution for disagreements between the government and private industry. (Protests are written objections by interested parties to a solicitation, proposed award, or award of a contract; see Chapter 12.)

COMPETITION IN CONTRACTING ACT OF 1984

The basic law governing contract formation is the Competition in Contracting Act (CICA) of 1984. It explicitly requires the government to use "full and open competition" in purchasing products and services. Accordingly, all responsible sources must be allowed an opportunity to compete for government contracts, meaning that acquisition officials do not have the luxury of buying from sources based on past good business relations.

Also, procurement officials may not restrict their sources to suppliers known for quality products and on-time delivery. This regulation is in marked contrast to the selection criteria of commercial and private sector businesses, which return to favorite vendors repeatedly rather than risk disappointment by using a vendor with which they have no business experience.

CICA specifies seven exceptions to the "full and open competition" requirement. These exceptions come into play if:

- Only one responsible source (or vendor) is available, and no other supplies or services will satisfy the agency's requirements.
- An unusual and compelling urgency (such as a war) exists.
- Vital supplies or facilities are needed for national emergencies.
- An international agreement between the United States and a foreign government regulates the conditions of a contract.
- A statutory requirement (such as the Small Business Act) calls for an exception.
- Disclosure of the government's needs would threaten national security.
- "Full and open competition" contradicts the public's best interest.

CICA does not apply to simplified acquisition procedures or purchases under $150,000 (see Chapter 10). Different rules on competition also apply for small businesses eligible to participate in preference programs (see Chapter 5).

BUY AMERICAN ACT

Except for a few exceptions identified in FAR Part 25, the Buy American Act requires the federal government to buy domestic articles, materials, and supplies for public use. An article, material, or supply is considered domestic if:

- It is an unmanufactured end product mined or produced in the United States.
- It is an end product that is manufactured in the United States (i.e., if the costs of its components mined, produced, or manufactured in the United States exceed 50 percent of the cost of its components).

The primary purpose of this act is to discourage the government from buying foreign products. There are six exceptions to the Buy American Act:

- Items to be used outside the United States.
- Domestic items that are unreasonably priced. (Unless an agency determines otherwise, the offered price of a domestic item is considered unreasonable when the lowest acceptable domestic offer exceeds the lowest acceptable foreign offer by more than 6 percent if the domestic offer is from a large business, or more than 12 percent if the domestic offer is from a small business.)
- Information technology that is a commercial item.
- Situations in which compliance with the Buy American Act would not be in the government's best interest.
- Items that are not mined, produced, or manufactured in the United States in sufficient and reasonably available commercial quantities.
- Items purchased specifically for commissary resale.

The Buy American Act does not apply to purchases under the micropurchase threshold of $3,000.

DoD and NASA have determined that it is inconsistent with the public interest to apply the restrictions of the Buy American Act to certain acquisitions. (See their respective FAR supplements for a detailed listing.)

TRUTH IN NEGOTIATIONS ACT

Congress enacted the Truth in Negotiations Act (TINA) to protect the government from unscrupulous contractors that falsify their cost proposals with erroneous information or defective pricing. When a contracting officer determines that TINA is appropriate for a particular acquisition (see below), contractors will be required to submit certified cost or pricing data with their proposals.

Cost or pricing data include more than just historical accounting data. They are facts and information that reasonably can be expected to contribute to the soundness of estimates of future costs and to the validity of costs already incurred. Examples of cost and pricing data include:

- Vendor quotations
- Cost trends
- Information on management decisions that could have a bearing on costs (such as changes in production methods)
- Make-or-buy decisions
- Data supporting projections of business costs.

The requirements of TINA generally apply to contracts greater than $700,000. However, the government may require cost and pricing data for negotiated contracts over $150,000.

Certified cost or pricing data are not requested when:

- The contracting officer determines there is adequate price competition.
- Prices are set by law or regulation.
- A waiver has been granted in unusual circumstances.
- Commercial items are being acquired (without modification).
- The amount involved is at or below the simplified acquisition threshold.

The head of a contracting activity may also waive the cost and pricing submission requirement in exceptional cases. The rationale for the waiver must be in writing. For example, if a contractor furnished cost or pricing data on previous production buys and the contracting head determines that such data are sufficient, a waiver may be granted.

If a contract is subject to TINA, the contractor and subcontractor must also certify, to the best of their knowledge and belief, that the data provided are current, accurate, and complete. If the cost and pricing data are not certified, the government may institute a defective pricing claim. Many contracts use the following certification:

Certificate of Current Cost or Pricing Data

> This is to certify that, to the best of my knowledge and belief, the cost or pricing data (as defined in section 2.101 of the Federal Acquisition Regulation [FAR] and required under FAR subsection 15.403-4) submitted, either actually or by specific identification in writing, to the contracting officer or to the contracting officer's representative in support of [*identify the proposal, quotation, request for price adjustment, or other submission involved, giving the appropriate identifying number (e.g., Solicitation No.______________)*] are accurate, complete, and current as of ____________. This certification includes the cost or pricing data supporting any advance agreements and forward pricing rate agreements between the offeror and the government that are part of the proposal.

Part V of this book details cost and pricing techniques used by many successful government contractors.

SERVICE CONTRACT ACT OF 1965

The Service Contract Act (SCA) was enacted to ensure that government contractors compensate their employees fairly and properly. It generally applies to federal contracts and subcontracts for services (performed in the United States) that exceed $2,500.

Service contracts must contain mandatory provisions regarding minimum wages and fringe benefits, safe and sanitary working conditions, and equivalent federal employee classifications and wage rates. The following services are generally covered by the SCA:

- Parking, taxi, and ambulance
- Packing and storage
- Janitorial, housekeeping, and guard services

- Food service and lodging
- Laundry services
- Repair and maintenance
- Data collection, processing, and analysis.

The SCA does not apply to:

- Contracts for construction or repair of public buildings
- Contracts for transporting freight or personnel
- Contracts subject to the Communications Act of 1934 (e.g., radio, phone, cable)
- Contracts for public utility services
- Any employment contract providing for direct services to a federal agency
- Contracts for operating postal contract stations for the U.S. Postal Service.

The Department of Labor defines the prevailing wage rates and fringe benefits by locality. The minimum wage requirement is specified in the Fair Labor Standards Act. All federal contracts are subject to this minimum wage. For more information on the Service Contract Act, see FAR 22.10.

FREEDOM OF INFORMATION ACT

The Freedom of Information Act (FOIA) is less a regulation to follow than it is an opportunity for contractors to get valuable information. Contractors are encouraged to use FOIA when they conduct market research. FOIA is particularly useful in obtaining information on federal agency buying trends and past contractual data. And yes, in many cases, even competitors' proposals can be obtained under FOIA.

> Author's disclaimer: Although competitors' proposals can be obtained under FOIA, they may be heavily redacted. Competitors are allowed to indicate, subject to government review, what portions of their proposals are "exempt under Rule 4" (essentially, proprietary). The courts have recently extended considerably the applicability of the exemption with regard to option prices for contract line items (CLINs). So please be judicious when making your FOIA requests.

FOIA was enacted on July 4, 1967, to give the public access to information that the federal government assembles, creates, and maintains. This act significantly changed the government's information disclosure policy. Before the enactment of FOIA, the individual bore the burden of establishing the right to examine government records or documents. No statutory guidelines or procedures existed to help individuals seeking federal information. In addition, no remedies (judicial or otherwise) were available for those denied access.

With the passage of FOIA, the burden of proof shifted from the individual to the government. The "right to know" doctrine replaced the "need to know" standard. Therefore, individuals who seek federal information no longer must show a need for the requested information.

The government must now justify the need for secrecy. FOIA further requires federal agencies to provide the fullest possible disclosure of information to the public, and it provides administrative and judicial remedies for individuals who are unjustly denied access to federal records.

FOIA applies to documents or records held by federal agencies in the government's executive branch. The executive branch includes cabinet departments, military departments, government corporations, government-controlled corporations, and independent regulatory agencies. FOIA does not apply to federally elected officials, including the president, vice president, senators, and members of Congress.

Each federal agency must have FOIA request and response procedures. Citizens may request any record in the possession of a federal agency that is not exempt under the provisions of FOIA. Exemptions include:

- Matters specifically required by executive order to be kept secret in the interest of national defense or foreign policy
- Matters related solely to the internal personnel rules and practices of a federal agency
- Matters specifically exempt from disclosure by statute
- Trade secrets and commercial information received by the government in confidence
- Internal memoranda related to the decision-making process of the federal agency
- Personnel or medical files

- Investigative records compiled for law enforcement purposes
- Geological data (such as maps).

In addition to these exemptions, there are other, commonsense reasons for which the government would reject a FOIA request. Perhaps, for example, the agency does not hold the requested record or the requested record does not exist. In general, if you request information that does not fall under one of the exemptions listed above, you are entitled to it.

Potential contractors should not have reservations about referencing FOIA for fear of being blackballed. Requesting information under FOIA is an accepted part of the procurement process. Actually, exhibiting an understanding of FOIA indicates a contractor's knowledge of the contracting process.

The first step in making a request under FOIA is to identify the federal agency that has the information. If you are unsure which agency has the information you seek, consult a government directory, such as the *United States Government Manual*. It lists all federal agencies, a description of their functions, and their addresses. The *Manual* is updated annually and is available online at www.usgovernmentmanual.gov.

Each federal agency must institute FOIA implementation procedures or instructions, which are contained in the agency's FAR supplement. Also, each agency has a FOIA officer, whose function is to ensure that vendors (or contractors) obtain the legitimate information they seek. The best way to get in touch with an agency FOIA center or officer is to visit www.foia.gov. If you prefer, you can contact USA.gov at **(800) FED-INFO.**

Your FOIA request should be in writing and addressed to the agency's FOIA officer. If you plan to mail your FOIA request, be sure to mark the envelope "Freedom of Information Act Request" on the bottom left corner to expedite the process. In your letter, identify the documents or records you need and state that your request is being made under the Freedom of Information Act.

When you make a request under FOIA, try to be as precise as possible. If you don't know the document title, describe what you seek as accurately as possible. A prospective contractor might say, "I would like the names of small businesses that were awarded contracts within the past six months for 5" x 12" white envelopes." Put your phone number on your request, so the agency employee can call you with questions. On the facing page is an example of a FOIA request to get you started.

Federal agencies typically charge you for the costs associated with obtaining and reproducing the FOIA information (usually between $10 and $30). If you request a small amount of information that is easy to obtain, the agency might provide it for free.

Federal agencies must respond to a FOIA request within 10 working days of receiving it. If an agency needs more time, it must acknowledge receipt of the request within 10 days and attempt to fulfill the request within 10 additional working days. The total response time of a federal agency should not exceed 20 working days.

Any FOIA request denial may be appealed to the U.S. District Court. Keep in mind that government records are public property and you have the right to this public information. For more detailed information on FOIA, obtain a publication called *Your Right to Federal Records* by calling the Federal Citizen Information Center at (888) 878-3256.

■ ■ ■

As a political entity and a vast business organization, the government must establish policies and procedures that not only represent good business judgment but also are fair to all concerned. This dual role has led to an extensive set of rules and regulations that govern the federal marketplace.

You should not look at these unique requirements as insurmountable barriers to the economically rewarding experience of doing business with the government. Just remember that the government is ready to do business with competent, qualified companies that can supply the products or services at reasonable prices.

■ ■ ■

FOIA Request Example

Date

FOIA Officer
Name of Agency
Address

RE: Freedom of Information Act Request

Dear [Name of FOIA Officer]:

Fairness, Inc., is hereby requesting under the Freedom of Information Act a copy of the winning technical proposal for Solicitation No.________________. Please forward the following information:

- Incumbent's name and address;
- Contract number; and
- Subsequent contract amendments.

If you deny all or any part of this request, please cite each specific exemption you think justifies your refusal and notify me of appeal procedures available under the law. Also, if there are any fees [greater than $30—*optional*] for copying or searching for the records, please let me know before you fill my request.

As prescribed under 5 U.S.C. section 552, Fairness, Inc., anticipates response within 10 working days upon receipt of this request. Portions of this request may be forwarded as you locate the documents.

If you have any questions, please feel free to call me at (800) 867-5309. Thank you for your cooperation.

Sincerely,

Joe Smith
President

CHAPTER 3

The Key Players

© 1999 Randy Glasbergen.
GLASBERGEN
"I'm paid $4,000,000 a year. You're paid $40,000. The only difference is a few zeros. Everyone knows that zero equals nothing. So what's the problem?"

What's in this chapter?

- Head of the contracting activity
- Contracting officer
- Competition advocates
- Small business specialists
- Requirements personnel

There's just no getting around it: the federal government is a gigantic bureaucracy. Currently, it has a payroll of more than two million employees and over 2,500 contracting activities (or buying offices) located throughout the United States. Therefore, it's imperative for prospective contractors to be familiar with its key players. This chapter highlights who's who in federal acquisition personnel.

HEAD OF THE CONTRACTING ACTIVITY

The head of the contracting activity (HCA) is the individual who has the overall responsibility for managing the contracting activity of a federal agency. Many agencies have several contracting activities. It's normally the HCA or his or her designee who appoints individuals as contracting officers.

Head of Agency

The head of agency (or agency head) has the responsibility and authority to contract for supplies and services needed to run an agency's mission requirements. In the Department of Defense (DoD), the secretary of the army, the secretary of the navy, and the secretary of the air force are also considered agency heads, in addition to the secretary of defense.

Each agency head must establish a system for selecting, appointing, and terminating contracting officers and must maintain a procurement career-management program. These selections and appointments must be consistent with the Office of Federal Procurement Policy's standards for skill-based training in performing contracting and purchasing duties.

In selecting a contracting officer, the appointing official considers the complexity and dollar value of the acquisitions to be assigned and the candidate's experience, training, education, judgment, and character. The appointing official will want to know whether the candidate has:

- Experience in government contracting and administration, commercial purchasing, or related fields
- Education or special training in business administration, law, accounting, engineering, or related fields

- Knowledge of acquisition policies and procedures
- Specialized knowledge in the particular assigned field of contracting
- Satisfactory completion of acquisition training courses.

CONTRACTING OFFICER

The federal government's "official buyer" is the contracting officer (CO). He or she enters into, administers, or terminates contracts and makes related determinations and findings. The contracting officer is the only person who can bind the government to a contract that is greater than the micropurchase threshold of $3,000. There are currently more than 28,000 contracting officers in the government (three-quarters of whom work at the Department of Defense).

When appointed, a contracting officer is issued a Certificate of Appointment, Standard Form 1402. This certificate is also referred to as a *warrant*. Each Certificate of Appointment identifies the contracting officer, the federal agency for which he or she works, and any limitations on his or her authority.

A contracting officer may bind the government only to the extent of the authority delegated. The Certificate of Appointment might, for example, limit a contracting officer's purchasing authority to supplies and services that cost less than $200,000. If you have any doubts about a contracting officer's authority, ask to see his or her warrant. Further, the contracting officer's name and agency or department must be typed, stamped, or printed on the contract.

Contracting officers ensure compliance with the terms of the contract and safeguard the interests of the government in its contractual relationships. If the contracting officer is unable to ensure that all requirements of law, executive orders, regulations, and all other applicable procedures, including clearances, have been met, he or she is prohibited from executing the contract. The contracting officer ensures that:

- Sufficient funds are available for the obligation.
- The price paid by the government is "fair and reasonable."
- The contractor receives impartial, fair, and equitable treatment.
- The contract meets the requirements of the applicable laws and regulations.

Certificate of Appointment

Under authority vested in the undersigned and in conformance with
Subpart 1.6 of the Federal Acquisition Regulation

Scott Stanberry

is appointed

Contracting Officer

for the

United States of America

Subject to the limitations contained in the Federal Acquisition Regulation and to the following:

Unless sooner terminated, this appointment is effective as long as the appointee is assigned to:

Contracts Division
(Organization)
General Services Administration
(Agency/Department)

(Signature and Title)
Head of Contracting Activity

NSN7540-01-152-5815
1402-101

10/15/08
(Date)

GSA-115
(No.)

STANDARD FORM 1402 (10-83)
Prescribed by GSA
FAR (48 CFR). 53.201-1

Example Certificate of Appointment

Because the contracting officer is the only government official with this responsibility, he or she is always under intense scrutiny from both contractors and government personnel. The Federal Acquisition Regulation is written specifically for the contracting officer, and it offers hundreds of options to consider. The contracting officer often requests the help of specialists in auditing, law, engineering, and other fields when making determinations.

Principal Contracting Officer or Procuring Contracting Officer

The principal, or procuring, contracting officer (PCO) is the individual responsible for issuing solicitations, accepting bids and proposals, and making the original award of the contract. If you have a problem with a solicitation before award, the PCO is the person to call.

By law, the PCO's name and phone number must appear on the cover of the solicitation and in the FedBizOpps synopsis. (FedBizOpps is where government buyers publicize their business opportunities on the Internet; see Chapter 8).

Depending on the situation, after the contract award is made, the PCO may delegate some contract management duties to the following specialists.

Administrative Contracting Officer

The PCO may delegate administrative responsibility for your contract to the administrative contracting officer (ACO). These functions typically include monitoring the contractor's performance, inspecting and accepting the contractor's supplies and services, and ensuring that the contractor is properly paid.

Administrative contracting officers are stationed around the country to keep a close eye on contractor performance. This practice allows the contracting officer to concentrate on awarding new contracts. The contracting officer still has the final authority on issues that have a significant impact on the contract.

Contracting Officer's Representative

Most federal agencies allow the contracting officer to appoint contracting officer's representatives (CORs) or contracting officer's technical representatives (COTRs). They assist the contracting officer in ensuring that the contractor's performance proceeds in accordance with the terms and conditions of the contract, especially on contracts for services. Typically, the COR will provide technical advice and guidance regarding the contract's specifications and statements of work.

The COR also keeps the contracting officer updated on the contract's status or progress by performing inspections and quality assurance functions. These functions include updating the contracting officer on any unusual circumstances, such as security violations, and monitoring metrics, such as whether the contractor has assigned adequate personnel to perform the contract's requirements.

The contracting officer appoints a COR to a contract in writing. This appointment letter must state the COR's duties and authority, along with any limitations placed on that authority. Only the contracting officer handles any changes involving unit cost, total price, quantity, or delivery schedules.

Normally only one COR is assigned to a contract, together with one alternate who can act only in his or her absence. One exception to this general rule is when there are large tasks awarded on a task order (indefinite delivery contract for services) contract. In that case, some agencies may appoint CORs for individual tasks.

In addition to the COR, other persons may be assigned to assist the contracting officer during the contract administration phase. These include quality assurance personnel, government property administrators, and others.

Termination Contracting Officer

For companies contracting with the government, the possibility that the contract may be terminated is a fact of life. In cases where a contract is terminated for the government's convenience or because of a contractor's default, a termination contracting officer (TCO) is typically used. FAR Part 49 contains the uniform policies and procedures on contract terminations.

In the event of a contract termination, the settlement process may be turned over to the TCO. A settlement proposal details the charges (or expenses) a contractor is seeking as reimbursement for work done to date. Once the contractor completes the settlement proposal, the TCO (with the help of government auditors) examines the proposal to verify its accuracy. When the TCO is satisfied with the settlement proposal, he or she signs the agreement and binds the government. The TCO may approve the settlement proposal without the contracting officer's approval.

COMPETITION ADVOCATES

The Competition in Contracting Act of 1984 requires each federal agency to appoint a competition advocate, who is responsible for promoting full and open competition. Competition advocates do this by challenging barriers to competition, such as restrictive statements of work, unnecessarily detailed specifications, and burdensome contract clauses.

Competition advocates also review the agency's contracting operations to ensure that appropriate actions are being taken to encourage competition and the acquisition of commercial items. For example, a competition advocate might examine solicitations expected to exceed $150,000 that are being conducted without full and open competition. The agency's senior procurement executive then reviews the findings.

The competition advocate is a member of the agency's executive staff. However, the competition advocate may hold no duties or responsibilities that would conflict with his or her primary responsibilities.

Competition advocates are always looking for ways to increase competition. If you find that a solicitation contains unnecessary restrictions, contact the contracting officer listed on the cover page. If you are not satisfied with the contracting officer's response, contact the competition advocate.

SMALL BUSINESS SPECIALISTS

Often, a small business's first government contract is the hardest one to get. For this reason, it is extremely important for small business owners to cultivate relationships with federal agencies in their area(s) of expertise. One of the best resources to gain this access is the Office of Small and Disadvantaged Business Utilization, or OSDBU. Each major federal agency and department has an OSDBU with at least one small business specialist. Within DoD, these offices are known as the Office of Small Business Programs (OSBP).

Small business specialists, also referred to as small and disadvantaged business utilization specialists (SADBUS), assist and counsel businesses on acquisition regulations and practices, finding buying offices for their supplies or services, and acquiring data on current or future procurements. They also ensure that their departments or contracting activities award a fair portion of their contracts to small businesses.

For instance, small business specialists review purchase transactions over the simplified acquisition threshold of $150,000 to determine whether they can be performed by a small business. If such purchase transactions are identified, the specialist may recommend to the contracting officer that the purchase be set aside for small businesses. Finally, a small business specialist can introduce you to the actual customer (or contracting personnel) who will purchase your supplies and services.

Small business specialists are an invaluable resource. For a current list of small and disadvantaged business utilization offices, visit www.osdbu.gov. For DoD small business programs, go to www.acq.osd.mil/osbp.

The Government Printing Office also has a publication called *Small Business Specialists*, which lists DoD small and disadvantaged business programs by state, including their addresses, phone numbers, and contacts. For information about this publication, contact:

Superintendent of Documents
Government Printing Office
Washington, DC 20402-9371
Phone (202) 512-1800

REQUIREMENTS PERSONNEL

As the term implies, requirements personnel, or end users, are the government employees responsible for determining which supplies and services a federal agency needs to run its operations. However, there is no universal title for these persons. The FAR encourages information exchanges among interested parties from the earliest identification of a requirement through receipt of proposals.

The following example should help clarify which government personnel would be considered requirements personnel. The Defense Advanced Research Projects Agency (DARPA) contracting activity must submit an annual budget for the items it will need to run its research projects. (DARPA is the central research and development organization for DoD.)

DARPA requires two separate groups to prepare budget requests. The first group consists of the agency's program managers (or head scientists), who prepare budgets for the supplies and services they will need to run their research projects during the upcoming fiscal year. The second group consists of the agency's logistics managers, who prepare budgets and make purchases for commonly used items like pens, computers, and office furniture.

Completed budgets are then submitted to the comptroller or equivalent person for approval. Once approved, they are sent to DARPA's budget office, where they are grouped together with the budgets of other buying offices to establish the total budget of the contracting activity.

In this example, there are two types of requirements personnel: program managers (or head scientists) and logistics managers. If you want to market your products or services to DARPA, you need to find out which program and logistics managers typically purchase your products. The best way to get in touch with a contracting activity's requirements personnel is to have the agency's or department's small business specialist set up an appointment for you.

When prospective contractors contact requirements personnel directly, it allows both parties to gain valuable information about each other. The requirements personnel find out which supplies and services are available to fulfill their needs. The contractor discovers the types of items the contracting activity typically purchases.

Meeting with an agency's requirements personnel is a great way to learn about a contracting activity's current and future needs. I can't think of a better way to get an insider edge on your competition than developing relationships with requirements personnel. Just as important: once an end user trusts your products and services, the chances for repeat business drastically increase.

■ ■ ■

These key players are not the only government personnel you will run into; they're just the ones who seem to pop up most frequently. The trick to being a successful contractor is to know who the key players are and to focus your attention and efforts on them. Pre-selling before a solicitation is announced publicly is not only allowed, it's encouraged!

■ ■ ■

How Your Business Size Offers Opportunity

Nobody puts Baby in a corner.

—Johnny Castle (played by Patrick Swayze)

By now you know that the federal government has an enormous impact on business. But are you aware that the government provides a variety of programs and services to assist small businesses, including technical, management, and financial assistance? In fact, the policy of the U.S. government is to give small businesses the maximum practical opportunity to participate in federal contracting. Congress has enacted numerous laws and regulations that promote the participation of small businesses in the federal contracting process.

What's more, mid-size to large companies can benefit from these small business programs by providing subcontracting opportunities to businesses that meet the government's criteria on their contracts.

Opportunities for Small Businesses/Independent Contractors

"We're the only company in the world that sells organic cookies made with goat urine, but the government isn't trying to break up *our* monopoly."

What's in this chapter?

- Small Business Act of 1953
- Government-wide goals
- North American Industry Classification System
- Size certification
- Small business affiliates
- Certificate of Competency
- Small business set-asides

Everyone knows that there is a big size difference between a major corporation like Microsoft and the mom-and-pop convenience store on your street corner. But how do you determine your actual business size? Is yours a small business? And if so, what happens when your business grows? When does your business cease to be small? These are very important questions because many of the government's programs and services are specifically targeted toward small businesses.

When competing in the federal marketplace, small businesses, especially certified small businesses, often operate with certain advantages.

Did You Know That . . .

According to the Small Business Administration (see www.sba.gov):

- There are more than 27.5 million small businesses operating in the United States?
- Small firms produce 16.5 times more patents per employee than large patenting firms?
- Business ownership is becoming more inclusive in the United States, with gains in ownership by women and minorities?
- During FY 2011, the government issued more than $100 billion worth of federal contracts to small businesses?

Small Businesses . . .

- Create nearly three out of every four new jobs
- Produce 51% of the gross national product
- Provide 55% of innovations
- Account for 53% of private-sector output
- Represent 96% of all U.S. exporters
- Account for 43% of new high-technology jobs
- Make 47% of all sales in the country
- Employ 51% of the private workforce
- Provide 67% of workers with their first jobs.

As you can see, the federal government offers tremendous opportunities for people looking to start new businesses or increase the size of their existing businesses. This chapter will help you determine your business size and discuss some of the advantages of being a small business.

SMALL BUSINESS ACT OF 1953

In the middle of the twentieth century, the government began to recognize that it had a problem with its procurement process. It seemed that a few large companies dominated some industries almost to the point of monopolization, and smaller companies were unable to compete for federal contracts. As a result, Congress passed the Small Business Act of 1953.

The Small Business Act requires the government to award a "fair proportion" of its federal contracts to small businesses. It also requires the government to provide small and small disadvantaged businesses with the maximum practical opportunity to participate in federal contracting. To help ensure these requirements are met, the act established the Small Business Administration (SBA).

GOVERNMENT-WIDE GOALS

Congress establishes government-wide goals for awards of federal contracts and subcontracts to small businesses. These goals are typically stated as percentages of the procurement dollars spent by the government each year. (See www.sba.gov for more details.)

Congress designated the following government-wide goals for FY 2012: 23 percent of all federal contracts should go to small businesses, 5 percent to small disadvantaged businesses (SDBs), 5 percent to small women-owned businesses (WOBs), 3 percent to small HUBZone businesses, and 3 percent to small service-disabled veteran-owned businesses (SDVOSB). Contract awards to small disadvantaged, women-owned, HUBZone, and service-disabled veteran-owned businesses each count toward the 23 percent goal for all small businesses.

SBA negotiates with each federal agency to determine an estimate for contract awards to small businesses. These estimates might be higher or lower than the government-wide goals, depending on the types of supplies and services being purchased. For example, a federal agency with a $40 million annual procurement budget might have the following agency goals:

Awards to SDBs	6%	x	$40,000,000 =	$2,400,000
Awards to small WOBs	4%	x	$40,000,000 =	$1,600,000
				$4,000,000
Awards to small businesses	15%	x	$40,000,000 =	$6,000,000
Total small business awards	**25%**			**$10,000,000**

SBA then compares each agency's estimates against its actual results to determine its success in meeting its goals. Federal agencies pay close attention to these results because they are given to Congress for review.

Agency goals provide two primary advantages for small businesses. First, they ensure that each federal agency has plans for awarding federal contracts to small businesses. Second, the goals give federal agencies a baseline against which to measure their progress yearly. If, six months into the year, a federal agency notices that it has awarded only 2 percent of its contracts to small disadvantaged businesses, government policy mandates that it concentrate on awarding contracts to SDBs over the next six months.

NORTH AMERICAN INDUSTRY CLASSIFICATION SYSTEM

SBA has taken the lead in defining what constitutes a small business in the eyes of the federal government. It issues a body of definitions called *size standards*, classified on an industry-by-industry basis. Size standards are generally defined by number of employees, average annual sales, or total electric output (for utility firms).

Small business size standards are also used for determining eligibility for various federal programs and services, such as financial assistance loans, 8(a) program participation, and participation in the Small Business Innovation Research (SBIR) program. See Chapter 5 for more details on these programs.

The North American Industry Classification System (NAICS, pronounced "nakes") is used to identify the various types of industries and establishments. On April 9, 1997, NAICS officially replaced the U.S. Standard Industrial Classification (SIC) system.

Why Switch from SIC to NAICS?

For more than 60 years, the SIC system served as the structure for collecting, aggregating, presenting, and analyzing data on the U.S. economy. It was developed in the 1930s, at a time when manufacturing dominated the U.S. economic scene. However, today's services-centered economy has rendered the SIC system obsolete because the system often fails to adequately account for new and emerging service industries.

Enter NAICS! NAICS focuses on how products and services are created, as opposed to the SIC system, which focuses on what is produced. This process-oriented classification methodology yields industrial groupings that are more homogenous and thus better suited for economic analysis.

NAICS groups the economy into 20 broad sectors:

<table>
<tr><th>Code</th><th>NAICS Sectors</th><th>Previous SIC Divisions</th></tr>
<tr><td>11</td><td>Agriculture, Forestry, and Fishing</td><td>Agriculture, Forestry, and Fishing</td></tr>
<tr><td>21</td><td>Mining</td><td>Mining</td></tr>
<tr><td>23</td><td>Construction</td><td>Construction</td></tr>
<tr><td>31-33</td><td>Manufacturing</td><td>Manufacturing</td></tr>
<tr><td>22</td><td>Utilities</td><td rowspan="2">Transportation, Communications, and Public Utilities</td></tr>
<tr><td>48-49</td><td>Transportation and Warehousing</td></tr>
<tr><td>42</td><td>Wholesale Trade</td><td>Wholesale Trade</td></tr>
<tr><td>44-45</td><td>Retail Trade</td><td rowspan="2">Retail Trade</td></tr>
<tr><td>72</td><td>Accommodation and Food Services</td></tr>
</table>

Code	NAICS Sectors	Previous SIC Divisions
52	Finance and Insurance	Finance, Insurance, and Real Estate
53	Real Estate and Rental and Leasing	
51	Information	Services
54	Professional, Scientific, and Technical Services	
56	Administrative Support/Waste Management Services	
61	Educational Services	
62	Health Care and Social Assistance	
71	Arts, Entertainment, and Recreation	
81	Other Services	
92	Public Administration	Public Administration
55	Management of Companies	(Parts of all divisions)

The shift to NAICS means a break in the historical time series. FedBizOpps is therefore retrievable under both the old SIC methodology (before April 9, 1997) and under NAICS (after April 9, 1997).

NAICS industries are identified by a six-digit code:

XX	Industry Sector (31–33 = Manufacturing)
XXX	Industry Subsector (321 = Wood Product Manufacturing)
XXXX	Industry Group (3219 = Other Wood Product Manufacturing)
XXXXX	Industry (32191 = Millwork)
XXXXXX	Country–U.S., Canadian, Mexican (321911 = Wood Window/ Door Manufacturing)

The NAICS coding system was developed to focus on the identification of high technology and new and emerging industries. Currently, NAICS has identified more than 350 new industries, including pet supply stores, casinos, interior design services, convenience stores, and HMO medical centers.

Visit www.census.gov/eos/www/naics/ for more information on NAICS codes.

Is Your Business "Small" Enough? (SBA Size Standards)

As a general rule, for businesses that regularly deal in products (e.g., manufacturing or wholesaling), the size standard is based on the average number of employees. A computer wholesaler, for example, is considered a small business if it has fewer than 500 employees averaged over a 12-month period. An aircraft manufacturer, NAICS code 336411, has a small business size standard of 1,500 employees.

On the other hand, if you're in a service industry, your company's average annual sales usually determine its size. An accounting firm, for instance, is considered a small business if it has less than $19 million in average gross revenue. A company providing engineering services on military equipment (NAICS code 541330_a) has a small business size standard of $35.5 million. Companies with multiple business lines may, in certain circumstances, qualify as small businesses when proposing for a particular requirement.

You probably think that these classifications are too high for most small businesses—and you're probably right. The government's aim is to let small businesses grow into thriving medium-sized businesses before taking away the small business benefits or perks. The government wants to make sure that a small business is self-sufficient before it graduates from the small business program.

You can match your NAICS code(s) with the table of small business size standards at www.sba.gov/size/, or contact:

Small Business Administration
Size Standard Division
(202) 205-6618
sizestandards@sba.gov

Suppose SBA is issuing a small business solicitation for construction services, and you want to determine whether your firm is eligible to bid. As a general construction contractor, your NAICS code is 236210:

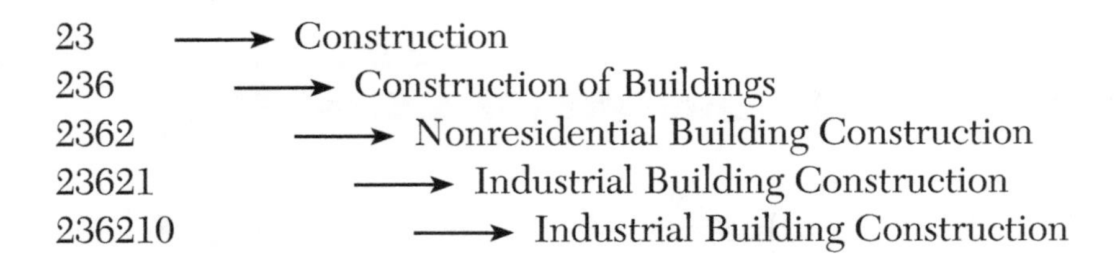

23 → Construction
236 → Construction of Buildings
2362 → Nonresidential Building Construction
23621 → Industrial Building Construction
236210 → Industrial Building Construction

A quick check of SBA's size standards table by NAICS code (www.sba.gov/size/) shows any company that is independently owned and operated with $33.5 million or less in average revenues could submit a bid or proposal.

SBA makes these size determinations annually, so be sure to check back often enough to ensure that you fit the size standard for your NAICS code.

Know Your NAICS Codes!

The government certainly likes to assign seemingly random numbers to everything. In the federal contracting landscape, however, NAICS codes are how buying offices determine what your company does and if they have a need for your particular products or services. One misplaced digit and your company could go from plumbing to event catering! Also, there are NAICS codes that qualify your business for various set-asides or preference programs.

Not only do most federal agencies list their procurement needs according to NAICS code, but contracting activities rely heavily on them when searching government databases. And even though you are required to enter only one valid code when you register, be sure to list *all* the codes that apply to your supplies and services. Do your homework. Firms that have not done a thorough job identifying all of the NAICS codes that apply to their business will often find themselves on the outside looking in when it comes to finding government contracting opportunities.

You may need to experiment a little, because not every business can be pigeonholed into a single NAICS category. In fact, for newer industries, a specific NAICS code may not even exist, which means you'll have to use your judgment and find codes similar to what your business does. But be careful not to go overboard: stick to the primary products and services your company offers.

SIZE CERTIFICATION

In most cases, a contractor self-certifies that it is a small business. It is the responsibility of the contracting officer to accept this certification or request that SBA formally determine the company's size. Competitors for a particular solicitation may also compel the contracting officer to make a formal size determination by submitting a timely protest. (A protest is a written objection by an interested party to a solicitation, proposed award, or award of a contract.)

A competitor may protest an award to a small business on several grounds. For example, a protest may arise if the winning business:

- Is affiliated with or controlled by a large business
- Has an agreement with a large business to be purchased
- Is actually a large business, based on proper consideration of the time period and methodology for measuring annual receipts
- Will not be materially participating (that is, performing at least 50 percent of the work) in the contract performance.

Note that if a company's owners intentionally misrepresent the company's size when bidding on a federal procurement, it might be subject to fines.

Protests must be submitted to the contracting officer within five working days of notification of the winner or ten working days of being notified of the competitive range. If the protest is not made in that period, SBA's findings will apply only to future purchases.

SMALL BUSINESS AFFILIATES

The most significant stumbling block for determining whether you qualify as a small business is your affiliations. Business concerns, organizations, or individuals are considered affiliates of each other, directly or indirectly, if either one has the power to control the other, or if a third party controls or has the power to control both.

Affiliates must combine their respective incomes and employees when determining their status as a small or large business. SBA's rule for affiliation is that "size determinations shall include the applicant concern and all its domestic and foreign affiliates."

Most business owners think of affiliates as divisions or subsidiaries, but SBA looks at an affiliation in terms of substance rather than mere form. SBA looks at who has the control. If a company can directly or indirectly control (or has the power to control) another company, the two are considered affiliates, and SBA treats them as one company. Whether the controlling company actually exercises its power is of no consequence as long as the ability to control is present.

CERTIFICATE OF COMPETENCY

SBA also manages the Certificate of Competency (COC) program. This program's primary purpose is to assist small businesses in obtaining federal contracts for which they were determined to be the lowest responsive and responsible bidder when the award decision was based on price alone. If your business is the low bidder on a federal contract and the contracting officer questions your ability to perform the contract, you may apply to SBA for a COC.

Here's how the program works:

1. Upon determining and documenting that an apparently successful small business lacks certain elements of responsibility, the contracting officer withholds the contract award for a period of 15 business days. Elements of responsibility include, but are not limited to, capability, competency, credit, and integrity. The documented areas of nonresponsibility are then referred to the appropriate SBA regional office.
2. SBA informs the small business that it has been determined nonresponsible and offers the business an opportunity to apply for a COC.
3. Once SBA receives an acceptable COC application, an authorized SBA representative visits the small business and reviews the areas of nonresponsibility cited. SBA also performs an onsite survey of the firm's facilities,

management, performance record, and production capacity in relationship to the contract in question. The SBA representative then sends his or her findings to the SBA regional director.

4. The regional director decides whether to issue a COC.
5. If the regional director decides to issue a COC, the contracting officer usually awards the contract to the small business. (The regional director's decision may not be appealed if the award is valued at $150,000 or less.) If the contracting officer disagrees with the determination, he or she appeals the case to SBA headquarters in Washington, D.C.

SMALL BUSINESS SET-ASIDES

All simplified acquisitions, other than micropurchases, are by law set aside for small business and may be awarded to a large business only if a small business cannot provide the supply or service at a reasonable price (see Chapter 10). Set-asides ensure that a fair proportion of the government's procurements go to small and small disadvantaged business concerns. All solicitations involving set-asides must specify the applicable small business size standard and product classification.

The contracting officer is responsible for reviewing acquisitions to determine whether they can be set aside for small business. Small business set-asides may be conducted using simplified acquisition procedures, sealed bidding, or negotiated procurement procedures (see Part IV).

Rule of Two

The "rule of two" states that purchases (other than federal supply schedules purchases—see Chapter 7) with an anticipated dollar value exceeding $150,000 must be set aside exclusively for small business participation if there is a reasonable expectation that:

- Offers will be received from at least two responsible small business concerns.
- Awards will be made at fair market prices.

If the contracting officer receives no acceptable offers, the set-aside requirement may be withdrawn and the procurement resolicited on an unrestricted basis.

When you see a FedBizOpps synopsis released for market research purposes, it is most often being done to establish a basis for determining if the acquisition is legitimately a sole-source procurement or if the acquisition should be set aside for small businesses. However, when applied literally, it can be a straitjacket to an acquisition official who wants to consider large businesses in the procurement process.

Also, where the "rule of two" applies to more than one business category, the FAR provides an equal preference for competitive HUBZone, 8(a), and service-disabled veteran-owned small business (SDVOSB) set-asides over small business set-asides alone. (See Chapter 5 for a detailed discussion of these set-aside programs.)

Set-Asides vs. Simplified Acquisition Procedures

Don't confuse small business set-asides with simplified acquisition procedures (see Chapter 10). The main difference between them is that set-asides typically are used for purchases greater than $150,000. The following example should clarify this difference.

Suppose a major computer manufacturer and a regular dealer work together to sell computers to the government. The manufacturer is considered a large business and the regular dealer a small business. A firm qualifies as a regular dealer if:

- It regularly maintains a stock of products (computers, in this case) for which it claims to be a dealer.
- The stock maintained is true inventory from which sales are made.
- Sales to the public are made regularly in the usual course of business.
- Sales are made regularly from stock on a recurring basis.
- The business is established and ongoing.

Now, let's assume the contracting officer plans to make two separate purchases using small business set-aside procedures. The first purchase is for 35 computers with an anticipated value of $124,000. This purchase would fall under simplified acquisition procedures because it's less than $150,000. Under these procedures, a small-business regular dealer may furnish any domestically manufactured products, regardless of the manufacturing company's size. In this example, then, the regular dealer would be eligible for this solicitation.

The second purchase is for 40 LaserJet printers with an anticipated value of $238,000. When a small business set-aside is greater than the simplified acquisition threshold, the regular dealer and the manufacturer must both qualify as small businesses. The regular dealer, therefore, would not be eligible for the solicitation because the manufacturer is a large business.

Partial Set-Asides

Partial set-asides enable the contracting officer to set aside a portion of a contract for small businesses. They may be used when:

- A total set-aside is not appropriate. (Suppose the Defense Advanced Research Projects Agency has issued a research and development (R&D) contract to study the atmosphere on Mars. Because this contract requires sophisticated equipment, it cannot be performed exclusively by a small business. Therefore, the contracting officer decides to set aside the reporting requirements of the study for a small business.)
- The procurement can be split into two or more economic production runs.
- One or more small business concerns are expected to have the technical competence and production capacity to satisfy the set-aside portion of the requirement at a fair market price.
- More than one large and one small business are expected to submit bids or proposals.

To set aside a portion of an acquisition, the contracting officer divides the requirement into a set-aside portion and a non-set-aside portion. The non-set-aside portion is awarded using normal contracting procedures.

To be eligible for the set-aside portion of the procurement, a small business must submit its bid and proposal at the time bids and proposals for the non-set-aside portion are due. Once all the awards have been made on the non-set-aside portion, the contracting officer negotiates the set-aside portion with the eligible small business concerns. The small business that submits the lowest responsive bid or proposal is awarded the contract. Partial set-asides may be conducted using sealed bidding or negotiated procedures.

Class Set-Asides

A class set-aside is the reservation of particular classes of products and services for small businesses to provide. For example, a buying office might decide to create a class set-aside for foodstuffs. Accordingly, if a particular buying office set up a class set-aside to provide Oreo cookies, only small businesses would be eligible to bid.

■ ■ ■

The Small Business Act requires the government to award a fair share of its contracts to small businesses. Therefore, to take advantage of those opportunities, you must ensure that your business size standard accurately reflects your company's business size. For more detailed information on small business size standards, size status, and size protests, visit www.sba.gov/size or consult a size determination specialist in one of SBA's Offices of Government Contracting.

■ ■ ■

Small Business Preference Programs

"You and Steve were both qualified for the promotion, but Steve's shirts are whiter and brighter and smell springtime fresh."

What's in this chapter?

- Definition of small disadvantaged businesses
- Evaluation preference for SDBs
- 8(a) business development program
- Status of preference programs
- Women-owned small businesses
- Service-disabled veteran-owned small businesses
- Labor surplus area set-asides
- SBA HUBZone Empowerment Contracting Program
- Small Business Innovation Research program

The government encourages small business participation in the federal marketplace through a series of preference programs. The laudable goal of these programs is to level the playing field for disadvantaged businesses and help ensure every U.S. citizen has an opportunity to compete for federal contracts. This chapter details some of the more common preference programs available today.

DEFINITION OF SMALL DISADVANTAGED BUSINESSES

To qualify as a small disadvantaged business (SDB), a firm must be a small business that is at least 51 percent owned by persons belonging to a socially and economically disadvantaged group. Socially disadvantaged persons are those who have been subjected to racial or ethnic prejudice or cultural bias based on their identity as a member of a particular group. Disadvantaged groups include:

- Asian Americans
- Black Americans
- Hispanic Americans
- Native Americans.

Economically disadvantaged persons are those whose ability to compete in the free market system has been impaired as a result of diminished capital and credit opportunities, compared with others in the same or a similar line of business. In determining the degree of economic disadvantage affecting a person, the government considers:

- Personal financial condition of the disadvantaged individual. (Program participants must have a net worth of less than $750,000—some of us are more disadvantaged than others!)
- Business financial condition.
- Access to credit and capital.
- Comparisons with other companies in the same or a similar line of business.

Disabled persons are not presumed to be socially and economically disadvantaged. See FAR 19.001 for a more detailed definition of small disadvantaged business concerns.

EVALUATION PREFERENCE FOR SDBS

The Federal Acquisition Streamlining Act of 1994 allows federal agencies to use an "evaluation preference" when evaluating offers received from SDBs on unrestricted solicitations. This preference allows an SDB to receive a contract even if its bid or proposal is higher than that of its competitors, up to a limit of 10 percent of the proposed contract price. This helps federal agencies attain the government's goal of awarding 5 percent of its contract dollars to SDBs. Set-asides, however, are still subject to the rule of two (discussed in the previous chapter).

To be eligible for an evaluation preference, a contractor must submit a certification, obtained within the past three years, stating that one or more socially or economically disadvantaged persons own and control the business. Businesses owned by persons who are not members of the statutorily presumed groups can qualify as SDBs by submitting evidence demonstrating their social and economic disadvantage.

An evaluation preference may not be used if the acquisition is:

- 100 percent set aside for SDBs
- Partially or totally set aside for small businesses
- Made pursuant to the 8(a) program or the labor surplus area program (which are discussed later in this chapter)
- Under the simplified acquisition threshold of $150,000
- Under the U.S. Trade Agreement Act.

> It should be noted that SDB preferences do not apply to all federal agencies. See FAR 19.11 for further clarification.

This example should help clarify how the evaluation preference works. Let's assume the National Aeronautics and Space Administration (NASA) plans to award a contract that has an evaluation preference of 10 percent for SDBs. Two businesses, one of which is an SDB, are competing for the contract. The firms make the following bids:

Regular business bid	$475,000
SDB bid	$500,000

Assuming the contract will be awarded on price-related factors alone, which contractor do you think would win? Let's do the math.

Regular business bid	$475,000	
	× 10%	SDB evaluation adjustment
Evaluation adjustment	$47,500	

The evaluation preference adjustment gives the regular business the following bid price:

Regular business bid	$475,000
Evaluation adjustment	$47,500
Regular business bid (after adjustment)	$522,500
SDB bid	$500,000

In this example, the SDB would win the contract because its bid is $22,500 lower after adjustment than that of the regular business.

8(a) BUSINESS DEVELOPMENT PROGRAM

Certified small disadvantaged businesses (SDBs) may also qualify or be eligible for the 8(a) business development program. This program fosters business ownership by persons who are socially and economically disadvantaged. This is a major preference program, and it permits agencies to award (sole source) contracts directly to eligible small businesses. It is named for the section of the Small Business Act from which it derives its authority.

SBA is responsible for awarding these noncompetitive contracts to eligible program participants. Participants in the 8(a) program can receive sole-source contracts worth up to $4 million for goods and services and up to $6.5 million for manufacturing. More than 8,000 companies currently participate in the program.

8(a) Qualifications

Unfortunately, 8(a) certification is not for everyone; the eligibility requirements exclude all but the neediest businesses.

Step one in qualifying for the 8(a) program is for a firm to demonstrate that it is owned by socially or economically disadvantaged persons. A small business qualifies as socially and economically disadvantaged if it is at least 51 percent owned by one or more persons who are black, Hispanic, or Native American. Members of any other group may qualify for the 8(a) program by establishing social disadvantage based on a "preponderance of evidence."

Applicants to the 8(a) program must have been in operation for at least two full years, as evidenced by business tax returns that show operating revenues in the applicant's primary industry. Applicants can obtain a waiver from this two-year requirement if they meet the following five conditions:

- The person or persons upon whom eligibility is based have substantial business management experience.
- The applicant firm can demonstrate the technical expertise to carry out its business plan.
- The applicant firm has adequate capital to sustain its business operations.
- The applicant firm has a record of successful performance on contracts from governmental or nongovernmental sources in its primary industry.
- The applicant firm can demonstrate that it has the ability to obtain the personnel, facilities, and equipment needed to perform on the contracts, in a timely manner, if admitted to the 8(a) program.

Eligibility Constraints

The conditions governing the definition of socially and economically disadvantaged persons impose constraints on the way in which an 8(a) business organization is structured and operated. Transactions that are routinely permissible for non-8(a) companies could jeopardize an 8(a) contractor's continued program participation. If your enterprise is to maintain its program eligibility, you must be aware of these constraints.

If a business is organized as a corporation, it must comply with the unconditional ownership requirement, as evidenced by at least 51 percent ownership of each class of voting stock by socially and economically disadvantaged persons. The business must maintain this level of ownership throughout its participation in the program.

The 8(a) program can be a powerful tool for assisting disadvantaged persons and their companies in the federal marketplace. A thorough understanding of the program's qualifications and requirements can help contractors avoid situations that could jeopardize their continued program eligibility.

Program Participation and Duration

The overall goal of the 8(a) program is to help firms transition into thriving businesses in the competitive marketplace. Program participation is therefore divided into two stages: the developmental stage and the transitional stage.

The developmental stage lasts for four years and helps 8(a) firms overcome their economic disadvantage through business development assistance. During this stage, SBA wants participants to achieve the following objectives:

- Maintain an existing business base
- Develop and implement a business plan and marketing strategy to facilitate the achievement of non-8(a) revenues.

During the transitional stage, which lasts five years, participants prepare to leave the 8(a) program. SBA encourages contractors to increase their non-8(a) support levels during the transitional stage. For example, total non-8(a) revenue should reach the targets shown below.

Transitional Stage	Total Non-8(a) Revenue
Year	
1	15%–25%
2	25%–35%
3	35%–45%
4	45%–55%
5	55%–75%

If your company is to survive or prosper, you need to develop an exit strategy from the 8(a) program as soon as possible. That strategy might include developing a mix of government and commercial contracts and establishing long-term business partnerships with major prime contractors.

On an interesting note, an 8(a) firm in its, say, final (ninth) year of eligibility for preference can be awarded a contract lasting up to five years under this program. For contracts lasting longer than five years, an agency cannot claim credit toward its small business goals if, after the fifth year of the contract, the firm no longer qualifies for 8(a) status even though the contract may still remain in effect.

Here's an example of how the 8(a) business development program works. Typically, three parties are involved in the process:

- The federal agency that awards the contract
- SBA, which receives the contract (the party that receives the contract is referred to as the *prime contractor*)
- The 8(a) firm that performs the contract (in this scenario, the 8(a) firm would be considered the subcontractor).

Suppose that the General Services Administration (GSA) plans to award a contract for security services. The contract is for two years at an estimated contract value of $2 million per year. After reviewing the plans for the job, the contracting officer decides it would be perfect for an 8(a) firm and contacts SBA. To help meet their agencies' goals, contracting officers are always on the lookout for 8(a) opportunities.

SBA then looks for qualified 8(a) firms to perform the contract. Several 8(a) firms are selected and told to submit competitive bids or proposals for the work. The contract is then awarded to the 8(a) firm with the lowest offer, without any negotiations.

Once SBA selects a qualified 8(a) firm to perform the contract, the firm negotiates a price for the contract with the contracting officer. When the parties agree, the contracting officer mails the solicitation to the 8(a) firm and awards the contract to SBA. SBA then awards a subcontract to the 8(a) firm, and the 8(a) firm begins the work.

During contract performance, the 8(a) firm deals directly with the federal agency that awarded the contract. Payments are also made directly from the federal agency to the 8(a) firm.

Nowadays, many federal agencies, under an agreement with SBA, award contracts directly to 8(a) firms. Also, 8(a) firms can, and very often do, get agencies to go directly to the SBA and request authorization to make an award to them. Why might agencies do this? Because if they're comfortable with the 8(a) firm, they can avoid going through a lengthy competitive process and can negotiate a contract directly with the firm.

Other Assistance

Financial assistance in the form of loans and advance payments is available to 8(a) program participants. SBA also offers a wide range of management assistance, including counseling and seminars.

Reporting Requirements

SBA annually reviews 8(a) firms for compliance with eligibility requirements. As part of the annual review, each participant firm submits the following items:

- Certification that the company meets the 8(a) program eligibility requirements
- Certification that no changes that could adversely affect the participant's program eligibility have been made
- Personal financial information for each disadvantaged owner

- Record of all payments, compensation, and distributions (including loans, advances, salaries, and dividends) made by the company to each of its owners, officers, and directors, or to any person or entity affiliated with such individuals
- IRS Form 4506, Request for Copy or Transcript of Tax Form
- Other information SBA deems necessary.

If a participant fails to provide this information for the annual review, SBA may initiate termination proceedings.

How to Apply for 8(a) Status

Any individual or business has the right to apply for section 8(a) assistance, regardless of whether it appears to be eligible. To get an application, contact:

SBA Answer Desk
(800) U-ASK-SBA (800-827-5722)
www.sba.gov

Once you complete your application, you will need to file it at the SBA field office that serves your company's principal place of business. (SBA has more than 100 field offices.) Your principal place of business is the location of your books and records and the office at which the people who manage the company's day-to-day operations work.

Once your application has been submitted, the regional Division of Program Certification and Eligibility (DPCE) has 15 days to review it for completeness. If the application is incomplete, you will have 15 days to provide the additional information and resubmit it. If DPCE determines the application is complete, SBA will make a final decision regarding your 8(a) program eligibility within 90 days.

If your application is rejected, you may request that SBA reconsider it. During the reconsideration process, you may submit additional or revised information. If your application is declined after reconsideration, you must wait a year from the date of reconsideration to submit a new application.

How Do the SDB Program and 8(a) Program Differ?

The purpose of the SDB program is to encourage minority-owned businesses, including contractors that graduated from the 8(a) program, to seek federal contracts. The SDB program, therefore, provides an alternative to SBA's 8(a) program for small minority-owned businesses seeking to participate in the economic mainstream. Here are the primary characteristics that differentiate the two programs:

The eligibility requirements for the SDB program are less stringent than those for the 8(a) program.

An SDB may self-certify that it meets the definition of an SDB, whereas an 8(a) firm must be certified by SBA to receive an 8(a) contract.

STATUS OF PREFERENCE PROGRAMS

Preference (or affirmative action) programs are always under intense scrutiny and change with the nation's mood or political climate. Are they fair? Do they do enough to help disadvantaged U.S. citizens? Are they constitutional? Is there a way to make everyone happy? What does the future hold for these preference programs?

These are some questions that affirmative action programs evoke, and unfortunately there really isn't a definitive answer to any of them. However, if there is any indication of what the future holds for these preference programs, it would have to be the Supreme Court case of *Adarand Constructors, Inc. v. Pena*.

On June 12, 1995, the Supreme Court made a decision that had a profound impact on affirmative action programs. The case of *Adarand Constructors, Inc. v. Pena* involved a Department of Transportation (DOT) contract clause that rewarded the prime contractor on the job for exceeding an SDB subcontracting goal. The contract clause stated the following:

> Monetary compensation is offered for awarding subcontracts to small business concerns owned and controlled by socially and economically disadvantaged individuals. . . . Compensation is provided to the Contractor to locate, train, utilize, assist, and develop SDBs to become fully qualified contractors in the transportation facilities construction field. The contractor shall also provide direct assistance to disadvantaged subcontractors in acquiring the necessary bonding, obtaining price quotations, analyzing

> plans and specifications, and planning and management of the work. . . . The Contractor will become eligible to receive payment under this provision when the dollar amount . . . of the DBE subcontract(s) awarded exceeds [10% for Colorado] of the original [prime] contract award.

In other words, the government would pay a prime contractor a 1.5 percent bonus if it awarded more than 10 percent of its subcontracts to SDBs.

Adarand Constructors, Inc. (owned by a white male) submitted the low bid for a guardrail subcontract. The prime contractor (Mountain Gravel) awarded the guardrail subcontract to the second lowest bidder, a certified SDB, to collect the contract bonus. Adarand filed suit against the government, claiming that it had violated the 14th Amendment of the Constitution, which guarantees "every citizen equal protection under the law."

Adarand claimed that because the contract was awarded on class-based, noncompetitive grounds, the company did not receive equal protection under the law. All the lower courts ruled against Adarand's lawsuit, and the case was sent to the Supreme Court. The Supreme Court found DOT's subcontractor clause to be neither constitutional nor unconstitutional. Rather, it used the case to set a standard of review that courts must follow when evaluating such preferences.

The Supreme Court altered the playing field in some important respects, holding that "all racial classifications, imposed by whatever federal, state, or local governmental actor, must be analyzed by a reviewing court under strict scrutiny." In other words, preferences or programs based on racial classifications are constitutional only if they are narrowly tailored measures that further compelling governmental interests.

Although the Supreme Court raised the bar that affirmative action programs must clear, the strict scrutiny standard does not necessarily spell the end of preference programs. Seven justices expressed continued support for affirmative action, and the Supreme Court emphasized that the government is not disqualified from acting in response to the lingering effects of racial discrimination. The SBA interprets these guidelines by limiting the preferences offered to SDBs bidding in industries that show the ongoing effects of discrimination.

WOMEN-OWNED SMALL BUSINESSES

Not only are women-owned small businesses (WOSBs) growing in number, range, diversity, and earning power, but they're also outpacing male-owned firms in job creation. Here are a few incredible statistics SBA has gathered on women business owners:

- Women create new businesses and new jobs at nearly twice the national rate. Seventy-five percent of new businesses started by women succeed, compared to only 25 percent of those started by men.
- About a third of all businesses are now owned by women.
- Over the past 20 years, the number of women-owned businesses has nearly doubled.

Clearly, women are changing the face of America's businesses as they contribute to the growth of our national economy. However, despite this growth, women-owned small businesses still employ only 6 percent of the U.S. workforce and continue to be underrepresented in the federal contracting marketplace.

To help remedy this situation, the SBA launched the Women-Owned Small Business (WOSB) Program and Economically Disadvantaged Women-Owned Small Business (EDWOSB) Program. The EDWOSB program is also known as the 8(m) program, in honor of the authorizing legislation.

Effective February 2011, contracting officers were officially authorized to set aside solicitations in underrepresented industries for competition solely amongst women-owned small businesses to help achieve the statutory goal of awarding 5 percent of all federal contracts to women-owned small businesses.

In FY 2011, the government awarded well over $500 billion in federal contracts. Federal agencies were therefore under the gun to award more than $26 billion in contracting dollars to women-led companies. (Ladies, please understand government agencies need your help, and we're talking serious dollars!)

Eligible businesses must meet three types of requirements:

1. **Size:** WOSBs must meet SBA's small business size standards.

2. **Ownership:** WOSBs must be at least 51 percent directly or unconditionally owned by one or more women who are U.S. citizens.
3. **Management:** WOSBs must have a woman manage the day-to-day operations.

To be an eligible EDWOSB, a company must:

- Be a WOSB that is at least 51 percent owned by one or more American women who are "economically disadvantaged." (A woman is generally presumed economically disadvantaged if she has a personal net worth of less than $750,000.)
- Have an economically disadvantaged woman manage the day-to-day operations of the small business.

The program specifically identifies 83 industries (by NAICS code) where women-owned small businesses are "underrepresented" or "substantially underrepresented" in federal contracting. EDWOSBs will have access to set-asides in both the underrepresented and substantially underrepresented categories, while WOSBs will have access to set-asides in just the substantially underrepresented category.

Also, EDWOSBs qualify for all three business categories: small business, small disadvantaged business, and small women-owned business. Federal agencies look for firms with this particular combination because contracts awarded to such firms can be applied to all of their small business goals.

For more information on SBA's programs for women-owned small businesses, visit www.sba.gov/content/contracting-opportunities-women-owned-small-businesses.

SERVICE-DISABLED VETERAN-OWNED SMALL BUSINESSES

If you are a veteran or a service-disabled veteran, the federal government is committed to providing you the maximum practicable opportunity to compete for federal contracts. In fact, the central feature of Executive Order 13360 calls for all federal agencies to develop a strategic plan to significantly increase their contracting and subcontracting with small businesses owned and controlled by veterans and service-disabled veterans. It also directs a government-wide goal of awarding 3 percent of all federal contracts to small businesses owned by service-disabled veteran-owned small businesses (SDVOSB).

To be eligible for this set-aside program, a SDVOSB concern must meet the following criteria:

- The service-disabled veteran (SDV) must have a service-connected disability that has been confirmed by the Department of Veterans Affairs or the Department of Defense.
- The SDV must unconditionally own 51 percent of the small business concern.
- The SDV must control the management and daily operations of the small business.
- The SDV must hold the highest officer position in the small business.

There are roughly 5 million veteran-owned businesses (VOBs) and approximately 500,000 SDVOSBs in the United States.

Federal agencies have had a difficult time meeting their goals in contracting with SDVOSBs. This has been due in large part to the lack of identified SDVOSBs in the marketplace.

SBA and the Office of Veterans Business Development are required to track and annually publish the percentage of federal procurement awards to veteran and service-disabled veteran businesses. This helps focus procurement activities on veterans and service-disabled veterans as a special group. Also, all veteran and service-disabled businesses are required to register with the Center for Veterans Enterprise at www.vetbiz.gov.

LABOR SURPLUS AREA SET-ASIDES

The Labor Surplus Area Program restricts competition to businesses that agree to perform most (at least half) of the contract work in areas that have higher than average unemployment, even if their headquarters are not located in the designated areas. This program directs government contract dollars into areas of severe economic need.

Labor surplus area set-asides are applied only when enough qualified businesses are expected to bid, so that SBA can award contracts at fair and reasonable prices. The government also encourages contractors to place subcontracts with businesses located in labor surplus areas.

The U.S. Department of Labor defines and classifies labor surplus areas. It puts out this information in a monthly publication called "Metropolitan Area Employment and Unemployment," which is available from the Government Printing Office.

SBA HUBZONE EMPOWERMENT CONTRACTING PROGRAM

This program encourages economic development in historically underutilized business zones (HUBZones) by establishing preferences for awarding federal contracts to small business concerns located in such areas. A HUBZone is an area with an unemployment rate that is at least 140 percent of the state's average or that has an average household income of no more than 80 percent of the nonmetropolitan state median. The HUBZone Empowerment Contracting Program was enacted into law as part of the Small Business Reauthorization Act of 1997.

Under this statute, SBA:

- Determines whether small business concerns are eligible to receive HUBZone contracts
- Maintains a list of qualified HUBZone small business concerns for use by acquisition agencies in awarding contracts under the program
- Adjudicates protests of eligibility to receive HUBZone contracts
- Reports to Congress the degree to which the HUBZone Empowerment Contracting Program has yielded increased employment opportunities and investment in HUBZones.

All federal agencies participate in the HUBZone program. Currently, Congress has established a government-wide goal of awarding 3 percent of all federal contracts to small HUBZone businesses.

Qualifications

For a small business to qualify for this program, at least 35 percent of its employees must reside in a designated HUBZone area. Small business concerns must be certified by SBA as meeting the HUBZone requirements. Metropolitan areas qualify as HUBZones based on census tract criteria. Nonmetropolitan counties must fulfill a specific income or unemployment test. Lands within the external boundaries of an Indian reservation also qualify.

The Census Bureau estimates that approximately 9,000 census tracts (out of 61,000) and 900 nonmetropolitan counties (out of 3,000) are HUBZones. SBA estimates that approximately 30,000 firms will apply to become certified HUBZone small business concerns. For more details on the HUBZone Empowerment Contracting Program, visit www.sba.gov/hubzone.

Program Benefits

HUBZone awards take precedence over small business set-asides. Contracting officers must set aside acquisitions over $150,000 for HUBZone small business concerns if two or more HUBZone small businesses make fair market offers. If a sole-source HUBZone contract is made, it must be greater than $150,000 but less than $3 million ($5 million for manufacturing contracts), and the award must be at a fair market price.

Small business concerns located in HUBZone areas receive a 10 percent price evaluation preference in full and open procurements. This evaluation preference works just like the SDB evaluation preference. The price offered by a HUBZone small business is considered lower than the price offered by a non-HUBZone firm as long as the HUBZone business's price is not more than 10 percent higher than the price offered by the otherwise lowest responsive bidder.

The HUBZone preference may not be used when price is not a selection factor (as in certain architectural-engineering contracts) or when the successful bidder is a non-HUBZone small business. Another significant provision of this program is that a firm that is both a HUBZone small business concern and an SDB can receive the evaluation preference for each qualification.

Suppose Sandy's Script Services is located in a HUBZone area and is owned by a socially and economically disadvantaged person. Sandy Spellman, the owner, wants to bid on a Department of Agriculture (USDA) contract for editing services. USDA receives the following bids for this contract:

Sandy's Script Services	$300,000
Edit, Inc.	$250,000

This solicitation is subject to full and open competition, and Edit, Inc., is not eligible for any preferences. The final bids are calculated as follows:

Sandy's original bid price	$300,000
HUBZone preference ($300,000 x 10%)	–($30,000)
Sandy's bid price (after preference)	**$270,000**
Edit, Inc., bid price	$250,000
SDB evaluation adjustment ($300,000 x 10%)	+30,000
Edit, Inc., bid price (after preference)	**$280,000**

Assuming the contract is awarded on price-related factors alone, Sandy's Script Services would win because its recalculated bid is $10,000 lower than that of Edit, Inc.

Ranking the Small Business Programs

So . . . with all these small business programs, what discretion does a contracting officer have when restricting an acquisition? Or better yet, what's the relationship among all the small business programs?

Thankfully, the Small Business Jobs Act of 2010 (Section 1347) was implemented to help clarify the process. Accordingly, the FAR was amended to add Section 19.203, which currently states:

(a) There is NO order of precedence among the 8(a), HUBZone, or service-disabled veteran-owned small business (SDVOSB) preference programs.

(b) At or below the simplified acquisition threshold of $150,000, the requirement to exclusively reserve acquisitions for small business concerns (small business set-asides) does NOT preclude the contracting officer from awarding a contract to a small business under the "preference programs" listed in (a).

(c) Above the simplified acquisition threshold, the contracting officer must first consider an acquisition for the 8(a), HUBZone, or SDVOSB preference programs before using a small business set-aside.

(d) Small business set-asides have priority over acquisitions using full and open competition.

SMALL BUSINESS INNOVATION RESEARCH PROGRAM

The federal government has seeded America's entrepreneurial economy for decades with various research and development (R&D) programs. In fact, the Internet was developed with funding from a government program similar to the Small Business Innovation Research (SBIR) program. Defense research has also given us satellite navigation, while National Institutes of Health (NIH) funding to map the human genome has had a powerful ripple effect throughout the scientific and medical communities.

The SBIR program is an extremely active and valuable program for the development of new ideas and innovative approaches. Federal agencies, especially the Department of Defense, award SBIR contracts for various R&D projects. Since SBIR was established in 1982, as part of the Small Business Innovation Development Act, it has helped thousands of small businesses compete for federal contracts.

Depending on an agency's budget size, SBIR solicitations are generally issued once or twice a year. An individual or firm can become involved with federal R&D projects in two ways:

- By responding to SBIR solicitations
- By initiating an unsolicited proposal (see Chapter 13).

The government also has an R&D program called the Small Business Technology Transfer Research (STTR) program, which works almost exactly like the SBIR program. For our purposes, these programs are treated as if they were the same.

Qualified small businesses are encouraged to propose innovative ideas through this program to meet the government's R&D needs. SBIR is designed to:

- Encourage small business participation in government research programs
- Foster and encourage participation by minority and disadvantaged persons in technological innovations
- Stimulate technological innovations
- Provide incentives for converting research results into commercial applications.

In FY 2011, the government spent more than $2.5 billion on R&D projects under this program. Obviously, SBIR is a major channel for obtaining research funding.

Participating Agencies

Federal agencies that fund more than $100 million in external R&D projects must participate in the SBIR program. These agencies currently include:

- Department of Agriculture
- Department of Commerce
- Department of Defense
- Department of Education
- Department of Energy
- Department of Health and Human Services
- Department of Homeland Security
- Department of Transportation
- Environmental Protection Agency
- National Aeronautics and Space Administration
- National Science Foundation.

Every year the participating agencies assemble solicitations that briefly describe the topics they are interested in. Most agencies allow potential contractors to propose subjects not included in their announcements as well. Proposals submitted in direct response to an SBIR solicitation are competitively evaluated on their scientific and technical merit.

SBIR Qualifications

A small business must meet certain eligibility criteria to participate in the SBIR program:

- The business must be American-owned and independently operated.
- The business must be a for-profit business.
- The principal researcher must be employed by the business.
- The company size is limited to 500 employees.

For most contractors, eligibility isn't a problem. Your primary challenge will be to communicate your idea and why it should be funded in 25 pages or less. A well-written proposal is paramount to your success in this program. Because only a small fraction of R&D funding actually results in a commercial product, the evaluators look for convincing arguments that describe the innovation, its use to the federal agency, and the contractor's qualifications. Only after the prospective contractor establishes its technical competence and the value of its idea do the evaluators consider the cost proposal.

The R&D Brochure

If your firm is interested in obtaining R&D contracts, you should consider preparing a brochure describing your organization and its capabilities. Obtaining R&D contracts requires marketing to the technical personnel of the appropriate contracting (or purchasing) activity. Experienced firms report that a well-thought-out brochure quickly establishes their basic qualifications and fields of endeavor.

At a minimum, an R&D brochure should identify work you have done or are doing, the type of work for which you are qualified, and the names and qualifications of technical personnel on your staff. When you contact a contracting activity, you should present your brochure to both the contracting and technical personnel.

The Three-Phase Program

SBIR uses a highly competitive, three-phase award system.

Phase I is the start-up phase. Phase I awards are typically in the neighborhood of $150,000 and last approximately six months. This phase is intended to determine the scientific or technical merit and feasibility of the ideas submitted.

If Phase I proves successful, the company is generally invited to apply for Phase II. Roughly 50 percent of Phase I award winners go on to Phase II.

Phase II is the performance phase. During this time, the R&D work is performed and the developer evaluates commercialization potential. Awards of up to $1 million for periods as long as two years allow contractors to expand their Phase I results. Phase II R&D projects result in a well-defined deliverable product or process.

Both Phase I and II contracts may include a profit or fee, since a small business is allowed to make a profit during these phases.

Phase III is the period during which Phase II innovation moves from the laboratory into the marketplace. No SBIR funds support this phase. The small business must find funding in the private sector, or federal agencies may award non-SBIR-funded follow-on contracts for products or processes that meet the mission needs of those agencies.

A major key in this program is the "fast track" process. When a Phase II award is appropriate and certain terms and conditions regarding private investment are met, the process is designed to accelerate the award of Phase II contracts. This helps to minimize the time lapse between the end of the Phase I contract and the beginning of Phase II. Experience has shown that when there's a sizable time lag, some businesses, even if they have meaningful ideas or projects, can't survive financially in the interim.

More than 40,000 SBIR awards have been made to date, and the Government Accountability Office (GAO) estimates that nearly a quarter of the awards have produced commercial products.

SBA's Role

SBA plays an important role as the coordinating agency for the SBIR program. It directs each participating agency's implementation of the SBIR program, reviews agency progress, and reports annually to Congress on the program's operation. Use it as your point of contact and information source.

SBA also collects solicitation information from participating agencies and publishes it in presolicitation announcements (PSA). PSAs provide contractors with the topics and anticipated release dates of potential acquisitions. These announcements are published periodically throughout the year and include the requesting agency's address and phone number.

For more information on the SBIR program, contact:

U.S. Small Business Administration Office of Technology
409 Third Street, SW
Washington, DC 20416
(202) 205-6450

www.sba.gov/content/small-business-innovation-research-program-sbir

■ ■ ■

Preference programs give small businesses a chance to compete with large firms for federal business. The contractor qualifications and restrictions of some of these programs require a little work to understand, but the effort certainly pays off in government assistance. It goes without saying that every eligible business should take advantage of the government's small business preference programs.

■ ■ ■

Chapter 6

Subcontracting Opportunities

"It is important to learn from your mistakes, Bob...but let's try not to learn quite so much."

What's in this chapter?

- Subcontracting plans
- Selecting a subcontractor
- Awarding a subcontract
- DoD Mentor-Protégé Program

For businesses new to federal contracting, getting your foot in the door tends to be the hardest task of all. In fact, the best—and often *only*—way to get your hands on Uncle Sam's cash is by serving as a subcontractor. That's generally because the big contracts go to the heavy hitters or fat cats who are better able to handle the notoriously arduous solicitation process.

Partnering or teaming with existing contractors allows new vendors to build valuable relationships with businesses in their particular field, while learning the ropes in dealing with the federal government. When a company enters into a contract to perform work for a customer (or the government) and another firm provides a portion of the goods or services necessary to fulfill the contract, the company is said to be subcontracting part of its contractual requirements.

A company's contract with the government is usually referred to as the *prime contract*, and its contracts with suppliers are referred to as *subcontracts*. The subcontractor does not have a direct contractual relationship with the government. Examples of major prime contractors include Lockheed Martin, Northrop Grumman, Cisco, General Dynamics, and Westinghouse.

The Small Business Administration (SBA) develops and promotes subcontracting opportunities for small businesses by referring small contractors to prime contractors. The market for subcontract work is nearly as large as the basic government market for contracting. As you can see in the figure below, during FY 2010, DoD prime contractors awarded more than $139.5 billion in subcontracts, $52.2 billion (or more than 36 percent) of which went to small businesses.

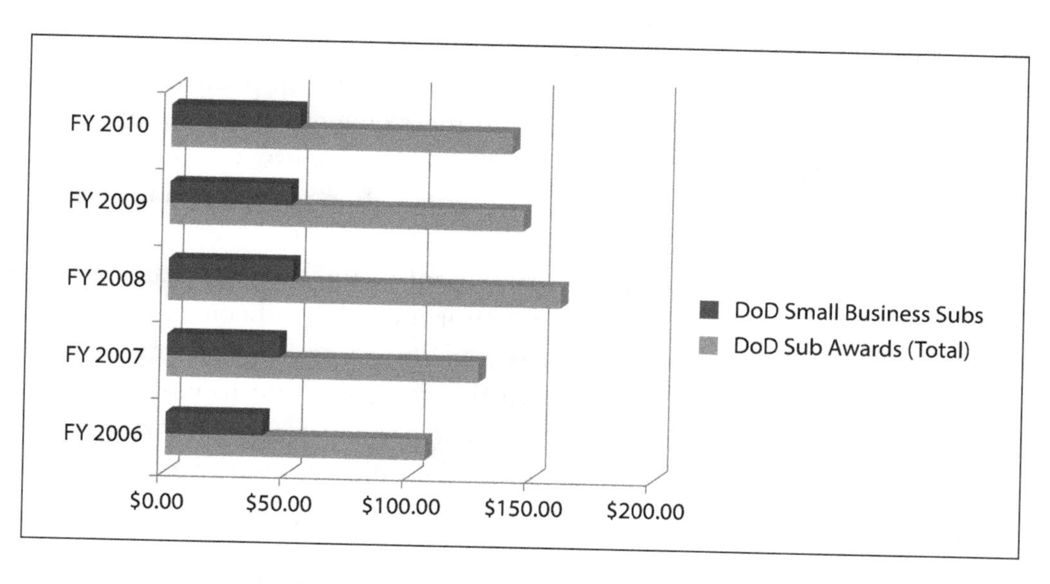

DoD Subcontract Awards (in billions)

Another good reason to look for subcontracting opportunities is to take advantage of contracts that are available only through prime contractors. Most construction projects, for example, are awarded as turnkey contracts. A turnkey contract is a contract that places the responsibility for completion completely on the winning contractor or prime contractor.

Suppose Weitz Construction was awarded a contract to build an office building. Weitz (the prime contractor) is unable to perform the air-conditioning portion of the building project. If an air-conditioning firm wanted to be part of this building project, it would need to get a subcontract for the work with Weitz.

SUBCONTRACTING PLANS

Why would a prime contractor want to subcontract, besides the obvious reason that few companies are able to offer a full spectrum of goods and services?

Well, in many cases prime contractors must subcontract certain portions of their work to small businesses in order to be eligible for a government contract of their own. In fact, SBA requires large businesses receiving contracts valued at over $650,000 ($1.5 million for construction) to develop plans and goals for awarding subcontracts to qualified small business concerns. This in turn forces federal contracting dollars to flow down to small businesses—while allowing agencies to avoid the paperwork that formal solicitation procedures require.

A subcontracting plan must include a statement of total dollars planned to be subcontracted, as well as percentage goals for awarding subcontracts to small, small disadvantaged, and women-owned small businesses. Descriptions of the needed supplies and services, along with the methods used to identify potential sources, are also included in the plan. The prime contractor is responsible for designating a small business liaison in the company who sources and/or works with subcontractors

When significant subcontracting opportunities exist, a contracting officer may publish in FedBizOpps the names and addresses of prospective prime contractors. In addition, the contracting officer synopsizes in FedBizOpps contract awards exceeding $25,000 that are likely to result in the award of subcontracts. Prime contractors and subcontractors also are encouraged to publicize subcontracting opportunities in FedBizOpps.

If a prime contractor fails to submit an acceptable subcontracting plan, it becomes ineligible for the contract. The government can also assess "liquidated damages" to a prime contractor that fails to make a good-faith effort to meet its subcontracting goals.

In negotiated acquisitions, a contracting officer may encourage prime contractors to offer subcontracting opportunities by providing monetary incentives, such as award fees, to primes. The amount of the incentive is negotiated and depends on the prime contractor's achieving its small business goals and the technical assistance and outreach programs it intends to provide.

Electronic Subcontracting Reporting System (eSRS)

Prime contractors must report their subcontracting efforts electronically via the Electronic Subcontracting Reporting System (eSRS). See www.esrs.gov for more information and insight.

SELECTING A SUBCONTRACTOR

With the subcontracting requirements discussed above, it's easy to see why prime contractors are always on the lookout for "good" small business partners. The process of selecting a sub, however, is more of an art than a science. Prime contractors consider a number of factors, including the:

- Degree to which the company's products or services fit the requirements of the contract
- Degree to which a mutually agreeable deal can be struck between the parties
- Size and socioeconomic status of the firm
- Company's asking price for its goods or services
- Technical superiority of the company's goods or services.

Basically, if you can make a prime's life easier by helping it hold up its end of the bargain with the government, you have a great chance of creating a long, rewarding relationship. It's a win-win.

Perhaps the most important consideration in a subcontracting relationship is that the contract clauses in the prime contractor's agreement with the government generally flow down to the subcontractor (i.e., are included in the subcontract). In other words, the subcontractor is equally bound to comply with the applicable acquisition rules and regulations. The solicitation enumerates the terms and conditions, and the potential subcontractor should understand their significance before entering into any agreement.

> There is no "privity of contract" between the government and any subcontractor. That is to say, the government's contractual relationship is with the prime contractor only. The subcontractor has no right to seek redress from the government but must do so with the prime contractor, even if it means filing a civil lawsuit to settle a disagreement.

AWARDING A SUBCONTRACT

Companies may negotiate and sign a subcontracting agreement at any point during the solicitation process. Generally, it is advantageous to the prime contractor if the agreement is signed prior to award because it locks in the subcontractor's terms and pricing. It also allows the prime contractor to calculate the total amount of risk it is taking on. Conversely, the subcontractor must devote resources to negotiating a subcontract that might, in fact, never be executed.

Subcontracting is a great way for small businesses to build up their resumes and make new industry contacts. But in many cases a subcontracting arrangement leads to misunderstandings and disputes between the parties. Having a rock-solid subcontracting agreement in place is the best way to protect against disagreements.

Once you receive the subcontracting agreement, be sure to look it over and go back to the prime contractor with any areas of concern. It is better to err on the side of caution beforehand than to sort out contracting disputes once the work has begun.

Most federal agencies publish a list of businesses that received contracts over $650,000 ($1.5 million for construction) and are subject to subcontracting goals. For example, DoD maintains a subcontracting directory at www.acq.osd.mil/osbp/doing_business. The directory lists DoD prime contractors alphabetically, including their addresses, phone numbers, and contacts and the products or services purchased.

SUB-*Net* and GSA's Subcontracting Directory

Although there is no single point of entry for subcontracting opportunities in the federal marketplace, SBA's SUB-*Net* (http://web.sba.gov/subnet) encourages prime contractors, federal agencies, state and local governments, and educational entities to post solicitations and notices online.

The General Services Administration (GSA) also maintains an excellent subcontracting directory at www.gsa.gov/subdirectory.

Small businesses are encouraged to contact prime contractors directly for subcontracting opportunities.

DOD MENTOR-PROTÉGÉ PROGRAM

The Department of Defense's Mentor-Protégé Program provides incentives to major contractors to help small disadvantaged businesses (SDBs) and qualified organizations that employ disabled persons enhance their capabilities for performing DoD contracts. The mentor assists the protégé by sharing its management expertise and technical skills to enhance the protégé's competitiveness.

Through such assistance, the program attempts to increase the participation of SDBs in DoD contracting. Many federal agencies (e.g., DOE, EPA, NASA) have their own mentor-protégé programs. Any prime contractor with an active subcontracting plan negotiated with DoD may participate as a mentor.

Contracting officers encourage mentors (prime contractors) to take a small business under their wing by providing such incentives as cost reimbursement, credit toward SDB subcontracting goals, or a combination of both. Mentors are also encouraged to strengthen and expand their own capabilities throughout their program participation.

Protégé Qualifications

To qualify as a protégé, a firm must be a small disadvantaged business, as defined by section 8(d)(3)(C) of the Small Business Act. This includes women-owned businesses and businesses owned and controlled by Indian tribes or Native Hawaiian organizations.

Any firm (excluding 8(a)-certified firms) that seeks eligibility as a small disadvantaged business for participation as a protégé must be certified by SBA. To qualify, contact your local SBA District Office for an application package. (Visit www.sba.gov to find the local office for your area.) Submit the completed application to SBA's Assistant Administrator for Small Disadvantaged Business Certification and Eligibility.

Finding a Mentor

You can identify a mentor by consulting *Subcontracting Opportunities with DoD Major Prime Contractors*. This publication lists most major DoD prime contractors that have negotiated subcontracting plans, including the names and phone numbers of their small business liaison officers and the firms' primary products or service lines. You can download this publication at http://www.acq.osd.mil/osbp/mentor_protege.

As a prospective protégé, you need to select as a mentor a firm with the technical capabilities you seek and a similar business focus. Look for one that might become the best future partner for teaming relationships. Keep in mind that a mentor might want to establish a subcontracting relationship before negotiating a mentor-protégé agreement. Be prepared to market your firm's capabilities and address what you will bring to the table.

To participate in the program, the mentor and the protégé must formalize their relationship through a letter of intent and a mentor-protégé agreement. These documents set forth the duration of the mentor-protégé relationship and detail the developmental assistance to be provided. Although DoD must approve these documents, it will have a limited oversight role during the program.

Mentor Responsibilities

The mentor can provide a broad array of assistance to the protégé, but the protégé must perform its own contracts and subcontracts. DoD will not give credit for or reimburse the mentor for any costs related to direct work the mentor performs on the protégé's contracts. The program aims to produce viable SDBs capable of performing contracts that require high-technology skills.

Visit www.acq.osd.mil/osbp/mentor_protege for more information about this program.

■ ■ ■

Both large and small companies can benefit from establishing subcontracting agreements. Mid-size to large companies can strengthen and expand their own capabilities while meeting their goals for providing opportunities for small, small disadvantaged, and women-owned small business concerns. As a result, federal contracting dollars flow down to small business concerns.

■ ■ ■

Federal Supply Schedules and GSA Schedules

© 1999 Randy Glasbergen.
www.glasbergen.com
GLASBERGEN
"To conform to government safety regulations, no one may climb the ladder of success without wearing a harness and special non-slip shoes."

What's in this chapter?

- Federal Acquisition Service
- Multiple Award Schedule
- GSA e-Library (formerly Schedules e-Library)
- Getting on a GSA Schedule
- GSA Advantage
- *MarkeTips* magazine
- Government-wide acquisition contracts
- Problems with federal supply schedules

Over the years I've been constantly asked, "What's the best and quickest way to get started? How can I get my commercial products and services to federal buyers? How can I get my hands on those federal dollars?"

If you're new to federal contracting or looking for an entry point to the government marketplace, the Federal Supply Schedule program is for you. A schedule contract is the only practical way a small business can obtain a preapproved federal price list for its products and services. In fact, *not* having a schedule contract actually excludes your company from many federal sales!

Federal supply schedules are the government's fastest-growing procurement method, especially for services. Only commercial items are solicited through schedule contracts. Currently, these schedules offer more than 30 million commercial products and services from over 21,000 suppliers. Historically, this program accounts for close to $40 billion in federal purchases each year, as shown in the figure below.

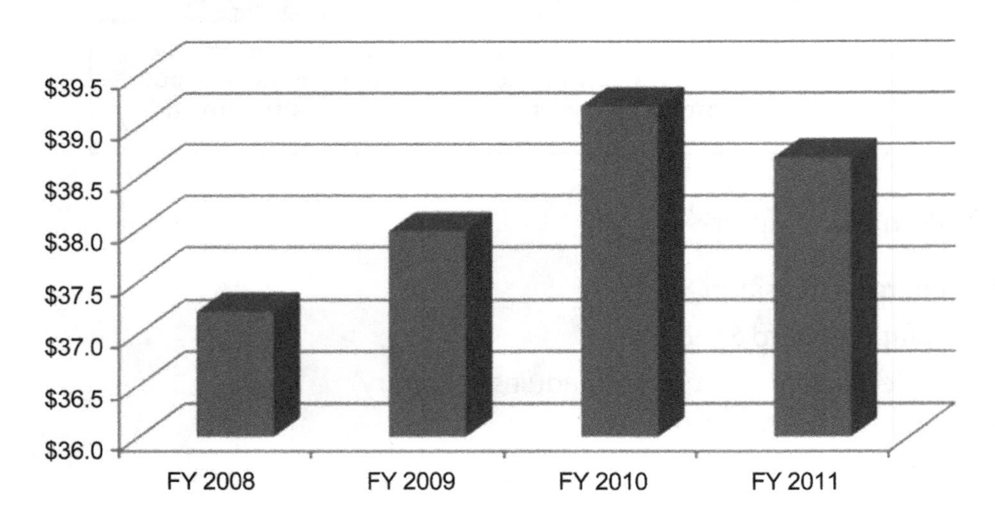

GSA Schedule Sales (in billions)

Designed to closely mirror commercial buying practices, federal supply schedules streamline the buying process for contracting activities (or buying offices). Both buyers and sellers benefit from the program, thanks to its shorter lead times, lower administrative costs, and reduced inventories. The buying power of the government also allows for volume discounts on its purchases.

Although a GSA schedule is an official federal contract, it is not automatically funded. Only when orders are placed by a federal agency does the funding occur. In the simplest terms, a schedule contract is a stamp of approval for your company's listed products and services. Better yet, think of a federal supply schedule as a mechanism to close federal sales.

The disadvantages of GSA schedules also are discussed later in this chapter.

FEDERAL ACQUISITION SERVICE

The Federal Acquisition Service (FAS), a division of the General Services Administration (GSA), manages and operates the Federal Supply Schedule program. Its primary responsibility is to negotiate indefinite-delivery/indefinite-quantity, no-guarantee-of-sale contracts with commercial firms to provide products and services at stated prices for specific periods (usually three years). To be eligible for the Federal Supply Schedule program, a contractor must have its schedule contract approved by FAS.

GSA schedule solicitations are posted on FedBizOpps (see Chapter 8). FAS currently negotiates schedule contracts for 62 categories of products and services, ranging from furniture and off-the-shelf office supplies, to information technology, to financial services, to travel and transportation services. It awards contracts under negotiated procurement procedures (see Chapter 12). Product prices are negotiated on a unit basis, while services are negotiated at an hourly rate.

Once approved by FAS, the schedule contract is assigned a classification code and published in a catalog or listing called a federal supply schedule (or GSA schedule). Each schedule covers a particular product or group of products, or a particular type of service. For example, schedule group 76, Publication Media, includes publications, encyclopedias, instructional/technical books and pamphlets, medical guides, almanacs, and geographical maps and atlases.

Each federal supply schedule contains ordering information, including covered products and services, the eligible contractors and their contact information, terms and conditions, prices, maximum and minimum order sizes, and ordering instructions. Federal buying offices place their orders directly with the vendor or contractor. In many cases, federal agencies are required to use federal supply schedules as their primary source of supply.

It's crucial for a contractor to get on a schedule contract that accurately reflects its products or services. In some cases, a particular item may be covered under more than one schedule. Therefore, some companies may need more than one schedule to cover all their offerings.

Program Benefits

GSA schedules are like fishing licenses, authorizing companies to go after federal contracts. They offer program participants—both vendors and agencies—the following benefits:

- The number of vendors holding a schedule contract is "unlimited," and a vendor may submit a proposal at any time.
- Schedules expose a contractor's products and services to a vast number of contracting activities or buying offices throughout the government for at least one year and, in some cases, up to five years.
- Schedule holders are preapproved to contract with federal agencies, thus making it easier for buying offices to transact purchases with a company.
- Schedules enable the government to use its buying power to obtain volume discounts on purchases.
- State and local governments can purchase from Schedule 70—Information Technology. In addition, certain prime contractors are eligible to purchase from federal supply schedules (see Part 51 of the FAR).
- Eighty percent of the contractors participating in the Federal Supply Schedule program are small businesses.
- Formal solicitation procedures are not used for schedule items because FAS has already determined the prices to be fair and reasonable.
- When a schedule is mandatory, the federal agencies specified in the schedule must use it.

FAS may also authorize other federal agencies to award and publish schedule contracts. The Department of Veterans Affairs, for example, awards schedule contracts for certain medical items. DoD uses a similar system for military items that are not part of the FAS program. Approximately 25 states have their own versions of federal supply schedules as well.

MULTIPLE AWARD SCHEDULE

The most common federal supply schedule type is the multiple award schedule (MAS). It is a list of contracts the government establishes with more than one vendor/contractor for the same types of products and services. Each year, federal agencies spend billions of dollars through MASs, buying everything from desks and paper clips to computers and software.

MAS contracts are awarded on a variable basis, meaning that contractors can respond to MAS solicitations at any time. There are no government specifications for the items listed in an MAS schedule. Any responsible contractor may submit offers in response to a solicitation for MAS contracts.

Each contractor on the MAS submits a different price list for its products and services and may offer specific options and features. An agency buying office selects the contractor that best meets its particular needs. For the most part, contractors do not participate in head-to-head competition, although agencies may hold competitions among schedule holders.

MAS contract holders must provide the government with prices that are at least as good as the prices they offer commercial clients. This negotiation objective is commonly known as *most favored customer pricing*. Moreover, contractors can offer additional discounts to make their schedule more competitive. Their MAS prices represent a ceiling price. Once a schedule price is approved, it can be changed only by GSA approval.

Contracting officers must follow negotiated procurement procedures when issuing MAS contracts. After the MAS contract is issued, the contractor prepares and distributes a catalog, price list, or both to the various ordering offices. Agency buying offices then use the catalogs, along with the MAS, to purchase needed products and services. Contractors must accept payment using the government-wide purchase card (see Chapter 10).

Buying offices may not purchase commercial products and services that are available under an MAS. As a result, if a company has a schedule contract, it is likely to have a competitive advantage over contractors that do not participate in the MAS program.

> The Small Business Jobs Act of 2010 officially authorizes federal agencies to set aside or reserve multiple-award contracts for small businesses. This interim rule amends FAR 8.4 to make clear that set-asides may be used in connection with the placement of orders under federal supply schedules.

GSA e-LIBRARY (FORMERLY SCHEDULES e-LIBRARY)

If you plan to go after business on the GSA schedule, you'll need to become familiar with the GSA e-Library, at www.gsaelibrary.gsa.gov. This site is the official online source for federal supply schedule information. It contains complete schedule listings, basic ordering guidelines, and details on schedule program changes. A search engine allows you to search by keyword, schedule number, item number, contractor name, and contract number. It is updated daily to ensure access to the latest award information.

Federal Supply Classification Codes

As a government contractor, it is useful to know the Federal Supply Classification (FSC) codes assigned to each of your products. Buying offices use FSC codes to identify products and services. FSC codes currently consist of 78 groups, which are subdivided into 646 classes.

Although contractors are not required to use FSC codes when registering with the government, they are encouraged to include the codes that apply to their products and services. FSC codes help buying offices identify a contractor's capabilities more accurately.

The FSC code uses a four-digit structure. The first two digits identify the group, such as:

Group	Title
70	Data Processing Equipment
71	Furniture
75	Office Supplies and Devices
81	Containers, Packaging, and Packing Supplies

The last two digits of the code identify the classes within each group. For example, group 71, Furniture, currently has the following classes:

FSC	Title
7125	Cabinets, Lockers, Bins, and Shelving
7105	Household Furniture
7195	Miscellaneous Furniture and Fixtures
7110	Office Furniture

For more information on FSC codes, visit www.dlis.dla.mil/h2.

GETTING ON A GSA SCHEDULE

To become an approved supplier under a GSA schedule, a business must go through an application process that can take months to complete. Therefore, it's never too soon to begin the application process and approval.

Here's a general outline to help you get your products and services listed on a GSA schedule and obtain your own GSA contract number.

1. Review "Getting on a GSA Schedule" at www.gsa.gov/gettingonschedule.
2. Identify the federal supply schedule that covers your products or services at the GSA e-Library (www.gsaelibrary.gsa.gov). There are currently more than 40 different federal supply schedules. Here are the schedule IDs for a few of them:

FAS Schedule	Schedule ID
Financial and Business Solutions (FABS)	520
Furniture	71
Leasing of Autos and Light Trucks	751
Professional Engineering Services	871
Environmental Services	899

(Note that hardware and software schedules generally require the contractor to offer support, such as maintenance or repair service.)

Each GSA schedule has a point of contact that can provide specific information about individual GSA schedule items.

3. Go to FedBizOpps (www.fbo.gov) to search for and download a copy of the current GSA schedule solicitation for your particular products or services.
4. Obtain a Dun & Bradstreet (D&B) reference check. For more information on reference checks, call Dun & Bradstreet at (800) 234-3867, or apply at www.dnb.com.
5. Complete all information in the solicitation. Each solicitation has different requirements, so be sure to read it carefully.
6. Be prepared to offer a competitive price.

The GSA Vendor Support Center maintains a library of federal supply schedules and authorized contractor catalog price lists. It is also a receiving point for customer and vendor questions regarding FAS products and services. For more information on the GSA Vendor Support Center, visit http://vsc.gsa.gov, or call (877) 495-4849.

Once a contract is successfully negotiated, the business is assigned a GSA contract number and placed on a list of approved suppliers for that particular schedule.

Now What?

You've just been awarded your first schedule contract. Congratulations! So now you're ready for all those orders to pour in. Unfortunately, having a schedule contract does not guarantee that you will receive government orders. It indicates only that you are an eligible contractor and that your products and services are reasonably priced. Therefore, while the ink is drying on your contract, you should immediately turn your attention to marketing your new award.

The first step in marketing your schedule contract is to develop your contract price list. A contract price list is a "catalog" that lists the items you have been awarded and identifies the terms and conditions of the contract. Your price list is your initial face to the customer. When designing your price list, be sure to make it user-friendly. A one-page flyer covering only the required items specified in your contract usually is best; see the example GSA schedule price list on the facing page for an example.

Buy My Stuff, Inc.

Price List

Contract # GS-35F-0213M

Products:		
Part #	**Product Description**	**GSA Price**
DS01	GEMS	$80,607.00
PS01	mCAT!	$6,525.36
CA01	LaserCat	$4,310.00

Software Maintenance:		
Part #	**Software Maintenance Description**	**GSA Price**
DS01-2	GEMS Year 2	$19,521.24
DS01-3	GEMS Year 3	$21,258.47

Labor/Service Rates:						
Cat #	**Labor Category**	**Year-1**	**Year-2**	**Year-3**	**Year-4**	**Year-5**
L001	Program Manager	$116.03	$120.56	$126.33	$133.08	$138.63
L002	Senior Network Engineer	$85.68	$93.04	$95.57	$100.35	$106.37
L003	Software Engineer	$59.38	$62.27	$65.43	$68.65	$73.09
L004	Database Administrator	$55.51	$59.31	$62.41	$65.77	$66.54
L005	Financial Analyst	$54.97	$58.32	$61.85	$64.21	$66.54
L006	Network Engineer	$53.05	$57.48	$60.82	$63.37	$66.54
L007	Technical Writer	$51.06	$53.78	$55.21	$57.97	$61.35
L008	Admin Support	$23.43	$25.55	$26.82	$28.13	$29.61

Buy Now Using GSA Advantage!

For more information, contact: 800-555-3000 ext. 101 or email: Joe@buymystuff.com

Example GSA Schedule Price List

Once your price list is completed, you'll need to distribute it to potential customers. For many schedules, GSA provides a mailing list of customers who have expressed an interest in the products and services on a particular GSA schedule. Be sure to ask your procuring contracting officer (PCO) if your schedule has a customer mailing list.

Although the government is moving toward a paperless environment, it's not there yet. Contractors should still take the time to mail a hard copy of their price list to prospective customers. Also, in your mailing be sure to include your company brochure and other literature about your products or services.

GSA ADVANTAGE

GSA Advantage is an online shopping service or ordering system for government buyers and is a major marketing tool for schedule holders. It provides access to several thousand contractors and millions of products and services. During FY 2011, GSA Advantage did more than $531 million in sales.

Your GSA schedule price list or company catalog needs to be posted to GSA Advantage no later than six months after contract award—the sooner the better! To post a company catalog, profile, or price list to GSA Advantage, go to http://vsc.gsa.gov. Click on the Getting on Advantage tab and go to the Schedule Input Program (SIP) instructions to begin.

Using words and phrases that accurately and effectively describe your products is critical to your marketing success. The SIP also allows contractors to post product photos to GSA Advantage. It is the contractor's responsibility to keep its GSA Advantage catalog/profile information current, accurate, and complete.

GSA Advantage gives contractors an opportunity to put a controlled marketing spin on their products and services by linking their company Web site to their catalog/profile. Be sure to make your Web site GSA-friendly. Put GSA's logo and your contract number on an easy-to-spot location on your Web site. Also, set up a separate email account for GSA schedule inquiries only.

Government buyers use GSA Advantage to:

- Search for items using keywords, part numbers, national stock numbers, supplier names, contract numbers, etc.
- Compare features, prices, and delivery options
- Configure products and add accessories
- Place orders directly online
- Review and choose delivery options
- Select a convenient payment method
- View order history.

Contractors use GSA Advantage to:

- Research the competition
- Check out the market
- Sell to the federal marketplace.

For more information on GSA Advantage, visit www.gsaadvantage.gov.

MARKETIPS MAGAZINE

Another way to market your products and services to potential customers is to supply advertisements to *MarkeTips*, a bimonthly publication for GSA customers. Advertising space in *MarkeTips* is free and is offered on a first-come, first-served basis. Because ad space is limited, vendors are generally restricted to two ads per year.

MarkeTips is sent to over 110,000 federal and military subscribers worldwide and is available via www.gsa.gov (search for "marketips").

> Getting a GSA schedule is just the tip of the iceberg when it comes to generating sales through your schedule contract. You must still aggressively market to agency buying offices that could potentially purchase your products and services. Call them. Send brochures. On your Web site, prominently list all the details of the GSA contract.
>
> Be sure to use GSA logos on all of your marketing materials. Remember, most federal supply schedules will have many suppliers, so you must find a way to get your products or services noticed!

GOVERNMENT-WIDE ACQUISITION CONTRACTS

Similar to GSA schedule contracts, government-wide acquisition contracts (GWACs) are prenegotiated, multi-agency contracts under which basic pricing for specified products and services is established. GWACs encourage long-term vendor agreements and focus solely on information technology (IT), such as computers and IT-focused support services.

However, unlike GSA schedules, GWAC proposals are generally accepted during a 30- to 60-day window, which is then closed at the end of the period. In addition, the number of vendors awarded GWACs is severely limited, thus restricting competition and favoring insiders (oh, no!).

The GSA Small Business GWAC Division manages a diversified portfolio of small business set-aside contracts for firms that specialize in providing innovative IT solutions. Major small business set-aside contract vehicles include:

- ***Alliant Small Business GWAC.*** The Alliant GWAC is designed to provide IT solutions to federal agencies while strengthening opportunities in federal contracting for qualifying small businesses. It is exclusively reserved for small firms. The maximum order period is up to ten years (five-year base contract, with a five-year option).
- ***Veteran Technology Services (VETS) GWAC.*** The VETS GWAC is a small business set-aside contract devoted exclusively to service-disabled veteran-owned small technology firms. VETS helps enable federal agencies to achieve small business goals through the purchase of IT solutions from small businesses owned by service-disabled veterans.
- ***8(a) STARS II GWAC.*** The Streamlined Technology Acquisition Resources for Services (STARS II) is a multiple-award, indefinite-delivery/indefinite-quantity (ID/IQ) contract vehicle designed to exclusively promote to federal agencies IT solutions provided by 8(a) small businesses. (The solicitation on this contract is currently closed. Interested parties may consider subcontracting opportunities or pursue an on-ramp in the future, if offered.)

For a comprehensive overview of each of the above GWACs, visit www.gsa.gov/portal/category/25281.

A word of caution: in most cases, unlike contracts under the GSA Schedule program, GWACs are awarded to a limited number of companies and therefore tend to be much more competitive to get. There are several other key differences between GSA schedules and GWACs:

- GSA schedules cover a much broader range of products and services; GWACs are limited to IT products and services.
- GSA schedules have separate ordering procedures for supplies and services; GWAC ordering procedures are set forth in the contract.
- GSA schedules allow contractor teaming arrangements to be established; GWACs do not.
- GSA schedules allow an ordering activity to establish blanket purchase agreements (see Chapter 10); GWACs do not.

PROBLEMS WITH FEDERAL SUPPLY SCHEDULES

You would think federal supply schedules would be a goldmine for small- and medium-sized companies—and in many ways they are. However, selling or wholesaling common-use commercial products and services to the federal government is extremely competitive. Markups of 8 percent to 12 percent are the norm for many products. In the face of this competition, small businesses are at a disadvantage because they are unable to maintain a large enough sales volume to be profitable.

Suppose that your small business is a regular dealer of Dell equipment and your agreement allows you to purchase computers for $1,000 each. Assuming you put a 10 percent markup on products you sell, your sales price per computer on the FSS would be $1,100 (which would be considered the unit price of the computer). The unit price on the FSS must be inclusive.

After reading this book, you decide to apply to FAS to get your computer products on a federal supply schedule. You consult the GSA e-Library and determine that federal supply schedule 70, Information Technology Equipment, is appropriate for your computers.

Next, you obtain your Dun & Bradstreet (D&B) reference check and use FedBizOpps to obtain the solicitation for federal supply schedule 70. Finally, you complete the solicitation.

Let's assume the Department of Commerce plans to purchase 200 Dell computers and has selected your federal supply schedule. The contracting officer making this purchase does not need to be concerned about the price of the computers because FAS has already determined your schedule prices to be fair and reasonable. You will earn a total gross profit (or margin) of $20,000 on this transaction:

FSS unit price (w/ 10% markup)	$1,100
Dell computers ordered	× 200
Total sales price	**$220,000**

The next step is to apply your indirect costs against this sales transaction.

Indirect costs are expenses incurred by a contractor that cannot be attributed to any one particular contract. Lighting in a manufacturing area that houses the work of several contracts would be an example of an indirect cost.

Indirect costs are classified further as either overhead (O/H) expenses or general and administrative (G&A) expenses.

O/H expenses are general costs like indirect labor, rent, supplies, insurance, and depreciation.

G&A expenses are any management, financial, or other expenses incurred for the general management and administration of the company as a whole.

The following breakdown shows the indirect costs and profit of this sales transaction.

Total gross profit (or margin)	**$20,000**
LESS	
O/H expenses:	
Salaries	$ 3,500
Supplies	$ 750
Equipment rental	$ 500
Depreciation	$ 2,250

G&A expenses:	
Executive salaries	$ 4,000
Personnel costs	$ 1,500
Professional services	$ 1,750
Training costs	$ 1,250
Total (net) profit	**$4,500**

When you consider these indirect costs, you barely break even on this transaction. That's the main problem with serving as a small business regular dealer or wholesaler to the government. How can a small business survive with such a low markup on its sales? In addition, what happens to the small business if the government doesn't consistently buy its products or services?

The key to being a successful regular government dealer or wholesaler is to have a large sales volume. Because many indirect costs remain consistent, regardless of sales volume, a large sales volume allows a contractor to cover more indirect expenses, increasing total profit. These indirect costs are referred to as *fixed costs*.

Suppose Joe's Janitorial Services provides your office cleaning services for $1,000 per month. This expense would be considered a fixed cost because it remains the same regardless of sales volume. If you increase sales, you earn a greater total profit because your fixed costs remain at $1,000, even though you take in more sales. Large businesses enjoy a tremendous advantage because they can maintain lower markups with larger sales volumes.

Another problem for small business regular dealers is that there is not much incentive for a large business or manufacturer to use a regular dealer to sell products to the government. Why would a large manufacturer need to use the services of a regular dealer if the government ordering activities can contact the manufacturer directly? Think about it: if your company were a large manufacturer like Dell, wouldn't you want to sell your products directly to the government so you could charge a more competitive price?

> Whew! With each edition, this chapter gets harder to write, or perhaps it becomes harder to keep simple.
>
> The selection of the right contract vehicle for your company's products and services is absolutely essential to your success. And finding a way to keep track of them all will certainly give you and your company a competitive advantage.
>
> In researching this book, I found that the Interagency Contract Directory (ICD; www.contractdirectory.gov) was extremely helpful for finding out what contracting vehicles are already available. The site is a central database for indefinite-delivery vehicles/contracts awarded by federal agencies. It's very user-friendly. Just enter keywords or the contract number in the search box and off you go!

■ ■ ■

Once you've been granted a GSA schedule—your "fishing license"—and your preapproved price list is in place, you can close government sales more quickly because your business joins a list of preferred vendors. In fact, *not* having a GSA schedule can automatically exclude your company from many federal purchases, so get one as soon as possible.

The Federal Supply Schedule program is designed to closely mirror commercial buying practices. Schedule holders need to have adequate cash flow, an effective delivery system, and an aggressive marketing plan to be successful. All government buying offices—large or small, and even those in remote locations—receive the same services, convenience, and pricing.

For small businesses especially, the keys to profitability in dealing with GSA schedules are (1) to not overestimate anticipated sales volume, (2) control overhead and G&A expenses, and (3) market like mad!

■ ■ ■

How to Find Government Contracting Opportunities

> Everyone has a plan 'til they get punched in the mouth.
>
> —*Mike Tyson*

Okay, you've completed the required registrations, carefully identified your product and service code(s), and submitted your GSA schedule application. Now, let the selling begin!

- ✓ Dun and Bradstreet (D&B): www.dnb.com
- ✓ System for Award Management (SAM) registration: www.sam.gov
- ✓ Online Reps & Certs (ORCA): https://orca.bpn.gov
- ✓ North American Industry Classification System (NAICS) code(s): www.census.gov/eos/www/naics
- ✓ Get on a GSA schedule contract with a preapproved price list (this can take months to complete): www.gsa.gov/gettingonschedule

In some ways, marketing to the federal government is just like marketing to any other business: Find out who's buying what you sell and reach out directly to them. But as you'll see in the following chapters, marketing to the federal government has its own set of rules and requirements, which can be a blessing, a curse, or both, depending on your company's background and understanding.

How to Market to the Federal Government

"The number one rule in sales is:
'Find Out What The Customer Wants'.
The customer wanted me to go away."

What's in this chapter?

- Finding markets for your supplies and services
- Finding agencies online
- FedBizOpps
- Federal Supply Schedules/GSA Schedules
- *Federal Register*
- Federal agency acquisition forecasts
- TECH-*Net*
- Federal Procurement Data System
- Year-end procurements

You'd think marketing to the federal government would be an easy subject to write about. The government has more than 350,000 contractors, who receive more than $500 billion worth of contracts each year. But as I began asking successful contractors and government officials about marketing to the government, I was amazed at how little they actually knew about the subject. Don't get me wrong—they all had some good ideas, but in the end they all seemed to conclude that *who you know* is the deciding factor in getting government contracts.

Now I'm sure that to be successful in any business, who you know is very important. But my question is: who is it that I should get to know, and how do I get to know them? And that question has gotten me a lot of blank stares and answers like "You've just got to find a way." So that's what Part III of this book is all about: learning how to market to the federal government.

Marketing to the government differs from marketing to other types of industries because the government makes purchases with funds that are financed by the public (that is, tax dollars). This means that the government has a higher degree of accountability for the ways in which those funds are spent. Federal buying offices, for example, must allow full and open competition for their purchases. This mandate helps ensure that contractors can compete for federal contracts without having to belong to an exclusive country club.

The bottom line is there really is no one way to market your supplies or services to the government because each federal agency makes acquisitions in a different way. But understanding the government's procurement methods (or sources) and the support services it offers to contractors can surely help.

This chapter touches on a number of marketing methods. Hopefully, you will be able to incorporate some of them into your business marketing plans.

FINDING MARKETS FOR YOUR SUPPLIES AND SERVICES

An important thing to remember about federal contracting is that you do not have to be located near Washington, D.C., or a federal agency itself to compete for contracts. The government currently has more than 2,500 buying offices (or contracting activities) and countless federal facilities located throughout the country. Who knows—with a little research, you might be able to find a government contracting opportunity right in your backyard! And I'm sure that for social and political reasons, a local facility would much rather buy from a hometown company.

SBA has grouped the federal market into 10 regions, as shown in the figure below.

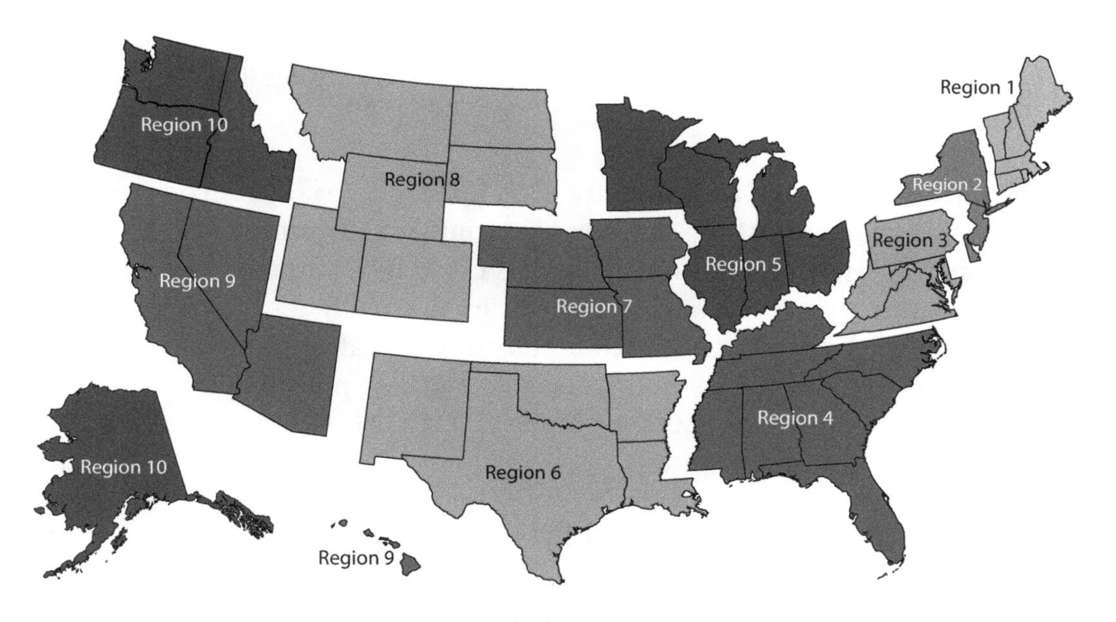

Regions of the Federal Market

To market successfully in the large and diverse federal marketplace, a contractor must focus on a specific area that offers the greatest opportunity for success based on available resources. The following questions might help you decide which markets to concentrate on:

- ***Where is your business located?*** Is it in a densely populated area like New York City or a rural area like Greenville, North Carolina? In a densely populated area, you can concentrate on using a business center that is close to your location because heavily populated areas tend to have larger government markets. On the other hand, in a rural area, you will probably use a business center that is farther away because these areas have fewer buying offices.

- ***What is your business type?*** If you are in a business that requires you to work at the job site, you should consider a smaller geographical area. For example, if you operate a construction company, most of your work will take place at the job site. It is therefore beneficial to work close to your home office.
- ***How much experience do you have?*** If yours is a relatively new business and you're still learning the ropes, you should probably look for opportunities near home. If you have been in business for many years and have a good share of the local market, you might consider expanding your market base.

At the outset, you should have a pretty good feel for how far your company can venture and still successfully perform the contract's requirements. Reaching out too far to perform government contracts could be a mistake that endangers your company's future business opportunities. Carefully identify the government market that you want to go after and stick to that plan. Once you determine your target markets, your next step is to locate opportunities within those markets. Visit www.sba.gov/about-offices-list/2 for a list of SBA offices by state.

FINDING AGENCIES ONLINE

The Web offers businesses unlimited marketing potential and is an essential component in doing business with the government. Each federal agency has its own Web site. One of the best ways to familiarize yourself with a particular agency is to browse its site. You'll quickly notice that most federal government Web sites end in .gov, an abbreviation for *government*.

Agencies typically use the short form of their names as their Web addresses. To find the Department of Energy's Web site, you would type:

www.doe.gov

If you wanted the Department of Health and Human Services, you would type:

www.hhs.gov

In the case of DoD agencies, their Web sites typically end in .mil, which is an abbreviation for *military*. The Defense Logistics Agency site is found at:

www.dla.mil

If an agency's Web address doesn't agree with its acronym, you can try to locate it using another agency's site. Easier still, just Google the agency.

FEDBIZOPPS

It's easier than ever to scope out federal contracts online. FedBizOpps (also known as FBO; www.fbo.gov) is the single government point of entry on the Web for federal procurements over $25,000. FedBizOpps helps level the playing field for small businesses by minimizing the effort and cost associated with finding government contracting opportunities.

> In the "olden days," solicitations were printed in a newspaper called the *Commerce Business Daily* (CBD). On January 4, 2002, FedBizOpps replaced the CBD as the official source for procurement opportunities and information.

Government buyers publicize their business opportunities by posting information directly to FedBizOpps via the Internet. Contractors looking to do business with the government are able to search, monitor, and retrieve opportunities solicited by the entire federal contracting community.

FedBizOpps lists synopses and notices of proposed contract actions, contract solicitations, amendments/modifications, subcontracting leads, contract awards, and other business opportunities. Although the General Services Administration (GSA) is responsible for the operation and maintenance of the Web site, the content of a notice is the sole responsibility of the buying office that issues or posts the notice.

Anywhere from 500 to 1,500 new notices are posted each business day. FedBizOpps currently supports more than 30,000 federal buyers in over 100 federal agencies and hosts more than 800,000 solicitation documents. Over 95 percent of all federal opportunities are listed on FedBizOpps.

Using FedBizOpps to Gain Market Knowledge

Federal buying activities frequently use FedBizOpps to:

- Solicit information for acquisition planning. Contractors are given an opportunity to comment on planned contracting actions.
- Announce opportunities for one-on-one meetings between government buyers and contractors for planning purposes.
- Announce small business conferences or fairs.
- Announce advance planning briefings for industry.

Federal procurement rules not only allow federal buyers to meet with contractors prior to the announcement of a solicitation, they actually encourage this. Meeting with agency acquisition officials or requirements personnel is a great way to gather advance information on their particular needs and introduce them to your company's products and services. I can't think of a better way to get an insider edge on your competition than using FedBizOpps to identify pre-selling opportunities.

Getting Started with FedBizOpps

Let's assume you want to identify opportunities for Facilities Support Services (NAICS code 561210) in the State of Arkansas.

1. Go to www.fbo.gov.

   Note: If you're new to FedBizOpps, be sure to read the User Guides located at the far right of this screen. Click the Vendor link.

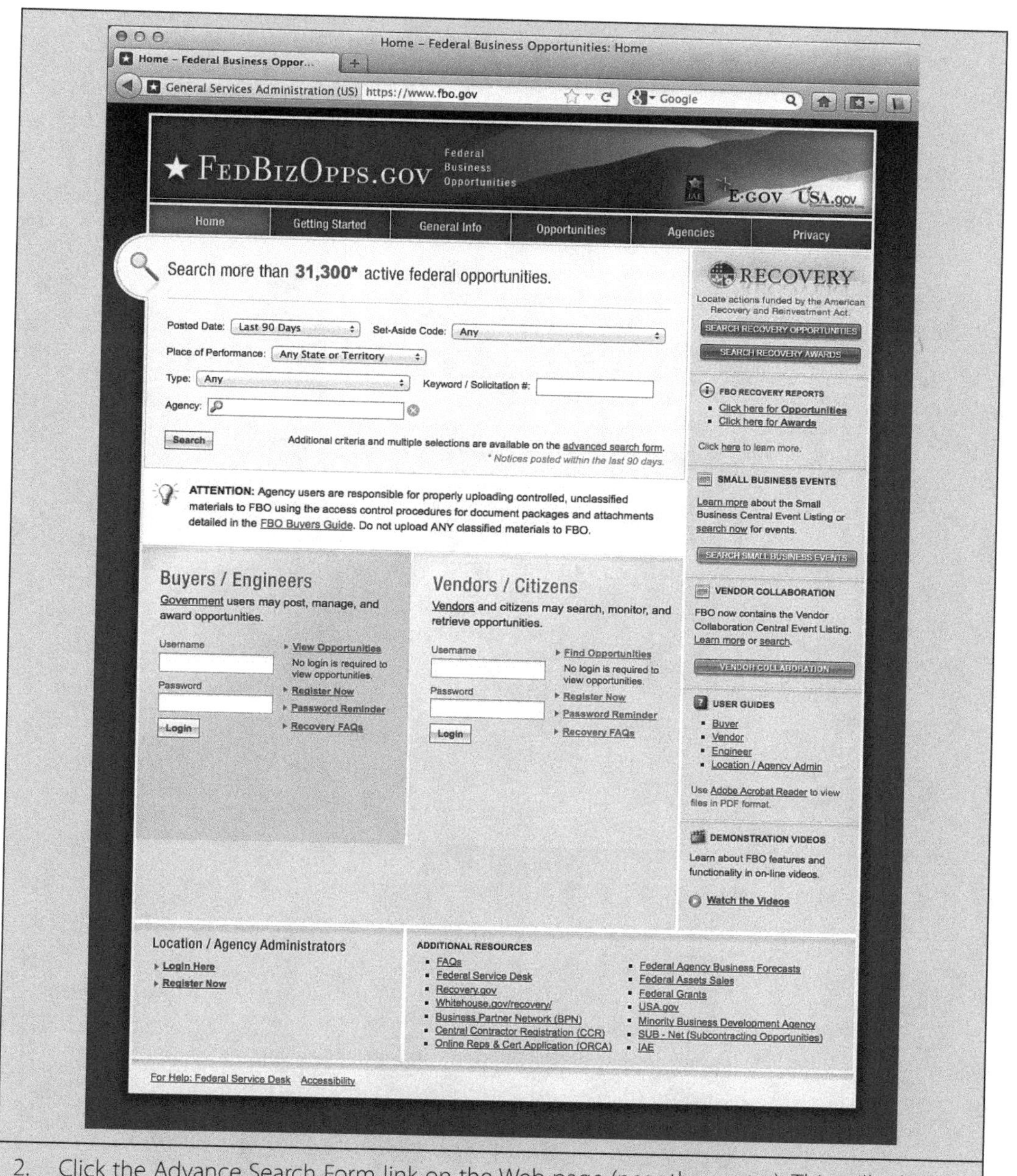

2. Click the Advance Search Form link on the Web page (near the center). This will take you to the FBO Synopsis/Awards Search page. FBO advanced search options include:
   - Posted Date
   - Place of Performance State and/or ZIP Code
   - Set-Aside Code
   - Opportunity/Procurement Type

- Agency/Office/Locations (begin typing to select from a list)
- Keyword or SOL# (solicitation number)
- NAICS Code (select from dropdown menu)
- Classification Code
- Statutory Authority requirements
- Date Ranges.

In this case, we are going to search the State of Arkansas for Department of Agriculture (USDA) opportunities under NAICS code 561210, Facilities Support Services. Once you have filled in the appropriate criteria, click the Search button.

3. Search results:

Search Results:

Opportunity	Agency/Office	Type/Set-Aside	Posted On
Facilities Maintenance Service AG-82A7-S-11-0100 Maintenance, repair, and alteration of real property	**Department of Agriculture** Forest Service R-2 Rocky Mountain Region	Combined Synopsis/ Solicitation / Total Small Business	May 04, 2015

In this case, a Combined Synopsis/Solicitation has been posted. To review the solicitation details, you'd click on the highlighted link (Facilities Maintenance Service).

Note: Many solicitations are reserved, or set aside, for small businesses, minority-owned businesses, women-owned firms, and veteran-owned businesses and are listed as such.

Facilities Maintenance Service

Solicitation Number: AG-82A7-S-11-0100
Agency: Department of Agriculture
Office: Forest Service
Location: R-2 Rocky Mountain Region

Solicitation Number:

AG-82A7-S-11-0100

Notice Type:

Combined Synopsis/Solicitation

Synopsis:

Added: May 04, 2015

It is the intent of this solicitation and any resultant contract to obtain Maintenance Services as specified herein for a base period of July 1, 2015 through June 30, 2016 plus four one-year options. Services will be performed at the Cass Job Corps Center.

Package #1

Posted Date:

May 4, 2015

AG82A7S110100Final.pdf

Description: It is the intent of this solicitation and any resultant contract to obtain Maintenance Services as specified herein for a base period of July 1, 2015 through June 30, 2016 plus four one-year options.

Contracting Office Address:

740 Simms Street
Regional Office
Golden, Colorado 80401

Place of Performance:

Cass Job Corps Center, located at 21424 N. Highway 23, Ozark, Arkansas 72949

Primary Point of Contact:

Len S. Patrick III,
Contract Specialist
lpatrick@fs.fed.us
Phone: 303-275-8534
Fax: 303-275-8594

Return To Opportunities List	Watch This Opportunity
Add Me To Interested Vendors	

To review the entire solicitation package, you'd click on the PDF attachment (AG82A7S-110100Final.pdf).

Be sure to click on the Watch This Opportunity box at the bottom of the solicitation and provide your email address. This is a subscription to a mailing list for all future announcements on this particular solicitation.

Vendor Notification Service

By registering for the Vender Notification Service (under Vendors /Citizens - Search, Monitor, and Retrieve Opportunities on the FedBizOpps homepage), vendors can register to receive procurement announcements by email. Vendors can specify notices they wish to receive by solicitation number, selected organizations, and product service classification. To date, more than 200,000 vendors are registered to receive business opportunities from FedBizOpps.

FedBizOpps allows users to join and view a published list of vendors interested in a particular solicitation. This is useful for vendors who are interested in teaming on procurement opportunities. The Add Me To Interested Vendors button will be on the listing page of the solicitation, if available. Eventually, federal agencies/buying offices will use this site regularly to receive proposals electronically.

Along the right side of the FBO Web page, there's special information about American Reinvestment and Recovery Act opportunities and awards, small business events, and a brand new category, Vendor Collaboration, for posting Industry Days and other events. Also, the FAQ page is quite informative.

Be Realistic

If you're new to the federal marketplace, it can be tempting to bid or propose on every federal contract that comes along, but your time and effort would be better spent targeting the best opportunities for your business. Look objectively at your company's resources. If the project seems too big, if you don't meet all of the solicitation's requirements, or if completing the proposal is going to put an unnecessary strain on your personnel, skip it and find another opportunity more suited to your specialties. In other words, don't burn that midnight oil if you don't have to.

FEDERAL SUPPLY SCHEDULES/GSA SCHEDULES

Not to be redundant, but every commercial contractor interested in selling to the federal government should be on a federal supply schedule—just your humble author's opinion! GSA schedules allow you to establish long-term government-wide contracts for your particular products and services. They are a great way to get your foot in the government's door.

Schedule holders are preapproved to contract with federal agencies, so your company joins a list of preferred vendors. GSA schedules thus provide government buying offices with a quick way to close federal sales while staying within the procurement rules for competition. Your approved prices or rates can also be used to validate your costs on other proposals you submit, thus helping keep the Defense Contract Audit Agency off your back.

Contractors looking for ways to diversify and/or complement their commercial sales base also should strongly consider getting on a schedule. Government business tends to complement your commercial business. Not only do schedule orders tend to be larger, but government buyers also tend to make purchases at different times of the year than do commercial buyers, often placing orders in September, when the government's fiscal year ends.

Chapter 7 goes into detail on the federal supply schedule program.

FEDERAL REGISTER

The daily newspaper that informs the public of congressional and federal enactments and regulatory activities is the *Federal Register*. It is the official publication used by the federal government to announce changes to the FAR. All changes to established agency regulations must be published in the *Federal Register*.

The National Archives and Records Administration is responsible for publishing the *Federal Register*. The publication varies in size from 200 to 600 pages (or more), depending on the number and length of announcements.

Paying careful attention to the *Federal Register* will help you anticipate the government's priorities and program changes. The *Federal Register* is available at www.gpoaccess.gov/fr/index.html.

Federal Register / Vol. 77, No. 91 / Thursday, May 10, 2012 / Rules and Regulations 27547

DEPARTMENT OF DEFENSE

GENERAL SERVICES ADMINISTRATION

NATIONAL AERONAUTICS AND SPACE ADMINISTRATION

48 CFR Parts 9 and 52

[FAC 2005–59; FAR Case 2012–013; Item I; Docket 2012–0013, Sequence 1]

RIN 9000–AM22

Federal Acquisition Regulation; Prohibition on Contracting With Inverted Domestic Corporations

AGENCY: Department of Defense (DoD), General Services Administration (GSA), and National Aeronautics and Space Administration (NASA).

ACTION: Interim rule.

SUMMARY: DoD, GSA, and NASA are issuing an interim rule amending the Federal Acquisition Regulation (FAR) to implement a section of the Consolidated Appropriations Act, 2012, that prohibits the award of contracts using appropriated funds to any foreign incorporated entity that is treated as an inverted domestic corporation or to any subsidiary of such entity.

DATES: *Effective Date:* May 10, 2012.

Comment Date: Interested parties should submit written comments to the Regulatory Secretariat on or before July 9, 2012 to be considered in the formulation of a final rule.

ADDRESSES: Submit comments identified by FAC 2005–59, FAR Case 2012–013 by any of the following methods:

- *Regulations.gov: http://www.regulations.gov.* Submit comments via the Federal eRulemaking portal by searching "FAR Case 2012–013". Select the link "Submit a Comment" that corresponds with "FAR Case 2012–013". Follow the instructions provided at the "Submit a Comment" screen. Please include your name, company name (if any), and "FAR Case 2012–013" on your attached document.
- *Fax:* 202–501–4067.
- *Mail:* General Services Administration, Regulatory Secretariat (MVCB), ATTN: Hada Flowers, 1275 First Street NE., 7th floor, Washington, DC 20417.

Instructions: Please submit comments only and cite FAC 2005–59, FAR Case 2012–013, in all correspondence related to this case. All comments received will be posted without change to *http://www.regulations.gov,* including any personal and/or business confidential information provided.

FOR FURTHER INFORMATION CONTACT: Mr. Michael O. Jackson, Procurement Analyst, at 202–208–4949, for clarification of content. For information pertaining to status or publication schedules, contact the Regulatory Secretariat at 202–501–4755. Please cite FAC 2005–59, FAR Case 2012–013.

SUPPLEMENTARY INFORMATION:

I. Background

This rule implements section 738 of Division C of the Consolidated Appropriations Act, 2012 (Pub. L. 112–74), which was signed on December 23, 2011. The same Governmentwide restrictions are already incorporated in the FAR for funds appropriated in Fiscal Years 2008 through 2010, under FAR Case 2008–009, which published as an interim rule in the **Federal Register** at 74 FR 31561 on July 1, 2009, and as a final rule which published in the **Federal Register** at 76 FR 31410 on May 31, 2011.

Section 738 of Division C extends to the use of Federal appropriated funds for Fiscal Year 2012, the prohibition against contracting with any inverted domestic corporation, as defined at section 835(b) of the Homeland Security Act of 2002 (Pub. L. 107–296, 6 U.S.C. 395(b)) or any subsidiary of such an entity.

An inverted domestic corporation is one that used to be incorporated in the United States, or used to be a partnership in the United States, but now is incorporated in a foreign country, or is a subsidiary whose parent corporation is incorporated in a foreign country. See the definition of inverted domestic corporation at FAR 9.108–1.

As in past consolidated appropriations acts that prohibited contracting with inverted domestic corporations, the prohibition does not apply when using Fiscal Year 2012 funds for a contract entered into before the date the funds were appropriated (December 23, 2011), or for any order issued pursuant to such contract. A paragraph has been added to FAR 52.209–10, Prohibition on Contracting with Inverted Domestic Corporations, to refer to the FAR 9.108–2 exceptions to the prohibition.

II. Executive Orders 12866 and 13563

Executive Orders (E.O.s) 12866 and 13563 direct agencies to assess all costs and benefits of available regulatory alternatives and, if regulation is necessary, to select regulatory approaches that maximize net benefits (including potential economic, environmental, public health and safety effects, distributive impacts, and equity). E.O. 13563 emphasizes the importance of quantifying both costs and benefits, of reducing costs, of harmonizing rules, and of promoting flexibility. This is not a significant regulatory action and, therefore, was not subject to review under section 6(b) of E.O. 12866, Regulatory Planning and Review, dated September 30, 1993. This rule is not a major rule under 5 U.S.C. 804.

III. Regulatory Flexibility Act

The Department of Defense (DoD), the General Services Administration (GSA), and the National Aeronautics and Space Administration (NASA) do not expect this rule to have a significant economic impact on a substantial number of small entities within the meaning of the Regulatory Flexibility Act, 5 U.S.C. 601, *et seq.,* because this rule will only impact an offeror that is an inverted domestic corporation and wants to do business with the Government. It is expected that the number of entities impacted by this rule will be minimal. Small business concerns are unlikely to have been incorporated in the United States and then reincorporated in a tax haven; the major players in these transactions are reportedly the very large multinational corporations. No domestic entities will be impacted by this rule. For the definition of "small business," the Regulatory Flexibility Act refers to the Small Business Act, which in turn allows the U.S. Small Business Administration (SBA) Administrator to specify detailed definitions or standards (5 U.S.C. 601(3) and 15 U.S.C. 632(a)). The SBA regulations at 13 CFR 121.105 discuss who is a small business: "(a)(1) Except for small agricultural cooperatives, a business concern eligible for assistance from SBA as a small business is a business entity organized for profit, with a place of business located in the United States, and which operates primarily within the United States or which makes a significant contribution to the U.S. economy through payment of taxes or use of American products, materials or labor." Therefore, an Initial Regulatory Flexibility Analysis has not been performed. DoD, GSA, and NASA invite comments from small business concerns and other interested parties on the expected impact of this rule on small entities.

DoD, GSA, and NASA will also consider comments from small entities concerning the existing regulations in subparts affected by the rule in accordance with 5 U.S.C. 610. Interested parties must submit such comments separately and should cite 5 U.S.C 610 (FAR Case 2012–013), in correspondence.

Example *Federal Register* Page

FEDERAL AGENCY ACQUISITION FORECASTS

Among the best sources a contractor can use to anticipate future contract actions or awards are federal agency acquisition forecasts. Each federal agency is required to compile and make available one-year projections of contracting opportunities that small and small disadvantaged businesses can perform.

Most federal agencies announce their acquisition forecasts online; visit www.acquisition.gov/comp/procurement_forecasts. An excellent source for future military programs can be found at http://comptroller.defense.gov/budget.html. Finally, the Office of Management and Budget offers overviews of agencies' budgets at www.whitehouse.gov/omb/budget/Overview.

As you review the budgeted procurement programs, be sure to look out for buying trends and potential teaming prospects.

TECH-*NET*

SBA's TECH-*Net*, the Technology Resources *Network*, is a search engine that features a database of high-tech small businesses. Business profiles are structured like executive business summaries, with specific data fields designed to meet the needs of researchers, investors, and other potential users. Small businesses can use their profiles to market their capabilities and accomplishments. TECH-*Net* also provides access to SBIR solicitations (see Chapter 5) and other technology procurement opportunities.

Businesses profiled on TECH-*Net* can be searched using NAICS code, key words, company name, ownership type, technology code, and contract award year. For more information on TECH-*Net*, visit http://web.sba.gov/tech-net/docrootpages.

FEDERAL PROCUREMENT DATA SYSTEM

Have you ever thought about which federal agencies typically buy your products and services? Or how much they bought? Or who the heck they bought them from?

When pursuing federal contracts, you'll need to identify market changes, analyze procurement history, and identify spending trends so you can pinpoint where to concentrate your sales efforts. Congress established the Federal Procurement Data System (FPDS) as a system for collecting, developing, and disseminating data on the more than $500 billion a year the government spends on supplies and services. It serves as a government-wide acquisition management information system.

FPDS provides unprecedented visibility into procurement and acquisition activities within federal agencies. Among its many features, FPDS:

- Provides the public access to federal data online and in real time
- Provides users with extensive online reporting capabilities, including reports with charts and graphs
- Collects data on over 16.5 million procurements valued at more than $3,000, including who bought what and from whom, the dollar amount of each transaction, when the contract was signed, and where the work was performed
- Maintains a historical trail of all transactions, including interagency transactions conducted through government-wide acquisition contracts (GWACs) and Federal Supply Schedule contracts (see Chapter 7)
- Enables government acquisition officials worldwide to input and access purchase data via the Internet.

Many of the dollar figures used in this book came directly from FPDS. The site is very user-friendly, and it's easy for anyone to set up an account. For more information on FPDS, visit www.fpds.gov.

Another excellent Web site for federal award information is www.usaspending.gov.

YEAR-END PROCUREMENTS

The federal government operates on the basis of a fiscal year that begins October 1 and ends September 30. As mentioned in Chapter 2, Congress appropriates funds to federal agencies to run their operations or meet their mission requirements. The appropriations can be for a single year, for multiple years, or on an unrestricted basis. Most appropriations are for a single year.

When Congress appropriates funds to a federal agency on a single-year basis, the agency must spend those funds during that particular fiscal year or lose the funding. Use it or lose it! This situation gives federal agencies no incentive to save money. In fact, it encourages agencies to spend all available funds.

Which quarter during the government's fiscal year historically has the highest level of procurement activity or acquisitions? If you guessed the fourth quarter, you're right. Why do you think this is? Maybe federal personnel go crazy from the heat. (Hey, it happens!) But more than likely it's because the majority of government funds expire on September 30. If you receive a solicitation during May or June, the agency might have to award the contract before midnight on September 30 or lose its funding.

It is a fact of life that year-end procurements tend to be a little frantic. Mostly this is the result of poor planning by the agencies, internal bickering, and politics. Procurements are often poorly thought out, poorly designed, and fraught with errors that must be corrected after the contract has been awarded. Knowing the government's situation at this time of the year gives you an advantage during the solicitation process.

There are, of course, exceptions to this requirement. Funds appropriated on an unrestricted basis (also referred to as *no-year money*) or funds appropriated for multiple years do not necessarily expire on September 30. Ask the contracting officer about the status of a contract's appropriated funds.

■ ■ ■

In spite of—or because of—the federal government's size and varied needs, no one way exists to market your supplies and services. There is no right answer or master guide that fits every need and situation. Each federal agency uses different acquisition methods; therefore, the best way to market your items is to contact specific federal agencies to determine exactly how their procurement processes work.

To be successful in marketing to the federal government, you must know your customer and be persistent. Visit each federal agency's Web site. Go to programs and workshops. Register your supplies and services with the agencies. Talk to each agency's small business specialist. Sign up for a federal supply schedule. Provide buying offices with brochures describing your company. In short, do whatever it takes to get your products and services noticed!

■ ■ ■

Support Programs and Services for Contractors

"Business is lousy. Maybe I should have done more market research first."

What's in this chapter?

- Small Business Administration
- Procurement Technical Assistance Centers (PTAC)
- DoD Office of Small Business Programs
- General Services Administration
- USA.gov
- National Contract Management Association

If there's one area that clearly differentiates the federal marketplace from the commercial world, it is the numerous resources the government has established to help small businesses participate in federal contracting. In fact, it is government policy for each federal agency to provide small businesses with information on procurements, guidance on solicitation procedures, and identification of subcontracting opportunities.

Many nonfederal sources offer support services as well. This chapter discusses many of the programs available to small contracting firms.

SMALL BUSINESS ADMINISTRATION

The world of federal contracting can be difficult to navigate, but small businesses have a resource and an ally in the Small Business Administration (SBA). The SBA offers a wide variety of programs and services, covering various business areas, including financial, technical, and management assistance, to small businesses. SBA is in business solely to help the small business owner.

Specifically, SBA offers five major programs:

- Business development assistance
- Procurement assistance
- Minority small business assistance
- Advocacy
- Financial assistance.

SBA also offers counseling services to business owners or potential business owners on all facets of small business matters.

The best place to locate up-to-the-minute information about SBA programs and services is www.sba.gov.

Did You Know That SBA . . .

- Partners with more than 8,000 private-sector lenders to provide capital to small businesses?
- Guaranteed more than 79,000 loans totaling $17 billion to small businesses during FY 2011?
- Maintains a portfolio guaranteeing more than $40 billion in loans to 220,000 small businesses that otherwise would not have such access to capital?
- Extended management and technical assistance to nearly one million small businesses through its 1,100 Small Business Development Centers and 10,500 Service Corps of Retired Executives volunteers?
- Provides loan guarantees and technical assistance to small business exporters through U.S. Export Assistance Centers?

SBA Answer Desk

The SBA answer desk is a toll-free information center that answers questions about starting or running a business and getting assistance. The toll-free number is (800) 8-ASK-SBA. The answer desk can give you a list of SBA district offices and their phone numbers. You can also obtain this information from www.sba.gov/content/find-local-sba-office.

Service Corps of Retired Executives

SBA developed the Service Corps of Retired Executives (SCORE) to provide one-on-one management counseling to aspiring entrepreneurs and business owners. SCORE's experienced business experts offer general advice on everything from marketing and writing a business plan, to managing cash flow/capital needs, to investigating the market potential for a product or service.

Counselors also give insight into how to start, operate, buy or franchise, and sell a business. SCORE services are free. Currently more than 10,500 volunteer business counselors are located at SBA field offices throughout the United States.

For a current list of SCORE locations, visit www.score.org, or call (800) 634-0245.

SBA Small Business Development Centers

Numerous studies have shown that most small businesses fail as a result of poor management. SBA established the Small Business Development Center (SBDC) program to provide management assistance to small business owners. This program coordinates efforts among universities across the country; local, state, and federal governments; and private-sector businesses to provide assistance with management techniques and technology to the small business community.

SBDC's services include assisting small businesses with financial, marketing, production, organization, engineering, and technical problems. In addition, SBDC offers specialized programs on international trade, business law, venture capital formation, and rural development.

Currently, there are 57 SBDCs—one in each state (Texas has four), the District of Columbia, Puerto Rico, Guam, and the U.S. Virgin Islands. In each state a lead organization sponsors and manages the SBDC program. The lead organization coordinates program services through a network of subcenters and satellite locations in each state, providing nearly 900 service locations. Subcenters are located at colleges, vocational schools, local government offices, and economic development centers.

The best way to locate an SBDC is to visit www.sba.gov/sbdc .

SBA Procurement Center Representatives

Procurement center representatives (PCRs) are located at major federal buying centers around the country as well as SBA area offices. They help increase the small business share of federal procurement awards by:

- Initiating small business set-asides
- Reserving procurements for competition among small firms
- Counseling and assisting small businesses in obtaining federal contracts.

Visit www.sba.gov/content/procurement-center-representatives for more information.

SBA Women's Business Centers

Women's Business Centers (WBCs) provide women with long-term training and counseling in all aspects of owning and managing a business. SBA has a network of more than 60 WBCs, with at least one representative in each state. For the phone number of the WBC in your state or district, visit www.sba.gov/content/womens-business-centers or contact the SBA answer desk at (800) 8-ASK-SBA.

The Office of Women's Business Ownership (OWBO), which oversees the network of WBCs, also provides comprehensive training, counseling, and information. Information about OWBO also can be found at the Women's Business Centers Web site noted above.

SBA Office of Advocacy

SBA's Office of Advocacy encourages policies that support small business development and growth. It works to reduce the burdens that federal policies impose on small businesses and to maximize the benefits small businesses receive. To accomplish these objectives, Congress has specified five statutory duties for the office:

- To serve as a focal point for receiving complaints, criticisms, and suggestions concerning federal policies that affect small businesses
- To counsel small businesses on ways to resolve problems in dealing with the federal government
- To represent small businesses before federal agencies whose actions affect them
- To recommend changes to better comply with the Small Business Act (see Chapter 4) and communicate such proposals to the appropriate agencies
- To work with federal agencies and private groups to examine ways in which small businesses can make better use of the government's programs and services.

The Office of Advocacy also provides statistics and research studies on small businesses. For more information, visit www.sba.gov/advocacy.

SBA Financial Assistance Programs

No matter how carefully you manage your company's cash flow, at some point you will have to borrow money. The two primary reasons a company borrows money are (1) to cover temporary cash-flow shortages and (2) to provide working capital for business growth. One of the best places for a small business to look for financial assistance is SBA.

SBA provides financial assistance in the form of loan guarantees to qualified small businesses that are unable to obtain credit elsewhere. These loans are available for many business purposes, such as acquiring real estate, buying equipment, raising working capital, buying or building inventory, or expanding. To be eligible for an SBA loan, a business must meet the size standards established by industry type (see Chapter 4).

SBA makes loans in conjunction with a bank or other lending institution, which provides the funds. It guarantees up to 90 percent of the loan. The major benefit to borrowers who obtain loans through SBA is the terms, which are typically longer than those available from commercial lenders. SBA does not provide grants to start or expand a business.

SBA offers many different types of loans, including:

- Minority prequalification loans
- Women's prequalification loans
- Physical disaster business loans
- Contract loans
- Surety bond guarantees
- Small business energy loans
- Microloans
- General contractor loans.

To be eligible for an SBA loan, you must first apply—and be rejected—for a loan from at least one qualified commercial lender. The reasons for rejection might include the following: the repayment period was too long, the business has not been in operation long enough, or the loan request was too large. If the lender rejects your loan request for any reason other than your ability to repay, ask if the lender would be willing to make the loan if SBA guaranteed it.

If the lender agrees to the SBA loan arrangement, it contacts SBA to determine whether the agency will guarantee the loan. Assuming that the loan meets SBA's criteria, it's up to the lender whether to make the loan. If the lender agrees, it makes the necessary arrangements to secure the guarantee with SBA. If the lender refuses to make the loan, the borrower must look for another lender.

Borrowers should be prepared to pay closing costs on SBA-guaranteed loans. Closing costs vary, but most tend to be 3 percent to 5 percent of the total loan amount.

PROCUREMENT TECHNICAL ASSISTANCE CENTERS

What can a Procurement Technical Assistance Center (PTAC) do for you?

- Determine if your business is ready for government contracting
- Help you register in the proper places
- See if you are eligible in any small business certifications
- Research contract opportunities.

Local, in-person counseling and training help small business owners sell products and services to federal, state, and/or local governments. Don't hesitate to find the PTAC near you by visiting www.dla.mil/SmallBusiness/Pages/ProcurementTechnicalAssistanceCenters.aspx.

Federal Procurement Conferences

Government-sponsored procurement conferences and trade shows give small businesses the opportunity to meet with acquisition specialists from military and civilian agencies, as well as prime contractors. Conferences are held at various locations throughout the country. For conference times and locations, visit www.acq.osd.mil/osbp/conferences.

Attendance lists at Vendor Industry Day Conferences are good for knowing who your competition might be. Most federal agencies post them routinely on FedBizOpps (www.fbo.gov).

DOD OFFICE OF SMALL BUSINESS PROGRAMS

The Office of Small Business Programs (OSBP) is the advocate for small businesses within the DoD community and provides guidance and technical assistance to help maximize the success of small firms and advance their needs. OSBP advises the secretary of defense on all matters related to small business.

The following programs are managed by OSBP:

- DoD Mentor-Protégé (see Chapter 6)
- DoD Small Business Innovation Research (SBIR) and Small Business Technology Transfer (STTR; see Chapter 5)
- Indian Incentive Program (This program compensates prime contractors that use Indian organizations on subcontracted work in accordance with DFARS Clause 252.226-7001).

Visit www.acq.osd.mil/osbp/ for more detailed information on the OSBP.

Military Opportunities

DoD has published an excellent handbook called *Doing Business with the DoD*, which furnishes general information about DoD contracting. If you plan to contract with DoD, this handbook will be very useful. The information can be found online at www.acq.osd.mil/osbp/doing_business.

GENERAL SERVICES ADMINISTRATION

The General Services Administration (GSA) is the government's landlord. GSA administers building leases—almost all of the larger ones. It also provides federal agencies with the tools necessary to perform their day-to-day operations. GSA spends several billion dollars annually to provide federal agencies across the country with:

- Workspace and security
- Furniture
- Phones and computers
- Travel services

- Motor vehicle fleet management
- Federal child care
- Historic building preservation
- Fine art management.

GSA's Web site, www.gsa.gov, has all kinds of useful information and downloadable forms; it is probably the best of the federal agencies' sites. Additional Web sites and contact details for gathering specific information appear in the box below.

GSA also distributes a handbook called *Doing Business with GSA*. Visit www.gsa.gov/portal/content/103249 to download it.

U.S. General Services Administration

Small Business Solutions

www.gsa.gov/osbu

Access to Government Contracting

GSA provides support and access for small businesses in a variety of industries.

Federal Acquisition Service

Commercial Products and Services

www.gsa.gov/fas
NCSCcustomer.service@gsa.gov
(800) 488-3111

Public Buildings Service

Construction, Architecture, Interior Design and Real Estate

www.gsa.gov/pbs
IndustryRelations@gsa.gov
(866) PBS-VEND

General Contracting Information

www.gsa.gov/howtoselltothegovernment
www.gsa.gov/smallbizhelp

Procurement Listings

www.fbo.gov
www.gsa.gov/smbusforecast

Partnering Opportunities and Other Contracting Support

www.gsa.gov/subdirectory
www.gsa.gov/mentorprotege
www.osdbu.gov/offices.html
www.aptac-us.org
www.sba.gov

Contracting Regulations and Policy

www.acquisition.gov

For GSA's Small Business Regional Representatives, Publications, Events, Free Training, and General Information

www.gsa.gov/osbu
www.gsa.gov/events
www.twitter.com/gsaosbu
interact.gsa.gov/groups/small-business-solutions

GSA Regional Centers/Small Business Utilization Centers

GSA Regional Centers serve as a front door for small businesses seeking to market their products and services to GSA. These centers advise and counsel people interested in contracting with GSA. Each center distributes federal directories, publication lists, references, and a variety of technical publications.

There are currently 11 Regional Centers throughout the country. Find the address and phone number of the Regional Center that serves your area or region at www.gsa.gov/sbu.

Each Regional Center is staffed by specialists who can provide information on how to:

- Introduce items for government purchase
- Learn about current opportunities with GSA
- Obtain copies of federal standards and specifications
- Review bid and proposal abstracts to learn the history of various contract awards (abstracts identify the names of successful contractors and the prices they bid)
- Obtain publications and other documents about government procurements
- Receive business counseling.

GSA Regional Centers play a central role in GSA's small business set-aside programs by challenging decisions not to set aside procurements for small business. They also review prime contracts to identify subcontracting opportunities for small and small disadvantaged businesses.

Office of Small and Disadvantaged Business Utilization

Each major federal agency and department must have an Office of Small and Disadvantaged Business Utilization (OSDBU). The OSDBU provides small businesses with information on procurement opportunities, guidance on procurement procedures, and identification of both prime and subcontracting opportunities. For a current list of OSDBU locations and addresses, visit www.osdbu.gov.

USA.gov

USA.gov is the federal government's one-stop shopping mall for all things government. By linking together government resources, USA.gov allows users to search popular topics; reference sources, such as news releases, forms, and laws and regulations; and identify services and benefits for citizens, businesses, and federal, state, tribal, and local governments.

Information specialists are also available to answer your questions directly, refer you to the correct office, or research your inquiry; call 1-(800) FED-INFO.

Federal Yellow Book

The *Federal Yellow Book* is an organizational directory of the departments and agencies of the federal government's executive branch. It lists the positions, addresses, and phone numbers of more than 40,000 federal officials. For more information about this publication, contact:

Leadership Directories, Inc.
(212) 627-4140
info@leadershipdirectories.com

www.leadershipdirectories.com

NATIONAL CONTRACT MANAGEMENT ASSOCIATION

The National Contract Management Association (NCMA) is a professional association in the field of contract management with more than 19,000 members. NCMA offers:

- Training programs
- *Contract Management* magazine
- *Journal of Contract Management*
- National and regional conferences
- Credential programs.

For more information about NCMA, contact:

National Contract Management Association (NCMA)
21740 Beaumeade Circle, Suite 125
Ashburn, VA 20147
Phone (800) 344-8096

www.ncmahq.org

■ ■ ■

In addition to the huge buyers like DoD and GSA, hundreds of lesser-known federal agencies buy from both large and small businesses. An excellent source of names and addresses for federal agencies is www.lib.lsu.edu/gov.

■ ■ ■

How the Government Issues Procurement Opportunities

> Congratulations on your promotion . . . From now on you will always eat well and never hear the truth again!
>
> —*Armedforcesjournal.com*

The government procures most of its products and services through "full and open competition." But how does the government determine who receives its awards? Is the winning contractor the one that submits the lowest bid, or is it the contractor with the best overall product or service? The answer: it depends on the solicitation type. The government primarily uses three methods to solicit contractors' offers:

- Simplified acquisition or small purchase procedures (FAR Part 13), discussed in Chapter 10
- Sealed bidding procedures (FAR Part 14), covered in Chapter 11
- Negotiated procurement procedures (FAR Part 15), discussed in Chapter 12.

Each solicitation method specifies the basis upon which the award decision will be made. Accordingly, step one of any solicitation you're considering is to carefully read through it and determine exactly what factors the government will use to make its award decision. If you're not 100 percent sure that you can make the deadlines or perform the work required, there's little point in spinning your wheels and being disappointed that you did not win that particular contract.

The Uniform Contract Format (UCF) is a format used by the federal government in solicitation packages sent to contractors. Chapter 13 walks you through the 4 parts and 13 sections of the UCF.

Simplified Acquisition or Small Purchase Procedures

"Unless we receive the outstanding balance within ten days, we will have no choice but to destroy your credit rating, ruin your reputation, and make you wish you were never born. If you have already sent the ninety-seven cents, please disregard this notice."

What's in this chapter?

- Micropurchases
- Simplified acquisition methods
  - Oral solicitation
  - Request for quotation
  - Government-wide commercial purchase card (credit card)
  - Blanket purchase agreement
  - Fast payment procedure

When the government makes major purchases (greater than $150,000), it follows an extensive set of procedures to ensure that the funds are spent fairly and wisely. However, the federal government cannot afford to spend the same amount of time and money on small purchases or commercial items. That's where simplified acquisition procedures come into play: they emphasize simplicity and reduced administrative costs.

Simplified acquisition procedures apply to purchases that cost $150,000 or less. This $150K limit is referred to as the *simplified acquisition threshold* (SAT). If an agency estimates that an acquisition will exceed the SAT, the acquisition must be handled using formal acquisition procedures (see Chapters 11 and 12). Simplified acquisition procedures represent 90 percent of the government's purchase transactions, although they account for less than 20 percent of the total procurement dollars.

By using simplified acquisition procedures, contracting officers avoid much of the red tape that slows down the purchase of supplies and services. These procedures also reduce the time and resources that a contractor spends in meeting peculiar government standards. The procedures, however, do not apply to orders from federal supply schedules (Chapter 7) or to delivery orders placed against existing contracts.

Federal agencies are required to use simplified acquisition procedures to the maximum extent practicable. In fact, acquisitions with an anticipated dollar value exceeding $3,000 but not over $150,000 are reserved exclusively for small businesses, provided there is a reasonable expectation of obtaining offers from two or more responsible small business concerns. If *that* doesn't convince you that government contracting offers exceptional opportunities for small businesses, nothing will.

MICROPURCHASES

Purchases that are $3,000 or less are referred to as *micropurchases*. (The micropurchase limit is $2,000 in the case of construction.) These purchases typically cover routine supplies and services. Micropurchases allow the government to keep less documentation, pay bills more quickly, and handle discrepancies less formally. They account for 70 percent of the government's purchasing actions.

Micropurchases use the following guidelines:

- Purchases must be distributed equitably among qualified suppliers to the maximum extent practical.
- Micropurchases may be awarded without soliciting competitive quotes if the price is deemed reasonable.

The requirements of the Buy American Act do not apply to micropurchases (see Chapter 2). Federal agencies may authorize employees who are not designated acquisition officials to make micropurchases, thus allowing the contracting officer to concentrate on major purchases. Micropurchases may be made from any type of seller, not just small businesses.

Micropurchases are most commonly made using the government-wide commercial purchase card. Contractors should direct their marketing to potential buyers (or contracting activities) through catalogs, ads, sales visits, and other conventional marketing techniques.

Acquisition Methods

$3,000 or less	Micropurchase procedures
$3,001 to $150,000	Simplified acquisition procedures
Over $150,00	Formal solicitation procedures

SIMPLIFIED ACQUISITION METHODS

Simplified acquisition procedures allow the government to use several authorized methods for entering into contracts. In most instances, contracts are made after obtaining quotes from at least two sources.

Oral Solicitation

Acquisition officials are first and foremost encouraged to solicit quotations "orally" when the transaction is under the simplified acquisition threshold and doing so helps expedite the purchase. Although the FAR does not have specific guidance on this subject, buying offices should have policies and procedures in place regarding their use of oral solicitations and the manner in which they are documented. It is always a good idea to document a contractor's price and the terms and conditions.

Request for Quotation

A request for quotation (RFQ) is a document (Standard Form 18) that the government uses to solicit prices for purchases that are under the simplified acquisition threshold of $150,000. The government typically uses RFQs when it wishes to obtain price, delivery, or other market information as the basis for preparing a purchase order.

Suppose James Statton, president of Answer Me, Inc., receives an RFQ for a phone answering machine and decides to submit a quote. James enters the price of the answering machine on Block 11 of SF 18, signs Block 14, and returns the form to Christine Edwards, the contracting officer, by the date specified on Block 10, as shown in the example on the facing page.

Government-Wide Commercial Purchase Card (Credit Card)

The quickest and simplest way to transact a federal purchase is to use a credit card. More than 3 million government employees currently hold one of these pieces of plastic money. They are typically used to buy supplies and services that fall under the micropurchase threshold of $3,000.

REQUEST FOR QUOTATION (THIS IS NOT AN ORDER)

THIS RFQ ☐ IS ☒ IS NOT A SMALL BUSINESS SET-ASIDE

PAGE 1 OF PAGES 6

1. REQUEST NO.: RFQ-DC-12-00082
2. DATE ISSUED: 05/29/2016
3. REQUISITION/PURCHASE REQUEST NO.: PR-DC-12-02905
4. CERT. FOR NAT. DEF. UNDER BDSA REG. 2 AND/OR DMS REG. 1 ▶ RATING

5a. ISSUED BY: US EPA - 1200 PENNSYLVANIA AVE. NW, WASHINGTON, DC 20460
6. DELIVER BY (Date): 07/30/2016

5b. FOR INFORMATION CALL (NO COLLECT CALLS)
NAME: CHRISTINE EDWARDS
TELEPHONE NUMBER: AREA CODE 202 NUMBER 564-2182

7. DELIVERY: ☒ FOB DESTINATION ☐ OTHER (See Schedule)

9. DESTINATION
a. NAME OF CONSIGNEE: US EPA - ERT-EAST
b. STREET ADDRESS: 2890 WOODBRIDGE AVE., BLDG 18
c. CITY: EDISON
d. STATE: NJ e. ZIP CODE: 08837-3679

8. TO:
a. NAME
b. COMPANY
c. STREET ADDRESS
d. CITY e. STATE f. ZIP CODE

10. PLEASE FURNISH QUOTATIONS TO THE ISSUING OFFICE IN BLOCK 5a ON OR BEFORE CLOSE OF BUSINESS (Date)

IMPORTANT: This is a request for information and quotations furnished are not offers. If you are unable to quote, please so indicate on this form and return it to the address in Block 5a. This request does not commit the Government to pay any costs incurred in the preparation of the submission of this quotation or to contract for supplies or service. Supplies are of domestic origin unless otherwise indicated by quoter. Any representations and/or certifications attached to this Request for Quotation must be completed by the quoter.

11. SCHEDULE (Include applicable Federal, State and local taxes)

ITEM NO. (a)	SUPPLIES/ SERVICES (b)	QUANTITY (c)	UNIT (d)	UNIT PRICE (e)	AMOUNT (f)
1	Digital Answering Machine	1		5,000.00	5,000.00

12. DISCOUNT FOR PROMPT PAYMENT ▶ a. 10 CALENDAR DAYS (%) | b. 20 CALENDAR DAYS (%) | c. 30 CALENDAR DAYS (%) | d. CALENDAR DAYS: NUMBER | PERCENTAGE

NOTE: Additional provisions and representations ☒ are ☐ are not attached.

13. NAME AND ADDRESS OF QUOTER
a. NAME OF QUOTER
b. STREET ADDRESS
c. COUNTY
d. CITY e. STATE f. ZIP CODE

14. SIGNATURE OF PERSON AUTHORIZED TO SIGN QUOTATION
15. DATE OF QUOTATION

16. SIGNER
a. NAME (Type or print)
b. TELEPHONE: AREA CODE, NUMBER
c. TITLE (Type or print)

AUTHORIZED FOR LOCAL REPRODUCTION
Previous edition not usable

STANDARD FORM 18 (REV. 6-95)
Prescribed by GSA-FAR (48 CFR) 53.215-1(a)

Example Request for Quotation (Standard Form 18)

Indeed, within DoD, use of the purchase card is mandated for most micropurchases. In fact, a written determination by a high-level official is required to not use the purchase card. During FY 2010, the federal government purchased over $30.2 billion worth of products and services using credit cards.

Federal agencies typically use MasterCard and Visa for their purchases. Anyone in possession of a government purchase card has procurement authority to use it (for purchases up to $3,000), based on the fact that he or she has the card. If you want additional verification that a buyer is eligible to use the card, ask to see his or her government identification card.

For purchases above the micropurchase level, the cardholder must be designated as a contracting officer.

Credit card sales are often referred to as the *hidden market* because there really isn't a convenient way to find out what local cardholders buy. Reaching out to cardholders using simple commercial marketing techniques—such as targeted emails, direct sales calls, and brochures—might be your best option. But, most important, ensure your business is able to accept credit card transactions, so you won't miss out on any quick sales opportunities!

Blanket Purchase Agreement

Blank purchase agreements (BPAs) further streamline the acquisition process. They are essentially charge accounts set up with qualified vendors. Contracting officers typically issue BPAs to several different vendors for the same types of supplies or services. This gives buying offices greater flexibility and choice when making purchase decisions.

The BPA may be limited to specific items, or it may cover all the products a vendor can furnish. Each BPA includes information about personnel who are authorized to place orders with the vendor, invoicing and payment procedures, delivery requirements, and fixed price(s) of the covered items. When a vendor establishes a BPA, it agrees to fill orders at or below the lowest price paid by its most favored private-sector customer.

A BPA may be established under the following circumstances:

- The agency purchases a wide variety of items in a broad class of supplies or services but does not know the exact quantities and delivery requirements in advance.
- There are no existing contract requirements for the same supply or service that the contracting activity is required to use.

BPAs may be established with:

- Multiple vendors for the same types of supplies or services to provide maximum practicable competition
- A single vendor from which numerous individual purchases (below the simplified acquisition threshold) will likely be made.

BPAs are usually established with local sources so that purchases can be made with minimal time and effort. Vendors are encouraged to contact buying offices to get their supplies and services listed on a BPA.

Once a buying office issues the BPA, the vendor must provide the authorized items upon request. BPAs are usually issued for a one-year period. With advance written notice (e.g., 30 days), either party may cancel a BPA. The majority of BPA orders are placed orally.

When a contracting officer makes a purchase using a BPA, he or she must still comply with small business set-aside requirements. Therefore, if two or more small businesses can perform the contract at reasonable prices, only small-business BPA vendors may be solicited.

Fast Payment Procedure

The fast payment procedure allows a contractor to be paid before the government verifies that supplies have been received and accepted. This procedure improves a contractor's cash flow by speeding up the payment process. The government may use these procedures for purchases of less than $30,000. In addition, on a case-by-case basis, agencies have the option to use this procedure for higher dollar amounts.

Fast payment procedures require a contractor to submit an invoice with the following certifications:

- The supplies were delivered to a post office, common carrier, or point of first receipt by the government.
- The contractor is responsible for replacing, repairing, or correcting the supplies not received, damaged in transit, or not conforming to purchase agreements.

Title to the supplies passes to the government upon delivery to the post office. Not all federal agencies use the fast payment procedure.

■ ■ ■

This chapter detailed the various types of and thresholds for simplified acquisition or small purchase procedures. You must be familiar with them so you will be aware of the policies and procedures that apply when you sell your supplies or services to the government.

■ ■ ■

CHAPTER 11

Sealed Bidding

"This is my final offer, Fred. I'll give you a 15% discount on all orders, free shipping for six months, two of my pickles, half of my fries **and** my little packet of crackers."

What's in this chapter?

- The solicitation process
- The sealed bidding (IFB) process
- Solicitation methods
- Preparing your bid
- Late bids
- Bid opening
- Bid evaluations
- Bid award

Sealed bidding is a rigid procurement process designed to protect the integrity of the competitive bidding system. It typically is used to purchase noncommercial products or services that are estimated to exceed $150,000. Although there is no dollar limit on the use of sealed bidding procedures, the federal government is authorized to use them only when:

- The government's specifications can be described clearly and accurately.
- Two or more bidders are expected to compete for the contract.
- There is adequate time to perform the sealed bidding process.
- The award will be made on the basis of price and other price-related factors.

Without these conditions, the contracting officer must use negotiated procurement procedures (see Chapter 12).

Price-related factors might include the costs or savings that could result from making multiple awards, taxes, inspection costs, and transportation differences. Sealed bidding procedures attempt to give all qualified contractors the opportunity to compete for government contracts while avoiding any favoritism.

THE SOLICITATION PROCESS

The sealed bidding process begins when a contracting officer publicizes a synopsis for a solicitation package, called an *invitation for bid* (IFB), in FedBizOpps. A synopsis briefly describes the scope of work for the project, and it is issued at least 15 days before the actual solicitation, although a shorter time frame is permissible for commercial items.

Information about obtaining a copy of the solicitation is included in the synopsis. Most solicitations can be downloaded directly from the Internet.

THE SEALED BIDDING (IFB) PROCESS

After the synopsis period, the contracting officer publicizes the actual IFB in FedBizOpps. The IFB contains everything a bidder must know to fulfill the contract, and it tends to be a sizable document. To be considered for an award, the bidder must agree to comply with all material respects of the IFB at the bid price.

The IFB is divided into sections and subsections, and it includes a transmittal sheet and table of contents. The transmittal sheet usually shows the solicitation number, the items to be acquired, the contract period, and other pertinent information. Do not submit the transmittal sheet with your bid.

An IFB should always include the following information:

- Description of supplies or services
- Specifications or statement of work
- Technical data
- Packaging requirements
- Inspection and acceptance criteria
- Delivery or performance schedules
- Deadline for submission of bids.

The contracting officer typically allows at least 30 days between the IFB's issuance and the bid opening for contractors to respond, unless combined synopsis/solicitation procedures are used. Sealed bidding always results in a fixed-price-type contract (see Chapter 14).

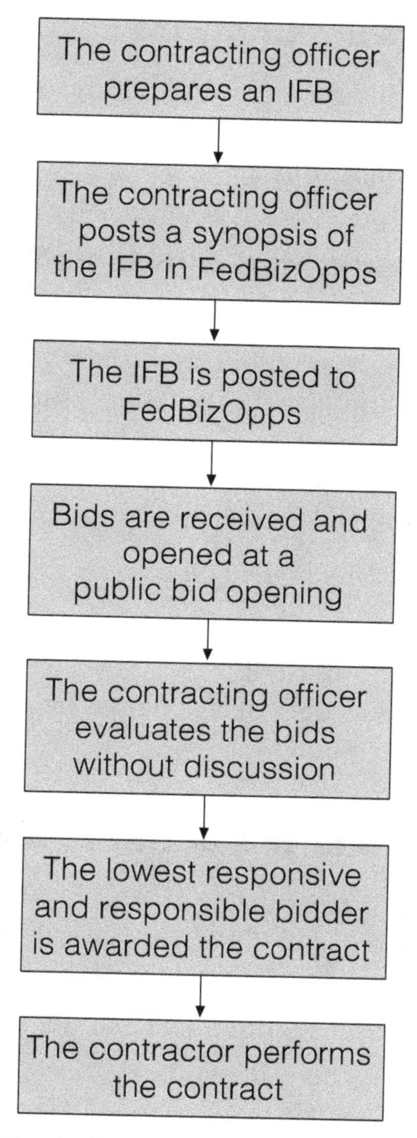
The contracting officer prepares an IFB
The contracting officer posts a synopsis of the IFB in FedBizOpps
The IFB is posted to FedBizOpps
Bids are received and opened at a public bid opening
The contracting officer evaluates the bids without discussion
The lowest responsive and responsible bidder is awarded the contract
The contractor performs the contract

Sealed Bidding (IFB) Process

SOLICITATION METHODS

A contracting officer uses one of four formats in preparing an IFB: (1) award/contract (Standard Form 26), (2) combined synopsis/solicitation, (3) Uniform Contract Format, or (4) Simplified Contract Format.

Award/Contract

Standard Form (SF) 26 is used when awarding sealed bid contracts for supplies or services and the bids were obtained on SF 33, Solicitation, Offer and Award (Block 18).

Combined Synopsis/Solicitation

To reduce the time required to solicit and award commercial-item contracts, agencies often use the combined synopsis/solicitation method. It combines the synopsis and solicitation issuance into a single document. This format is being used more and more because it allows for greater flexibility in preparing and organizing the IFB. The combined synopsis/solicitation is appropriate only for a relatively simple acquisition.

When this method is used, there are no prescribed times specified between the publication of the synopsis and the issuance of the solicitation, nor is a time prescribed for how long the solicitation should remain open. The FAR states only that potential bidders should be afforded a reasonable opportunity to respond.

Uniform Contract Format

For most major purchases, the contracting officer uses the Uniform Contract Format (UCF). In fact, all IFBs for noncommercial products and services must use the UCF unless:

- The Simplified Contract Format (SCF) is used.
- The solicitation is for construction, shipbuilding, ship repairs and maintenance, architect/engineering services, or items that require special contract forms.

See Chapter 13 for more detailed information about the UCF.

Simplified Contract Format

Because an IFB always leads to a fixed-price contract, contracting officers may use the SCF. The SCF should include the following information to the maximum practical extent:

- ***SF 1447, Solicitation/Contract.*** SF 1447 is the cover page. It includes the solicitation number, the issue date, the contracting activity, and a place for the signatures of the contractor and the contracting officer, as shown in the example on the next page.
- ***Contract schedule.*** The contract schedule includes the following: (1) contract line item number, (2) supplies or services description, (3) unit price and amount, (4) packaging requirements, (5) performance requirements, and (6) other information.
- ***Clauses.*** The clauses include those required by the FAR and those considered necessary by the contracting officer.
- ***List of documents and attachments.***
- ***Representations and instructions.*** These typically are divided into (1) representations and certifications; (2) instructions, conditions, and notices; and (3) award evaluation factors.

PREPARING YOUR BID

If your company decides to bid on a solicitation, you should start to work on your bid immediately upon receipt of the IFB. This is particularly important if the contract is large or if you must obtain and read several documents before bidding. Carefully examine the IFB's specifications, including all instructions and clauses. Questions about the IFB should be directed to the contracting officer named in the solicitation. Make no assumptions without authorized clarification.

The solicitation package should indicate where to obtain essential specifications and standards. If it doesn't, the contracting officer will provide that information. Bidders must meet the requirements of all the documents cited in the package.

Once you have read the IFB and the required documentation carefully, you should prepare a work plan and a delivery schedule. The work plan should detail the time and material costs of fulfilling the contract—information you'll need in determining your bid price. The delivery schedule should detail distances to the locations to which you'll ship the products.

SOLICITATION/CONTRACT
BIDDER/OFFEROR TO COMPLETE BLOCKS 11, 13, 15, 21, 22, & 27

1. THIS CONTRACT IS A RATED ORDER UNDER DPAS (15 CFR 700) | RATING | PAGE OF

2. CONTRACT NO. | 3. AWARD/EFFECTIVE DATE | 4. SOLICITATION NUMBER | 5. SOLICITATION TYPE ☐ SEALED BIDS (IFB) ☐ NEGOTIATED (RFP) | 6. SOLICITATION ISSUE DATE

7. ISSUED BY CODE
NO COLLECT CALLS

8. THIS ACQUISITION IS ☐ UNRESTRICTED OR ☐ SET ASIDE: % FOR:
☐ SMALL BUSINESS
☐ WOMEN-OWNED SMALL BUSINESS (WOSB) ELIGIBLE UNDER THE WOSB PROGRAM
☐ HUBZONE SMALL BUSINESS
☐ EDWOSB
☐ SERVICE-DISABLED VETERAN-OWNED SMALL BUSINESS
NAICS:
☐ 8(A)
SIZE STANDARD:

9. (AGENCY USE)

10. ITEMS TO BE PURCHASED *(BRIEF DESCRIPTION)*
☐ SUPPLIES ☐ SERVICES

11. IF OFFER IS ACCEPTED BY THE GOVERNMENT WITHIN ______ CALENDAR DAYS (60 CALENDAR DAYS UNLESS OFFEROR INSERTS A DIFFERENT PERIOD) FROM THE DATE SET FORTH IN BLOCK 9 ABOVE, THE CONTRACTOR AGREES TO HOLD ITS OFFERED PRICES FIRM FOR THE ITEMS SOLICITED HEREIN AND TO ACCEPT ANY RESULTING CONTRACT SUBJECT TO THE TERMS AND CONDITIONS STATED HEREIN.

12. ADMINISTERED BY CODE

13. CONTRACTOR OFFEROR CODE FACILITY CODE

14. PAYMENT WILL BE MADE BY CODE

TELEPHONE NUMBER ______ DUNS NUMBER ______
☐ CHECK IF REMITTANCE IS DIFFERENT AND PUT SUCH ADDRESS IN OFFER

SUBMIT INVOICES TO ADDRESS SHOWN IN BLOCK:

15. PROMPT PAYMENT DISCOUNT

16. AUTHORITY FOR USING OTHER THAN FULL AND OPEN COMPETITION ☐ 10 U.S.C. 2304 ( ) ☐ 41 U.S.C. 253 ( )

17. ITEM NO.	18. SCHEDULE OF SUPPLIES/SERVICES	19. QUANTITY	20. UNIT	21. UNIT PRICE	22. AMOUNT

23. ACCOUNTING AND APPROPRIATION DATA

24. TOTAL AWARD AMOUNT *(FOR GOVERNMENT USE ONLY)*

25. ☐ CONTRACTOR IS REQUIRED TO SIGN THIS DOCUMENT AND RETURN ______ COPIES TO ISSUING OFFICE. CONTRACTOR AGREES TO FURNISH AND DELIVER ALL ITEMS SET FORTH OR OTHERWISE IDENTIFIED ABOVE AND ON ANY CONTINUATION SHEETS SUBJECT TO THE TERMS AND CONDITIONS SPECIFIED HEREIN.

26. ☐ AWARD OF CONTRACT: YOUR OFFER ON SOLICITATION NUMBER SHOWN IN BLOCK 4 INCLUDING ANY ADDITIONS OR CHANGES WHICH ARE SET FORTH HEREIN, IS ACCEPTED AS TO ITEMS:

27. SIGNATURE OF OFFEROR/CONTRACTOR

28. UNITED STATES OF AMERICA *(SIGNATURE OF CONTRACTING OFFICER)*

NAME AND TITLE OF SIGNER *(TYPE OR PRINT)* | DATE SIGNED | NAME OF CONTRACTING OFFICER | DATE SIGNED

AUTHORIZED FOR LOCAL REPRODUCTION
PREVIOUS EDITION NOT USABLE

STANDARD FORM 1447 (REV. 2/2012)
Prescribed by GSA - FAR (48 CFR) 53.214(d)

Example Simplified Contract Format Cover Page (Standard Form 1447)

Some solicitations require bidders to submit a work plan and a delivery schedule as part of the offer. They might also require bidders to submit information about the company's financial stability and relevant experience. Your bid must address performance and delivery at least equal to the IFB's minimum standards.

Bidders should not substitute items that they deem just as good as the specified items. A bid must meet the exact specifications called for in the bid request, or the bid may be declared nonresponsive. Because price is the primary evaluation factor in sealed bidding, it is to your advantage to determine the price that the government paid for similar supplies and services in the past. Among the best sources are past bids.

After a contracting activity issues an IFB, but before bid opening, it may make changes to the IFB. Typical changes involve quantities, specifications, delivery schedules, or opening dates. Such changes are made through an IFB amendment (SF 30, Amendment of Solicitation/Modification of Contract).

Any amendments that a contracting officer makes to an IFB must be sent to each contractor that was sent a solicitation package. Upon submission of the IFB, bidders must acknowledge all issued amendments. Failure to do so may cause the bid to be declared nonresponsive.

Once you have completed your bid, review it for clarity, consistency, and accuracy. Compare your work plan, budget, and schedule to ensure that they agree. Double-check cost figures and computations to be sure that all information has been included.

If everything checks out, the next step is to submit your bid. Be sure to review the submission instructions and verify the address to which the bid should be sent to allow enough time to meet the deadline. Keep in mind that an IFB is a contractual document. If a prospective bidder submits an erroneous bid and is awarded a contract on that basis, the result could be little or no profit, or even serious financial loss.

LATE BIDS

If you receive a solicitation, the first thing to do is to note the date and time your bid is due. This is extremely important because the government will not accept bids that are even five seconds late.

This rule has a few exceptions. Late bids may be considered if the bid was:

- Mishandled by the government
- Sent by U.S. Postal Service Express Mail Next Day, no later than 5:00 P.M. at the place of mailing, two working days before the bid opening date
- Sent by registered or certified mail, postmarked no later than the fifth calendar day before the deadline
- Sent electronically and received by the government no later than 5:00 P.M. one working day before the bid opening date
- The only offer received.

The government may also, at any time, consider late modifications to an otherwise successful bid that make its terms more favorable to the government.

If hand-delivering the bid, be sure that you include the room number and meet any other special requirements for hand delivery. Security concerns can delay hand delivery of a bid, so be sure to allow extra time or use a bonded courier. When a bid is received late and cannot be considered, the government notifies the bidder and holds the bid unopened.

BID OPENING

All bids in response to an IFB are secured until the bid opening, which takes place in a public location at the time specified on the IFB. Anyone may attend a bid opening. At the time designated for opening, a bid opening officer publicly opens all unclassified bids.

A bidder may withdraw its bid at any time before the bid opening date. Once the bids have been opened, the contracting officer will allow withdrawals or corrections to bids only if the bidder substantiates a mistake, the manner in which it occurred, and the intended bid. An obvious clerical error, for example, may be corrected and the bid considered with the other offers if the contractor verifies the error and the intended bid.

BID EVALUATIONS

A bid opening officer, who is usually not the contracting officer, opens, announces, and records all the bids. They are recorded on a form called an *abstract of bids*. Interested parties may examine the bids at the time of recording but will be denied access to financial and other proprietary information of the bidders. Following the recording, the bid opening officer reveals the results to the contracting officer.

The contracting officer evaluates the bids, considering such items as price, options, economic price adjustments, transportation costs, and other areas controlled by regulations. Discounts, such as prompt payment discounts (see Chapter 17), are not considered during the evaluation of bids. Any discount that the bidder offers, however, becomes part of the contract award.

To be eligible for the award, the bidder must be both responsive and responsible.

- To be *responsive*, the otherwise successful bidder must not have taken exception to the IFB's specifications, work statement, or other terms. A bid usually will be rejected as nonresponsive if its prices are subject to change without notice.
- To be *responsible*, the otherwise successful bidder must be able to produce the products or services, meet the delivery schedule, follow the terms and conditions, and have adequate financial capabilities.

The contracting officer uses the following pre-award survey to determine whether a bidder is both responsive and responsible:

- Does the bidder have adequate financial resources to perform the contract?
- Can the bidder comply with the proposed delivery or performance schedule?
- Does the bidder have a satisfactory performance record?

- Does the bidder have the necessary production, technical equipment, and facilities?
- Is the bidder eligible to receive an award under the applicable laws and regulations?

The pre-award survey may be informal or formal. An informal pre-award survey includes a review of the bidder's capabilities, performance records, and previous contracts and/or phone inquiries of previous customers. The informal survey typically is used for small and straightforward contracts.

A formal pre-award survey, on the other hand, involves the assistance of another federal agency, the Defense Contract Management Agency (DCMA). The contracting officer may ask DCMA to review all or some of the following items: the bidder's technical capabilities, production capacity, quality assurance procedures, financial capability, transportation, security, environmental considerations, and any other areas of concern. Formal procedures typically are used for large contracts that involve a significant number of products or services.

If the apparent low or otherwise successful bidder is determined to be nonresponsive or nonresponsible, and it is a small business, the findings must be referred to SBA for further investigation. SBA then performs its own investigation to determine whether the small business can perform the contract.

If SBA determines that the small business is competent, it issues a Certificate of Competency, which binds the contracting officer for that particular procurement (see Chapter 4).

BID AWARD

The lowest bidder that meets the IFB's evaluation criteria is awarded the contract. Each bidder must keep its bid open (or available) during the evaluation period. The contracting officer conducts these procedures based strictly on the sealed bids. There are no discussions with the bidders. When two or more equal low bids are received, the contract is awarded in the following order:

1. Small business concerns that are also labor surplus area concerns (see Chapter 5).

2. Other small business concerns.
3. Other business concerns.

If two or more bidders still remain equally eligible, a drawing with the remaining bidders will be made.

The contracting officer may reject all bids received if he or she believes that this action is in the government's best interest. For example, if the bids were submitted in bad faith or were calculated in collusion by the bidders, the contracting officer may reject them.

Finally, the successful bidder receives a properly executed award document, or notice of award (NOA). The NOA has no specified format, but it should include the contract number, the contract's effective date, the authorized funding, the initial tasks that the bidder will perform, and the contracting officer's approval (or signature). An NOA serves as the bidder's go-ahead.

The contracting officer notifies the unsuccessful bidders in writing or orally, usually within three days of contract award. If an unsuccessful bidder requests additional information, the government must provide:

- The successful bidder's name and address
- The contract price
- The location of the abstract of bids that may be inspected.

Contracting officers must consider all contract award protests or objections, whether received before or after the award is issued. If a written protest is received "before award," the contracting officer will not award the contract until the matter is resolved, unless the items being procured are urgent or the performance will be unduly delayed by failure to make the award promptly.

■ ■ ■

In theory, the IFB allows for a shorter solicitation process, a fast evaluation, and a quick award at the lowest price. However, because the government must accept the lowest overall bid, this solicitation method is less likely to be used for state-of-the-art products and services.

The ability to use trade-off analysis to determine best value—that is, negotiated procurement—is therefore a significant factor in why sealed bidding isn't used more. In fact, some contracting activities never issue IFBs.

■ ■ ■

CHAPTER 12

Negotiated Procurements

"Lemont is our finest negotiator. Perhaps you've read his book, *The Art of Pouting.*"

What's in this chapter?

- Exchanges with industry before proposal receipt
- Presolicitation notices
- The solicitation process
- Preparing your proposal
- Oral presentations
- Late proposals
- Proposal evaluation
- Source selection processes and techniques
- Changes and discussions
- Final proposal revision and award
- Debriefings
- Protests

When it is desirable to consider the technical superiority of a contractor's products or services, the federal government uses negotiated procurement procedures. Unlike sealed bidding procedures, negotiated procurements permit bargaining and discussions with offerors before making a final source selection. They are the federal government's most flexible acquisition method, but it is also the most complicated.

Negotiated procurement procedures take many forms. They may call for competitive proposals, involve restricted competition, or even be sole source. Eighty percent of the contracts that exceed the simplified acquisition threshold of $150,000 use negotiated procedures. They are ideal for R&D projects, for which each contractor takes a different approach to meet the government's needs.

A request for proposal (RFP) is the solicitation document most often used under negotiated procurement procedures. It contains the information needed for prospective contractors to prepare proposals. Some contractors refer to all of the documents that make up the RFP as the *bid set*, but most government agencies do not, since the word *bid* is associated with sealed bidding and not negotiated procurements.

The RFP, like an invitation for bid (IFB), is a request for an offer. A contractor's response to an RFP represents an offer, which the government may accept without change or negotiation, resulting in a binding contract. The solicitation, however, must state whether the intent is that proposals will be evaluated and awarded (1) after discussions with offerors or (2) without discussions with offerors. (Even if the latter is indicated, the agency reserves the right to hold discussions.)

If the contracting officer intends to enter into discussions, he or she must conduct written or oral discussions with all responsible offerors that submit proposals within the competitive range. Price, technical requirements, performance, terms and conditions, and delivery schedules are all open to negotiation. During discussions, the contracting officer may also decide that the government's best interests might be better served by a contract that is significantly different from the original solicitation.

When a contracting officer uses negotiated procedures, the following conditions should be met:

- All contractors are treated fairly and impartially but need not be treated the same.
- The contract gives the winning contractor incentive to perform the contract on time and at the lowest possible cost to the government.
- The contract price is fair and reasonable.

EXCHANGES WITH INDUSTRY BEFORE PROPOSAL RECEIPT

The government encourages information exchanges among interested parties, from the earliest identification of a requirement through proposal receipt. These exchanges are intended to improve the understanding of government requirements and industry capabilities, thereby allowing potential offerors to determine whether or how to satisfy the requirements. Acquisition strategy, such as the proposed contract type and the feasibility of requirements, may also be addressed during the exchanges.

Interested parties typically include potential offerors, end users, acquisition personnel (such as the program manager), and others involved in the outcome of the procurement. The exchanges must be consistent with procurement integrity requirements. Some techniques that the government might use to promote these early exchanges include:

- Industry or small business conferences
- Public hearings
- Market research
- One-on-one meetings with potential offerors
- Presolicitation notices
- Draft RFPs
- Requests for information (RFI), which may be used when the government currently does not intend to award a contract but wants market information for planning purposes (RFIs never result in a binding contract)
- Presolicitation or pre-proposal conferences
- Site visits.

Active participation in these early exchanges will give you a great head start on your competition. Once the solicitation is issued or released, the contracting officer will be the focal point of exchanges among potential offerors.

> Acquisition reform in the 1990s provided for greater exchange of information between the government and prospective offerors prior to the release of the solicitation and the ability to seek clarification of minor issues without having these exchanges be considered discussions. This is important because the emphasis now is on award without discussions where possible; once discussions are held with one offeror, they must be held with all offerors.

PRESOLICITATION NOTICES

Buying offices invite potential offerors to provide feedback on a presolicitation notice, thus allowing acquisition officials to identify and evaluate viable contractors. At a minimum, the presolicitation notice contains sufficient information to permit potential contractors to determine whether to participate in the acquisition. Federal agencies evaluate each response based on the criteria stated in the notice.

A presolicitation notice might request information on proposed technical concepts or might be limited to a statement of qualifications. Federal agencies notify the respondents in writing if they are invited to participate in the resultant acquisition or if, based on the information submitted, they are unlikely to be viable competitors.

THE SOLICITATION PROCESS

The process of negotiation starts in a way that is similar to sealed bidding. The contracting officer publishes a synopsis of an RFP in FedBizOpps 15 days before issuing the solicitation. After this 15-day period, the actual RFP is published in FedBizOpps. If necessary, the contracting officer may hold a pre-proposal conference. (A pre-proposal conference is a briefing held by the contracting officer to explain complicated specifications and requirements to prospective offerors.)

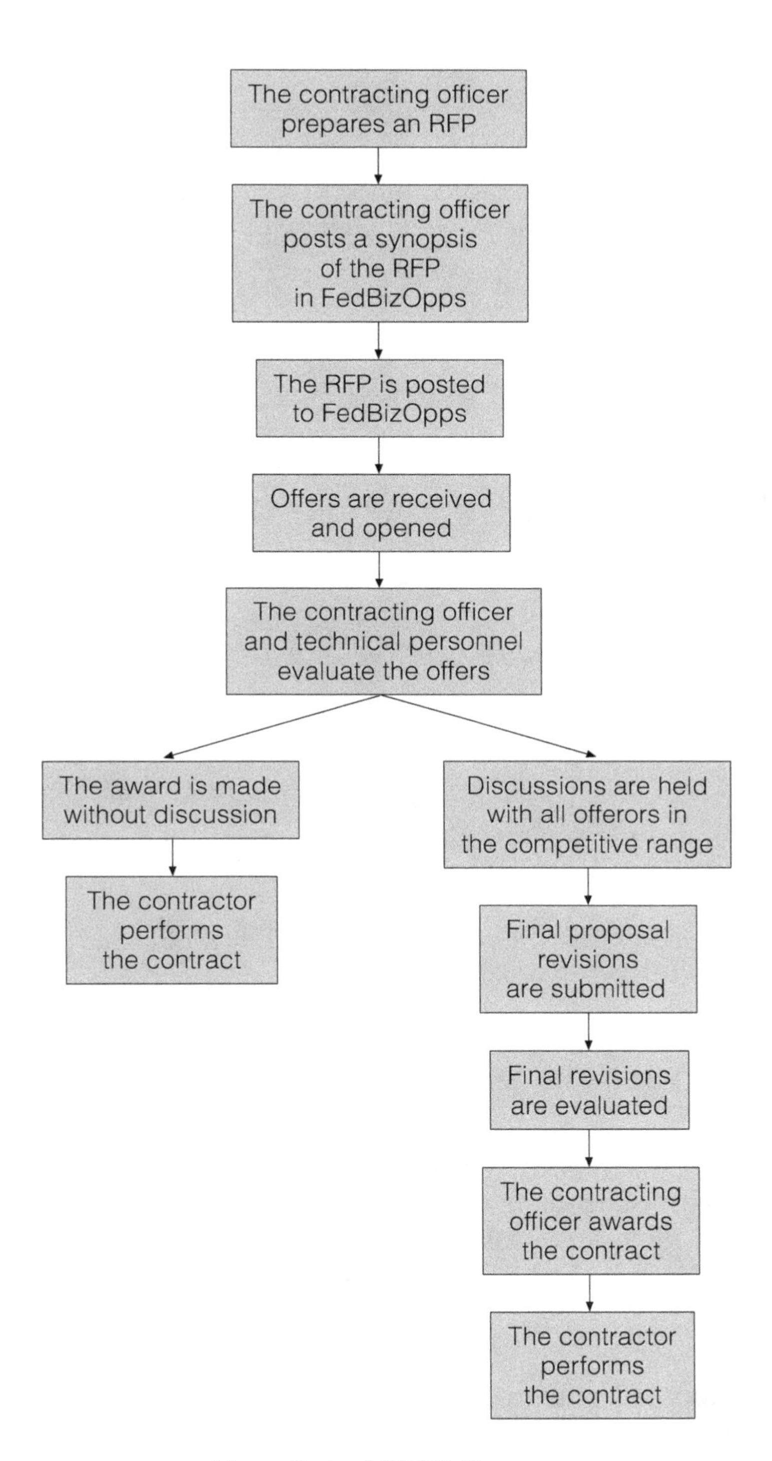

Negotiated (RFP) Process

Solicitation Methods

The contracting officer uses one of the following formats to prepare RFPs:

- Solicitation/Contract/Order for Commercial Items (SF 1449)
- Uniform Contract Format (SF 33; see Chapter 13)
- Simplified Contract Format (SF 1447).

At first glance, these solicitation methods look identical to those used for IFBs. Differences between IFBs and RFPs include the solicitation provisions, proposal preparation instructions, and evaluation factors. The quickest way to differentiate between them is to look at Block 4 of SF 33, Block 5 of SF 1447, or Block 14 of SF 1449 (see Chapter 13 and Chapter 11 for copies of the first two forms).

RFP Requirements

At a minimum, RFPs for competitive acquisitions must provide:

- The government's requirements.
- The contract's anticipated terms and conditions. (The solicitation may authorize offerors to propose alternative terms and conditions.)
- Information required for the offeror's proposal.
- Factors and significant subfactors that will be used to evaluate the proposal, and their relative importance.

PREPARING YOUR PROPOSAL

Word of caution: responding to a RFP requires considerable time and effort. Generally, the cost of preparing a winning proposal is 3 percent to 5 percent of the contract's total dollar value. Prospective offerors should examine each solicitation carefully to decide whether preparing a proposal is worth the effort and cost.

Evaluation factors tell potential offerors what considerations will be used to evaluate and grade proposals compared to the requirements set forth in the statement of work (SOW). Price is always an evaluation factor in any source selection. Other evaluation factors include:

- Technical requirements
- Management capabilities
- Relevant experience and past performance.

The contracting officer tailors the evaluation factors to each acquisition's characteristics and requirements. Selected factors enable the contracting officer to determine, based on the proposal submitted, how well the offeror understands—and the degree to which the offeror could successfully meet—the RFP's requirements. This includes applying a relative order of importance, assigning evaluation "scores" (which normally are non-numerical), or both.

The source selection authority's (SSA) award decision is based on a comparative assessment of the proposal against all source selection criteria in the solicitation. Offers are evaluated against the evaluation criteria, and then a comparative analysis of the offers is made based on their evaluation "scores."

Cost/Price Proposal

Offerors develop cost and pricing data to convince the government purchaser of the reasonableness of their proposed costs. (They are generally not required to provide proposed costs for competitive procurements.) Cost and pricing data include estimates of the expected costs of performance and the offeror's expected profit or fee (i.e., cost + profit = total price). The cost/price evaluation criteria differ for fixed-price, incentive, and cost-reimbursement contracts. Part V of this book details the various contract types.

For a fixed-price contract, the offeror's total proposed price is the main evaluation factor. Incentive contracts, on the other hand, are structured and evaluated as a package of cost factors, including target cost, share ratio, ceiling price, or maximum/minimum fee. Finally, cost-reimbursement contracts require federal agencies to use estimates of expected costs (plus a fee or profit) to measure the cost realism of the proposed contract costs. The RFP states the contract type to be awarded and its applicable terms.

Cost/price evaluation factors include:

- Proposed cost/price completeness
- Proposed cost/price reasonableness

- Proposed cost/price realism
- Cost/price risk assessment.

When an award is based on adequate price competition, a cost/price proposal may not be required.

> An independent government cost estimate or a cost realism analysis for cost proposals (including cost-reimbursement and T&M contracts) are generally conducted by government personnel before proposals are received to determine the "probable cost" of a contract. This probable cost may be quite different from the costs offerors propose. The award decision is made based on probable cost, not proposed cost.
>
> The question is, can an offeror get access to the government's "cost estimate" to help ensure its proposal pricing/costs are in accordance with acquisition officials' analysis? Having such information could be a tremendous advantage in preparing your proposal pricing!
>
> My take? There's certainly no harm in asking.

Technical Proposal

The primary purpose of the technical proposal is to assure the government that you possess the know-how and resources to perform the contract requirements. The RFP details specific technical criteria that your proposal must meet. Technical proposals are generally prepared according to the Instructions to Offerors section (section L) of the Uniform Contract Format (see Chapter 13).

In large, technically complex procurements, a representative from an agency's technical and operational areas might help develop the factors for award. In many cases, the technical proposal is the most significant evaluation factor. Technical evaluation factors might include:

- Soundness of proposed technical approach
- Innovativeness of proposed technical approach
- Requirement compliance
- Requirement understanding
- Key personnel or other resources
- Available facilities
- Technical risk assessment.

Federal specifications and standards are a prescribed set of rules, conditions, and requirements established to achieve uniformity in materials and products. They specify performance requirements and the quality and construction of materials and equipment needed to produce acceptable goods. The General Services Administration (GSA) issues and controls federal specifications, which all federal agencies must use.

The technical proposal may cover the RFP's management aspects, or the contracting activity may require separate technical and management proposals.

Management Proposal

A management proposal explains how the contractor intends to manage the proposed program if awarded the contract. The key element here is the description of your type of management. Specifically, your management proposal should explain the organizational structure, management capability, company controls, and assignment of key personnel to the contract. If you do not intend to form a specific management group, describe your overall operation method.

A management proposal is evaluated based on:

- Soundness of the proposed management plan
- Corporate resources for overseeing and performing the work
- Logical, timely pursuit of work schedules
- Quality plan
- Management risk.

Note that if resumes are to be submitted, be sure that personnel meet the qualifications required.

Developing the factors and determining their relative importance should be the joint responsibility of the requiring organization's contracting officer and the program manager or technical representative. Ideally, the evaluation factors should be developed as early as possible in the acquisition's planning phase.

ORAL PRESENTATIONS

To enhance or substitute for portions of the written proposal, the government may request that offerors perform oral presentations. The offeror's capabilities, past performance, work plans or approaches, staffing resources, and transition plans are all suitable topics. Oral presentations may occur at any time during the acquisition process and are subject to the same restrictions as written information regarding timing and content.

The major use of oral presentations has been to permit evaluators to receive information about the capability of the offeror—generally demonstrating its understanding of the work or describing how the work will be performed—directly from the key members of the offeror's team that will actually perform the work.

Substituting oral presentations for portions of a proposal streamlines the source-selection process and can greatly reduce the need for written material; sometimes information can be conveyed in a more meaningful and efficient way through verbal means.

Unless the RFP requires it, offerors do not have to discuss confidential information, such as technical approaches, during their oral presentations. Instead, offerors may provide the government with a written description of their planned approach for carrying out the work after completing their presentation. Prerecorded videotaped presentations that lack real-time interactive dialogue are not considered oral presentations, although they may be included in an offeror's submission when appropriate.

When a solicitation calls for oral presentations, it describes:

- Types of information to be presented orally and the associated evaluation factors
- Qualifications of the personnel who will give the oral presentation
- Requirements for, and any limitations on, written material or other media to supplement the oral presentations
- The oral presentation's location, date, and time
- Time restrictions for each presentation

- The scope and content of exchanges that may occur between the parties during the presentation, including whether discussions will be permitted.

The contracting officer maintains records of the oral presentations (e.g., video recording, audio recording, written records) and documents the evaluation factors for the source selection decision.

LATE PROPOSALS

Negotiated procurement procedures have no formal public bid opening, as with sealed bidding, but you must submit your proposal by the date and time stated on the RFP, the closing date. Late proposals will be considered only if:

- The government mishandled the proposal.
- You sent the proposal by U.S. Postal Service Express Mail Next Day, no later than 5:00 P.M. at the place of mailing, two working days before the proposal opening date.
- You sent the proposal by registered or certified mail, postmarked no later than the fifth calendar day before the deadline.
- You sent the proposal electronically and the government received it no later than 5:00 P.M. one working day before the proposal closing date.
- Only one proposal is received.

The government will also consider, at any time, late modifications to an otherwise successful proposal that make the proposal's terms more favorable to the government. If you hand-deliver the proposal, make sure you have the right room number and meet any other special requirements for hand delivery.

PROPOSAL EVALUATION

The time the government takes to perform an evaluation depends on the number of proposals received and the complexity of the items being evaluated. The process of selecting the winning contractor is called *source selection*. The purpose of source selection is to select the contractor whose proposal has the highest degree of credibility and whose performance is expected to best meet the government's needs at a reasonable price.

The selection process must be fair and reflect a comprehensive evaluation of each submitted proposal. Throughout the evaluation process, the contracting officer is typically designated as the source selection authority (SSA) and the government's exclusive agent with the authority to enter into and administer contracts.

The selection process typically includes the evaluation of technical and cost/price proposals, negotiations between the various parties, and preparation and selection of a best and final offer. When certain evaluation factors affect the selection decision more than others, the solicitation should clearly identify the weight of the factors and how the final scoring will be done. It is the responsibility of the offerors to understand the basis on which their proposals will be evaluated and how best to prepare them.

Contracting officers evaluate past performance in all RFPs that are expected to exceed $150,000. Your past performance helps indicate your ability to perform the contract requirements for which you submitted your proposal. The RFP allows you to provide references for similar contracts you performed.

When contractors lack relevant past performance information, the FAR currently states that they will be treated neither favorably nor unfavorably. Further, the Comptroller General has found on occasion that it is okay for a contracting officer to pay more for a contractor with good past performance than a contractor with no past performance who submits a lower-cost proposal. If the contracting officer determines past performance is not appropriate for a particular solicitation, he or she has the authority to remove it as an evaluation factor.

Technical proposals should not contain a total price reference; that way, price doesn't influence the technical evaluation. They should, however, include resource information, such as labor hours and categories, materials, and subcontracts, so that the offeror's understanding of the scope of work can be evaluated. Technical representatives/personnel are often used to help evaluate technical proposals.

RFPs are not opened publicly, so the competitive position of the various offerors is not disclosed.

> Price is always an evaluation factor in any source selection, even if the weighting accorded price is low.

SOURCE SELECTION PROCESSES AND TECHNIQUES

The following are some of the more common acquisition processes and techniques.

Best Value Continuum

In negotiated acquisitions, the contracting officer looks for the best overall value to the government. If the contract requirements are clearly definable and the risk of unsuccessful performance is minimal, price dominates the source selection. When successful contract performance is less certain and more development work is required, technical and past performance considerations might play a more important role. The solicitation should clearly identify the source selection factors.

Trade-off Process

If simply comparing the prices of proposals that meet the solicitation's requirements will not result in the best value to government, a trade-off process should be used. The trade-off process gives the source selection authority the flexibility to select the offer providing the best value, which might not be the lowest-priced offer or the one submitted by the highest technically rated offeror. This trade-off must be consistent with the RFP.

The trade-off process is appropriate when the government's requirements are difficult to define or complex. The perceived benefits of a higher-priced, higher-quality proposal must merit the additional cost.

Lowest Price, Technically Acceptable Process

The lowest price, technically acceptable source selection process is appropriate when the best value to the government is expected to result from selecting the technically acceptable proposal with the lowest evaluated price. For this method, the following requirements apply:

- The solicitation must set forth the evaluation factors and significant subfactors that establish the requirements of acceptability.
- Trade-offs are not permitted.
- Proposals are evaluated for acceptability but not ranked using the non-price factors.

CHANGES AND DISCUSSIONS

Unlike sealed bidding, negotiated procedures allow offerors to propose changes to the RFP's terms and conditions. It is common for offerors to propose changes to the statement of work, recommend alternative delivery schedules, or even suggest a different product or service. If, for example, a buying office issues a solicitation for red widgets, the offeror, for whatever reason, could submit a proposal for blue widgets.

However, unless alternate proposals are requested or allowed in the RFP, offerors who propose to change the government's requirements run a great risk of having their proposals immediately rejected as nonresponsive, and in some cases not even evaluated or "scored." Also, they take the chance that the government will award the contract without discussion to a competitor.

When discussions are necessary, the regulations require the contracting officer to conduct written or oral discussions with all responsible offerors in the competitive range. Information about competing proposals may not be disclosed during the discussions.

The competitive range consists of the most highly rated proposals. Considerations include:

- Strengths and weaknesses of each technical proposal.
- Past performance.
- The proposed price. (Price may never be excluded as an evaluation factor, and it must be considered in establishing the competitive range. Failure to do so, if the competitive range decision were to be protested, would cause the protest to be sustained.)

- Offeror's understanding of the contract requirements.
- Management proposal (if applicable) and any other special requirements of the RFP.

Offerors outside the competitive range are eliminated from further consideration.

FINAL PROPOSAL REVISION AND AWARD

At the conclusion of the discussions, the offerors that are still within the competitive range receive an opportunity to revise their proposals. The government then notifies all offerors to submit their final proposal revision (previously called the *best and final offer*) by a certain time and date. A final proposal revision is, in effect, an opportunity to enhance your proposal.

The late proposal rules also apply to final proposal revisions. So, to be purposely redundant, be sure to submit your final proposal revision on time.

A contracting officer will not reopen discussions with contractors after receiving final proposal revisions unless doing so benefits the government. For example, additional discussions would be necessary if it is clear to the contracting officer that the final proposal revisions received are inadequate to justify contractor selection and award.

The final source selection (or contract award) is based on the content of the final proposal revisions. Just as in sealed bidding, however, an offeror must be deemed "responsible" to receive the contract (see Bid Evaluations, Chapter 11). The contract is usually awarded in one of three ways:

- By sending the successful offeror a copy of the award contract. (If SF 33, Solicitation, Offer and Award [see Chapter 13], is used as the cover sheet for the RFP, the contracting officer would complete and sign the award section of this form.)
- By notifying the successful offeror by phone with written confirmation.
- By notifying the successful offeror by letter.

The contracting officer usually notifies unsuccessful offerors within three business days of contract award.

Sealed Bidding vs. Negotiated Procedures

Characteristics	Sealed Bidding	Negotiated Procedures
Initial solicitation document	IFB	RFP
Response (offer)	Bid	Proposal
Specification or requirements	Must be precise	Less precision required (discussions allowed)
Minimum prospective bidders	Two	May be sole source
Amendments to solicitation after closing	Not allowed	Allowed
Selection criteria	Lowest bidder	Award is made in accordance with the stated evaluation criteria
Types of contracts (see Part V of this book)	Fixed-price only	Fixed-price or cost-reimbursement

DEBRIEFINGS

Once the contract is awarded, unsuccessful offerors may request a debriefing with the acquisition officials. During a debriefing the contracting officer, along with other government personnel involved in the evaluation, discusses with the unsuccessful offeror why its proposal was not chosen for award. The debriefing should occur within five days after receipt of the written request. (Debriefings are conducted with only one offeror at a time.)

Successful offerors also can request a debriefing, and I encourage it. Why? Because if you're the winner, it's valuable to know what you did right and, for future proposal submissions, what you could have done to improve your proposal. Also, you can discuss possible contract opportunities in the future and when they might be coming down the pike. Winning offerors often don't take the time to go through a debriefing because they are too busy gearing up for the contract.

As part of the discussions with unsuccessful offerors, the contracting officer may provide details on the number of offers solicited and received, the name and address of each firm receiving an award, the quantities and prices of each award, and (in general terms) the reasons their proposals were not accepted.

Offerors excluded from the competitive range during the evaluation process may also request a pre-award debriefing.

A debriefing should foster an open, nonadversarial atmosphere. Please use this opportunity to learn what did and didn't work in your proposal. At a minimum, the debriefing should provide:

- The government's evaluation of the significant strengths and weaknesses of the offeror's proposal
- Overall evaluated price and technical rating, if applicable, of the successful offeror
- Summary of the rationale for award
- For acquisitions of commercial items, a description of the make and model of the item to be delivered by the successful offeror
- Reasonable responses to concerns about source selection procedures and applicable regulations.

The contracting officer will not provide point-by-point comparisons of the proposals. Also, the debriefing should not disclose proprietary information about other offerors, including:

- Trade secrets and confidential manufacturing processes and techniques
- Confidential financial information
- The names of individuals who provided past performance information.

Don't expect to be completely satisfied with the debriefing results. Some debriefings may be ineffective because government evaluators are naturally inhibited by the fear of triggering a protest. What most contracting activities have found is that well-done briefings that clearly explain the SSA's rationale for the source selection decision mitigate the possibility of protests.

PROTESTS

Sooner or later, the government will make a decision that you (the contractor) might not agree with, or to be more blunt, that you think is completely wrong. In that case, you might consider filing a protest.

First and foremost, protests should be filed no later than ten days after the date on which the basis for the protest was known or should have been known. For your protest to have any chance of success, it is critically important you adhere to this ten-day deadline.

Protests are written objections by "interested parties" to a solicitation, proposed award, or award of a contract. Interested parties include actual or prospective offerors whose direct economic interest would be affected by the award of or failure to award a particular contract. Additionally, contractors are encouraged to seek alternative dispute resolution (ADR) procedures for protests (see Chapter 17).

The contracting officer must consider all protests, whether submitted before or after contract award. It is important to note that a timely protest after award results in a stay of the award, which means that performance is suspended until the protest is resolved. For protests before award, normally the award is held in abeyance (a state of temporary suspension, for you non-lawyers). Successful protests can change a planned award or cause cancellation of an award already made.

Protests are usually initiated by a written filing with the Government Accountability Office (GAO) or, in some cases, the U.S. Court of Claims. A protest may also be submitted directly to the contracting officer or the buying agency.

If the protest is filed with GAO, the protester must provide a copy of it to the contracting officer no later than the next day. GAO's Office of General Counsel then requests a report on the matter from the contracting officer. When this report is received, a copy is provided to the protester, who is given the opportunity to comment.

Many times, GAO holds an informal conference to give the contractor an opportunity to present its views. GAO then considers the facts and issues raised by the protest and adjudicates a decision in the name of the Comptroller General.

Decisions are usually made within 100 days of initial receipt of the protest. This is a statutory requirement and, to the best of my knowledge, the GAO has never exceeded that time; in fact, most GAO decisions are rendered within 80 days.

Both the protester and the contracting officer receive a copy of the decision. If a protester disagrees with GAO's decision, it may appeal the decision to the Court of Appeals for the Federal Circuit. If the protester disagrees with that decision, it may appeal the matter all the way to the Supreme Court. FAR 33.1 provides detailed information on protests.

In federal contracting, protests are par for the course. If you feel you have a valid claim, do whatever it takes to protect your interests. Historically, protestors have obtained some form of relief for about one-third of protests filed.

> In fiscal year 2011, the number of protests filed with the Government Accountability Office was less than 2,400. Given the hundreds of thousands of procurements conducted annually, this is really a quite low number. Factors associated with acquisition reform may have contributed to this low protest figure—namely, the fact that multiple ordering contracts and federal supply schedules can now be placed simultaneously with several firms, a situation in which protests are generally not permitted during the ordering process. Also, a more refined and better structured negotiated contracting process exists, and debriefings are more substantive than they were previously.

■ ■ ■

Negotiated procurement procedures enable the government to evaluate desirable features and technical superiority. RFPs allow the government and industry to correct errors in understanding and specifications by permitting discussions and negotiations.

On the downside, RFPs may require a long-term effort. Multiple final proposal revisions tend to erode the integrity of the procurement process.

■ ■ ■

CHAPTER 13

The Uniform Contract Format

© 1997 Randy Glasbergen.
GLASBERGEN
"I haven't read your proposal yet, Bob,
but I already have some great ideas
on how to improve it."

What's in this chapter?

- Part I: The schedule
- Part II: Contract clauses
- Part III: List of documents, exhibits, and other attachments
- Part IV: Representations and instructions
- Amendments to the solicitation
- Typical proposal weaknesses and deficiencies
- Procurement instrument identification numbers
- Unsolicited proposals
- Contingent fees

Federal solicitations lay out a host of explicit instructions and conditions your company must follow to be eligible for a contract award. The Uniform Contract Format (UCF) is the most common solicitation format used by the federal government today. During FY 2011, the federal government issued the UCF for more than 100,000 solicitations.

Both invitations for bid (IFBs) and requests for proposal (RFPs) are completed using this solicitation format. Depending on the complexity of the procurement, a completed solicitation package can be anywhere from 20 to 5,000 pages in length.

Prospective contractors tend to be intimidated by the sheer volume or size of the UCF. Don't be! Once you become familiar with the UCF's organization, you will be able to anticipate and understand its content. Careful attention to the entire solicitation package is crucial to your success.

The 4 parts and 13 sections of the UCF are shown below.

Uniform Contract Format

Part I—The Schedule

Section A: Solicitation/contract form

Section B: Supplies or services and prices/costs

Section C: Description/specifications/statement of work

Section D: Packaging and marking

Section E: Inspection and acceptance

Section F: Deliveries or performance

Section G: Contract administration data

Section H: Special contract requirements

Part II—Contract Clauses

Section I: Contract clauses

Part III—List of Documents, Exhibits, and Other Attachments

Section J: List of attachments

Part IV—Representations and Instructions

Section K: Representations, certifications, and other statements of offerors or respondents

Section L: Instructions, conditions, and notices to offerors or respondents

Section M: Evaluation factors for award

The UCF need not be used for the following acquisitions:

- Construction and architect-engineering contracts
- Shipbuilding, ship overhaul, and ship repair
- Subsistence contracts
- Product or service contracts requiring special contract formats
- Letter requests for proposals
- Contracts exempted by the agency head
- Firm fixed-price or fixed-price with economic price adjustment acquisitions that use the Simplified Contract Format.

Contracting officers are encouraged to use the UCF to the maximum extent practicable. One of its primary benefits is that it ensures that the same general information appears in the same order in most federal solicitations. This familiar format enables the reader to focus on the proposal's content rather than its form. Federal agencies must ensure that the various sections of the solicitation are in agreement.

Any section of the UCF that does not apply to the particular solicitation may be deleted.

Part IV, Representations and Instructions, is usually not included in the resulting contract, but the contracting officer retains it in the contract file. Each solicitation package includes all the necessary forms, along with the date and time proposals must be received.

PART I: THE SCHEDULE

The purpose of the schedule is to explain the products or services being acquired, along with contractual requirements and specifications. The schedule provides details on the items being solicited; technical information about production, packaging, delivery, and inspection; and other information necessary to meet the contract requirements.

Before we talk about each section individually, let's quickly highlight a few details about the UCF first. A cheat sheet, if you will. . .

1. In Section A (usually the cover page), make note of the box with the due date. Now you know how much time you have to prepare your response.
2. Next, jump to Section L and pay special attention to how the proposal is supposed to be organized. Does it make sense? Is the outline doable?
3. Finally, go to Section M. Find out how the solicitation will be graded and what the agency thinks is important.

Decision time: Is this particular contract worth your company's time and effort, or would your interests be better served somewhere else? Remember, you can't focus on every opportunity, especially if you have a low probability of winning. In other words, don't burn that midnight oil if you don't have to!

Section A: Solicitation/Contract Form

Standard Form 33 (SF 33), Solicitation, Offer and Award, is typically the first page and serves as the cover sheet of the solicitation package (see facing page). It contains information about the time and place at which offerors should submit proposals. It also itemizes a table of required contents that each offeror must provide.

The offer section of this form, which the offeror completes, constitutes a legally binding offer. The award section is completed by the contracting officer after making the source selection or award decision. Once the contractor receives this signed solicitation package, the package becomes an executed contract.

If the contracting officer does not use SF 33, the cover sheet of the UCF must include the following:

- Name, address, and location of issuing activity (including room and building where proposals must be submitted)
- Solicitation type

Standard Form 33

SOLICITATION, OFFER AND AWARD

1. THIS CONTRACT IS A RATED ORDER UNDER DPAS (15 CFR 700) | RATING | PAGE OF PAGES

2. CONTRACT NUMBER | 3. SOLICITATION NUMBER | 4. TYPE OF SOLICITATION ☐ SEALED BID (IFB) ☐ NEGOTIATED (RFP) | 5. DATE ISSUED | 6. REQUISITION/PURCHASE NUMBER

7. ISSUED BY CODE | 8. ADDRESS OFFER TO *(If other than Item 7)*

NOTE: In sealed bid solicitations "offer" and "offeror" mean "bid" and "bidder".

SOLICITATION

9. Sealed offers in original and ______ copies for furnishing the supplies or services in the Schedule will be received at the place specified in Item 8, or if handcarried, in the depository located in ______ until ______ *(Hour)* local time ______ *(Date)*

CAUTION - LATE Submissions, Modifications, and Withdrawals: See Section L, Provision No. 52.214-7 or 52.215-1. All offers are subject to all terms and conditions contained in this solicitation.

10. FOR INFORMATION CALL: | A. NAME | B. TELEPHONE *(NO COLLECT CALLS)* AREA CODE / NUMBER / EXT. | C. E-MAIL ADDRESS

11. TABLE OF CONTENTS

(X)	SEC.	DESCRIPTION	PAGE(S)	(X)	SEC.	DESCRIPTION	PAGE(S)
		PART I - THE SCHEDULE				PART II - CONTRACT CLAUSES	
	A	SOLICITATION/CONTRACT FORM			I	CONTRACT CLAUSES	
	B	SUPPLIES OR SERVICES AND PRICES/COSTS				PART III - LIST OF DOCUMENTS, EXHIBITS AND OTHER ATTACH.	
	C	DESCRIPTION/SPECS./WORK STATEMENT			J	LIST OF ATTACHMENTS	
	D	PACKAGING AND MARKING				PART IV - REPRESENTATIONS AND INSTRUCTIONS	
	E	INSPECTION AND ACCEPTANCE			K	REPRESENTATIONS, CERTIFICATIONS AND OTHER STATEMENTS OF OFFERORS	
	F	DELIVERIES OR PERFORMANCE					
	G	CONTRACT ADMINISTRATION DATA			L	INSTRS., CONDS., AND NOTICES TO OFFERORS	
	H	SPECIAL CONTRACT REQUIREMENTS			M	EVALUATION FACTORS FOR AWARD	

OFFER *(Must be fully completed by offeror)*

NOTE: Item 12 does not apply if the solicitation includes the provisions at 52.214-16, Minimum Bid Acceptance Period.

12. In compliance with the above, the undersigned agrees, if this offer is accepted within ______ calendar days *(60 calendar days unless a different period is inserted by the offeror)* from the date for receipt of offers specified above, to furnish any or all items upon which prices are offered at the price set opposite each item, delivered at the designated point(s), within the time specified in the schedule.

13. DISCOUNT FOR PROMPT PAYMENT *(See Section I, Clause No. 52.232-8)* | 10 CALENDAR DAYS (%) | 20 CALENDAR DAYS (%) | 30 CALENDAR DAYS (%) | CALENDAR DAYS (%)

14. ACKNOWLEDGMENT OF AMENDMENTS *(The offeror acknowledges receipt of amendments to the SOLICITATION for offerors and related documents numbered and dated)*: | AMENDMENT NO. | DATE | AMENDMENT NO. | DATE

15A. NAME AND ADDRESS OF OFFEROR | CODE | FACILITY | 16. NAME AND TITLE OF PERSON AUTHORIZED TO SIGN OFFER *(Type or print)*

15B. TELEPHONE NUMBER AREA CODE / NUMBER / EXT. | ☐ 15C. CHECK IF REMITTANCE ADDRESS IS DIFFERENT FROM ABOVE - ENTER SUCH ADDRESS IN SCHEDULE. | 17. SIGNATURE | 18. OFFER DATE

AWARD *(To be completed by Government)*

19. ACCEPTED AS TO ITEMS NUMBERED | 20. AMOUNT | 21. ACCOUNTING AND APPROPRIATION

22. AUTHORITY FOR USING OTHER THAN FULL AND OPEN COMPETITION: ☐ 10 U.S.C. 2304(c) ( ) ☐ 41 U.S.C. 253(c) ( ) | 23. SUBMIT INVOICES TO ADDRESS SHOWN IN *(4 copies unless otherwise specified)* | ITEM

24. ADMINISTERED BY *(If other than Item 7)* CODE | 25. PAYMENT WILL BE MADE BY CODE

26. NAME OF CONTRACTING OFFICER *(Type or print)* | 27. UNITED STATES OF AMERICA *(Signature of Contracting Officer)* | 28. AWARD DATE

IMPORTANT - Award will be made on this Form, or on Standard Form 26, or by other authorized official written notice.

AUTHORIZED FOR LOCAL REPRODUCTION
Previous edition is unusable

STANDARD FORM 33 (REV. 9-97)
Prescribed by GSA - FAR (48 CFR) 53.214(c)

Example Solicitation, Offer and Award (Standard Form 33)

- Solicitation number (each federal agency uses its own contract numbering system)
- Issuance date
- Closing date and time
- Number of pages
- Requisition or other purchase authority
- Brief description of item or service
- Requirement for the offeror to provide its name and complete address
- Offer expiration date.

SF 33 also has a section for any price discounts you're willing to offer.

The Prompt Payment Act (see Chapter 17) requires the government to make payments within 30 days of receipt of a properly prepared invoice. If, however, a contractor wants a faster payment turnaround, it may offer the government a prompt payment discount. For example, the contractor may offer a 1 percent discount on the invoice amount if the government makes payment within 15 days. Prompt payment discounts are not considered in determining the low offeror.

An authorized company representative must complete and sign the requested information above. Do not use a transmittal letter to forward an offer unless the contracting officer specifically requires you to do so. Any such letter attached to an offer will be considered part of the offer. Stock phrases, such as "prices subject to change without notice," or even letterhead slogans, could invalidate an offer.

Section B: Supplies or Services and Prices/Costs

Oh boy, pricing . . . better go talk to Bob in accounting!

Section B is basically the government's order form. Anything the government intends to buy should show up here, along with the bid or proposal price. This includes a brief description of the offered products and services, including item number; stock/part number (if applicable); and quantities. Each unique item or service is generally placed on a separate line and given a contract line item number (CLIN).

The Federal Acquisition Regulation (FAR) lists no specific structure requirements for this section, but the Department of Defense, for example, would use the following price/cost format to purchase 30 office desks:

Item No.	Supplies/Service	Quantity	Unit	Price	Amount
0001	Office Desk	30	EA	$2,000.00	$60,000.00

DoD uses a four-digit CLIN. If chairs were also purchased with this solicitation, CLIN 0002 would be the item number.

When the purchased item has separate parts, different prices, or different delivery schedules, they are further subdivided. Here is a breakdown for a computer system being purchased by DoD:

Item No.	Supplies/Service	Quantity	Unit	Price	Amount
0001	Computer System		EA		
0001AA	Monitor	5	EA	$300.00	$1,500.00
0001AB	Keyboard	5	EA	$50.00	$250.00
0001AC	CPU	5	EA	$800.00	$4,000.00
0002	Setup	As required			$500.00
0003	Maintenance Agreement	As required			$1,000.00

Subline items receive a two-digit alphanumeric identifier, such as 0001AA. This further CLIN breakdown helps in monitoring or administering contract performance.

Section B may require price lists, catalogs, or GSA schedule contracts to justify prices/costs for the commercial items solicited. Service contracts, on the other hand, are based on estimated hours, and the offerors propose loaded rates. Chapter 15 of this book details various costing methods.

Section C: Description/Specifications/Statement of Work

This section includes further descriptions and specifications of the government's requirements as laid out in Section B. The FAR provides no specific structure for this section. Section C also describes minimum or mandatory requirements. If a contractor fails to satisfy any of the stated requirements, the government may reject the proposal as nonresponsive—so please read this section carefully.

The description of the products or services may reference specifications, standards, technical data packages, or other descriptive resources. If the contract is for products, Section C includes purchase descriptions or specifications that the products must meet. For services, the statement of work describes the tasks to be performed.

For procurements with a large number of specifications, the specifications may be grouped together and listed in Section J as an exhibit. Section J is typically used to inventory large documents or attachments, including performance work statements.

Section D: Packaging and Marking

This section is pretty self-explanatory. Contractors must preserve, pack, and mark all items in accordance with standard commercial practices or other special requirements if the products are subject to a more hostile environment. Packaging and marking requirements may exceed the cost of the unit itself, so be sure to include these costs in your proposal or bid price. If there are no packaging and marking requirements, as in service contracts, this section is omitted from the proposal.

Section E: Inspection and Acceptance

Before any product is accepted, the government verifies that the materials meet all contractual requirements. Section E contains the contractor inspection and acceptance instructions, as well as quality assurance and reliability requirements. The standard inspection requirement directs the contractor to maintain an inspection system that is acceptable to the government, maintain records of inspections conducted, and allow the government to make its own inspections.

This section may also identify specific tests that the contractor must conduct during the manufacturing process or, if the contract is for services, during specific phases of the work. The government has the right to require a contractor to replace or correct defective products. Rejections, late deliveries, and other performance failures are recorded in the contract file. Contracting officers review this file before making new awards to the contractor.

> Other inspection and acceptance requirements may also be found in Section C and Section I.

Section F: Deliveries or Performance

For products, the delivery (or performance) schedule usually states the calendar date or a specified period after the contract has been awarded. It also lists the place of delivery, usually stated as F.O.B. (free on board) origin or F.O.B. destination. Service deadlines are usually specified by a contractual period (or period of performance).

An F.O.B. origin contract requires the government to pay shipping costs and to assume the risk of loss or damage to the goods en route. The contractor is responsible only for delivering the goods to a common carrier or to the U.S. Postal Service. Delivery is complete once this occurs.

With F.O.B. destination, the contractor is responsible for the arrival of goods to the location specified in the contract. The contractor pays all shipping costs and retains the risk of loss or damage to the goods until they arrive at their destination.

Section G: Contract Administration Data

Section G supplements the administrative information contained in Section A. This information typically includes:

- The contracting officer's name and address, the contract's technical representative, and the administrative officer
- Accounting and appropriation data

- Procedures for preparing and submitting invoices
- Seller's payment address
- Contract administration office instructions.

This section becomes important as a company tries to collect payment.

Section H: Special Contract Requirements

Customized clauses that do not fit elsewhere in the UCF are contained in Section H. Policies concerning placement of these clauses vary among federal agencies and even among the buying offices within an agency. Such clauses might include:

- Option terms
- Economic price adjustment provisions
- Government-furnished property or facilities
- Foreign sources
- Multiyear provisions
- Limitations on the federal government's obligations
- Service Contract Act wage determinations
- Payment of incentive fees
- Technical data requirements.

The contracting officer has numerous clauses and provisions to choose from when drafting Section H. Every clause included in this section must be there for a reason—either a regulation requires it or the administration of the contract necessitates it. Careful judgment should be used when selecting clauses because they add to the contract cost and tend to raise objections by contractors.

PART II: CONTRACT CLAUSES

Part II of the UCF contains a variety of contract clauses.

Section I: Contract Clauses

The circumstances of the proposed contract predetermine the clauses in this section, although the contracting officer may include any additional clauses that he or she expects to apply to the resulting contract. As a general rule, only clauses included in FAR Part 52 (and a federal agency's FAR supplement, Part 52) are included in this section.

These laws or regulations are commonly referred to as *boilerplate clauses*. The contracting officer has little or no leeway in preparing this section. Each clause derives its authority from the FAR or from a public law, statute, or executive order.

Most clauses included in this section are referenced by the clause number, title, date, and regulation source. Instead of printing an entire clause within a contract, an agreement may merely refer to the clause, such as FAR 52.203-3, Gratuities. (This is called *incorporation by reference* in the FAR.) Contractors are still liable for the legal consequences of the clause's terms, even if the clause is not expressly quoted or spelled out.

Clauses must be written out or incorporated in full text if:

- The FAR or an agency regulation specifically requires full text
- The seller must complete the clause
- The contracting officer's boss directs it.

Most clauses included in Section I must "flow down" to subcontractors. In other words, the same clauses that apply to the prime contractor also apply to the subcontractor. If you are unfamiliar with a referenced clause, be sure to obtain a copy of it so you will know exactly what the government requires of you.

The easiest way to obtain a copy of a referenced clause is to download it directly from the FAR at www.arnet.gov/far.

Provisions do not typically appear in this section. How does a provision differ from a clause? A *clause* is a term or condition that is used in both contracts and solicitations that can apply *before and after* the contract award, such as a clause requiring a contractor to maintain a drug-free workplace. A *provision* is used only in solicitations and applies only *before* contract award, such as procedures for handling late proposals. Provisions provide direction to the seller and are typically found in Section K, L, or M.

PART III: LIST OF DOCUMENTS, EXHIBITS, AND OTHER ATTACHMENTS

Part III contains a variety of attachments.

Section J: List of Attachments

Requirements that do not fit into any other sections of the UCF appear in Section J. It's essentially an inventory of documents. The FAR provides little guidance on the format or content of these attachments. The contracting officer, however, is directed to provide a list of the title, date, and number of pages for each attached document. Attachments might include:

- System requirements and specifications
- Architectural drawings
- Exhibits
- Work statements
- Government-furnished property.

When you receive an IFB or RFP, be sure that it includes all the attachments listed in this section. If you're unable to obtain all the attachments, strongly consider a "no bid."

PART IV: REPRESENTATIONS AND INSTRUCTIONS

This part includes instructions for preparing your bid or proposal, along with questions you must answer (or a questionnaire you must fill out) for your bid or proposal to be considered. Items ranging from definitions of contracting terms to statements about contract conditions are contained in this section.

Part IV is not included in the final contract award, but the contracting officer retains the winning contractor's representations and certifications. Be sure to fill in and sign all sections as required; if you don't, you might be considered nonresponsive and your bid or proposal might be rejected.

Section K: Representations, Certifications, and Other Statements of Offerors or Respondents

To be eligible for federal contracts, an offeror must provide information about itself and certify that it complies with all applicable laws and regulations in FAR 52.3. These representations and certifications (sometimes called *reps and certs*) usually require fill-in-the-blank answers.

- Is the offeror's workplace drug-free?
- Is the offeror a small business?
- Is the offeror minority-owned?
- Has the offeror performed the requirements for Certification of Procurement Integrity?

Online Representations and Certifications Application

Vendors are now required to submit their representations and certifications online using the System for Award Management (SAM) registration system. SAM is a federal Web-based system that aggregates and standardizes the collection of representations and certifications found in solicitations. Prior to the Online Representations and Certifications Application (ORCA), vendors were required to submit reps and certs for each individual contract award over $150,000 (captured in Section K provisions of solicitations). ORCA is now part of SAM.

This site not only benefits contractors by allowing them to maintain accurate records but also benefits contracting officers as they can view records, including archives, with a click of the mouse. SAM records are considered public information, meaning anyone with your DUNS number can search your records.

Once your company is in the database, you can access and update your information at any time. Vendors must update their information in SAM at least annually to maintain an active status. When responding to a solicitation, you'll either certify that your reps and certs are current as of the date of your signature, or list any changes.

For more details about SAM, visit www.sam.gov.

Section L: Instructions, Conditions, and Notices to Offerors or Respondents

Section L spells out how the proposal should be prepared. The instructions are designed to facilitate the evaluation process. This section, for example, might specify a limitation on the number of pages or volumes in the proposal, require that a certain font size and margins be used, and lay out the order of presentation.

Once you understand all the conditions listed in this section, check to see if comparable instructions found in Section C and Section M are consistent. Read carefully: a misunderstanding could lead to your bid or proposal being summarily rejected.

Section L also contains information on the various conditions and circumstances that might affect the proposal, such as:

- Whether the proposal is set aside for small businesses
- The expected contract type
- Procedures for handling late proposals.

In general, Section L should include information that facilitates offerors' submitting their best possible proposal and provides the source-selection team with sufficient data to make an award decision.

If the solicitation instructions are ambiguous, get clarification from the contracting officer (preferably in writing).

Section M: Evaluation Factors for Award

The federal government's criteria for evaluating proposals and selecting the winner are identified in this section. Section M must include and adequately describe all factors the government will consider in making the selection. The solicitation also informs offerors of minimum requirements that apply to particular evaluation factors, such as the requirement that the contractor's proposal be technically sound.

In sealed bidding, the evaluation criteria are limited to price and price-related factors. Cost/price is always an evaluation factor in any source selection. However, negotiated procurements allow the contracting officer to evaluate price, terms and conditions, technical requirements, delivery schedules, and management proposals.

Section M often shows each factor's relative weight in the evaluation process. The technical requirements, for example, might be twice as important as the management proposal. Government evaluators will consider only the factors specified in this section. Understanding the weight attached to each solicitation component will allow you to tailor your proposal responses to maximize your potential for selection.

If no relative importance of evaluation factors is given, the Comptroller General has held that offerors have a right to assume they are equal in importance. However, to be on the safe side, you may want to contact the contracting office for confirmation. Usually when the factors are meant to be equal in importance, Section M will state that they are indeed equal in importance.

> To help ensure that your proposal addresses all the elements of Section C, Section L, and Section M, you might consider preparing a compliance matrix that identifies where each item is addressed in the proposal.

AMENDMENTS TO THE SOLICITATION

In many cases, the contracting officer will issue amendments to a solicitation. An amendment might, for example, clarify ambiguities, add requirements to the statement of work, or delete requirements. Amendments should be taken very seriously because their content could dictate significant changes to the original solicitation, as well as the time allowed for performance. Now that most solicitations are available online, contractors should be sure to check FedBizOpps daily for any amendments.

To amend a solicitation, the contracting officer may furnish SF 30, Amendment of Solicitation/Modification of Contract, to prospective offerors. (The example on the next page shows an amendment to extend the date that proposals are due from April 5, 2016, to April 19, 2016.) Offerors acknowledge receipt of the amendment by completing Blocks 8 and 15 on SF 30 and returning the form with the bid or proposal.

AMENDMENT OF SOLICITATION/MODIFICATION OF CONTRACT

1. CONTRACT ID CODE | PAGE 1 OF PAGES 1

2. AMENDMENT/MODIFICATION NO.: 0001

3. EFFECTIVE DATE: 03/19/2016

4. REQUISITION/PURCHASE REQ. NO.: 01-12NN63100.000

5. PROJECT NO. *(If applicable)*

6. ISSUED BY — CODE: MA-542

U.S. Department of Energy
Headquarters Office of Procurement Services
1000 Independence Ave., SW
Washington, DC 20585

7. ADMINISTERED BY *(If other than Item 6)* — CODE

8. NAME AND ADDRESS OF CONTRACTOR *(No., street, county, State and ZIP Code)*

Happy's Office Furniture
850 Taylor St.
Fort Worth, TX 76102

CODE — FACILITY CODE

(X) [X] 9A. AMENDMENT OF SOLICITATION NO.: DE-RP01-12NN63100

9B. DATED *(SEE ITEM 11)*: 03/03/2016

[ ] 10A. MODIFICATION OF CONTRACT/ORDER NO.

10B. DATED *(SEE ITEM 13)*

11. THIS ITEM ONLY APPLIES TO AMENDMENTS OF SOLICITATIONS

[X] The above numbered solicitation is amended as set forth in Item 14. The hour and date specified for receipt of Offers [X] is extended, [ ] is not extended.

Offers must acknowledge receipt of this amendment prior to the hour and date specified in the solicitation or as amended, by one of the following methods: (a) By completing items 8 and 15, and returning 2 copies of the amendment; (b) By acknowledging receipt of this amendment on each copy of the offer submitted; or (c) By separate letter or telegram which includes a reference to the solicitation and amendment numbers. FAILURE OF YOUR ACKNOWLEDGMENT TO BE RECEIVED AT THE PLACE DESIGNATED FOR THE RECEIPT OF OFFERS PRIOR TO THE HOUR AND DATE SPECIFIED MAY RESULT IN REJECTION OF YOUR OFFER. If by virtue of this amendment your desire to change an offer already submitted, such change may be made by telegram or letter, provided each telegram or letter makes reference to the solicitation and this amendment, and is received prior to the opening hour and date specified.

12. ACCOUNTING AND APPROPRIATION DATA *(If required)*

13. THIS ITEM ONLY APPLIES TO MODIFICATION OF CONTRACTS/ORDERS. IT MODIFIES THE CONTRACT/ORDER NO. AS DESCRIBED IN ITEM 14.

CHECK ONE	
[ ]	A. THIS CHANGE ORDER IS ISSUED PURSUANT TO: *(Specify authority)* THE CHANGES SET FORTH IN ITEM 14 ARE MADE IN THE CONTRACT ORDER NO. IN ITEM 10A.
[ ]	B. THE ABOVE NUMBERED CONTRACT/ORDER IS MODIFIED TO REFLECT THE ADMINISTRATIVE CHANGES *(such as changes in paying office, appropriation date, etc.)* SET FORTH IN ITEM 14, PURSUANT TO THE AUTHORITY OF FAR 43.103(b).
[ ]	C. THIS SUPPLEMENTAL AGREEMENT IS ENTERED INTO PURSUANT TO AUTHORITY OF:
[ ]	D. OTHER *(Specify type of modification and authority)*

E. IMPORTANT: Contractor [ ] is not, [ ] is required to sign this document and return ______ copies to the issuing office.

14. DESCRIPTION OF AMENDMENT/MODIFICATION (*Organized by UCF section headings, including solicitation/contract subject matter where feasible.)*

The purpose of this amendment is to extend the date that proposals are due from April 5, 2016 to April 19, 2016. Accordingly, Part II, Section L, Provision L.8 - Time, Date and Place Bids/Proposals are Due is revised to reflect the following: 1:00 p.m. on April 19, 2016.

Except as provided herein, all terms and conditions of the document referenced in Item 9A or 10A, as heretofore changed, remains unchanged and in full force and effect.

15A. NAME AND TITLE OF SIGNER *(Type or print)*: Happy Gilmore, CEO

16A. NAME AND TITLE OF CONTRACTING OFFICER *(Type or print)*: David J. Smith, Contracting Officer

15B. CONTRACTOR/OFFEROR — *(Signature of person authorized to sign)*

15C. DATE SIGNED: 03/19/2016

16B. UNITED STATES OF AMERICA — *(Signature of Contracting Officer)*

16C. DATE SIGNED: 03/19/2016

NSN 7540-01-152-8070
Previous edition unusable

STANDARD FORM 30 (REV. 10-83)
Prescribed by GSA FAR (48 CFR) 53.243

Example Amendment of Solicitation/Modification of Contract (Standard Form 30)

If the offeror does not acknowledge or sign the amendment, its bid or proposal may be disqualified as nonresponsive.

Don't confuse amendments to a solicitation with modifications to a contract. Amendments generally add new requirements, change requirements, clarify discrepancies in the solicitation, or delete something before the proposal's due date. Modifications, on the other hand, are changes to an awarded contract.

TYPICAL PROPOSAL WEAKNESSES AND DEFICIENCIES

Whether you're new to government contracting or have enough past performance references to fill a book, making a mistake in your bid or proposal can cost you a contract. It's essential that you give yourself plenty of time to read through the entire solicitation. Did you answer all the questions? Are all the requested prices and quantities filled in? Missing even a single piece of information can disqualify you, so it's worth your time to triple-check everything.

Here's a list of common proposal weaknesses and misteaks:

(Oops! How many of you immediately noticed I misspelled the word *mistakes*? Lesson one: misspellings, wordiness, an unclear writing style, and grammatical errors are by far the most common deficiencies in proposals.)

- Noncompliance with the solicitation's specifications and requirements
- Unrealistic cost estimates (either too high or too low)
- Insufficient understanding of the contract's requirements
- Poor proposal organization
- Unsubstantiated rationale for the proposed approach
- Insufficient resources to accomplish the contract's requirements
- Incomplete response to the solicitation.

To avoid these problems, it might be a good idea to set up a checklist of solicitation requirements as you read through the IFB or RFP. Then, during your final proposal review, make sure you've properly covered everything identified on the checklist.

PROCUREMENT INSTRUMENT IDENTIFICATION NUMBERS

Each solicitation issued by the government receives a procurement instrument identification number, known as a PIIN, which typically consists of 13 digits (or positions).

> DoD refers to PIINs as Department of Defense Activity Address Codes (DODAACs). Why create such a scary acronym? You'll need to talk to DoD about that one!
>
> Here are a few DODAAC buying offices:
>
> **Major Army Buying Offices:**
>
> | | |
> |---|---|
> | Contracting Command, MICC | W911S8 |
> | National Guard Bureau | W912MM |
>
> **Major Navy Buying Offices:**
>
> | | |
> |---|---|
> | Office of Naval Research | N00014 |
> | Naval Air Systems Command | N00019 |
>
> (It sure would be nice to have a DODAAC directory on the Web. Anyone?)

The first six digits identify the contracting activity (or buying office) issuing the solicitation. The next two digits in the PIIN identify the fiscal year. The ninth character identifies the solicitation type being used, such as an invitation for bid (B) or a request for proposal (R). The remaining digits identify the particular solicitation or contract.

The following is the PIIN for a request for proposal issued in FY 2016 by the Office of Naval Research.

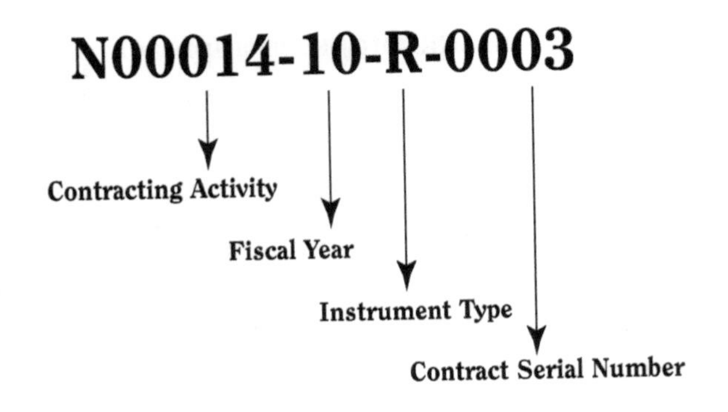

On an interesting note, the 13-alphanumeric-character PIIN for a solicitation will not be the same as the PIIN for a contract. The first six characters will be identical, but the seventh may not be if the contract is awarded in a later fiscal year than when the solicitation was issued. The eighth character will be different because different letters are used to identify different kinds of solicitations and contracts, and the four characters in positions 10 through 13 are numbers normally issued in sequence, starting most often with 0001 at the beginning of each fiscal year.

UNSOLICITED PROPOSALS

So you or your company have come up with a new and innovative idea that might benefit the government—what do you do? In that case you can create an opportunity for yourself by submitting an unsolicited proposal.

An unsolicited proposal is a written offer submitted to a federal agency on the contractor's initiative to obtain a contract. It is not submitted in response to a formal or informal solicitation request. A major advantage of submitting an unsolicited proposal is that your offer is typically one of a kind. That is, you probably won't have competition.

The government typically encourages the submission of new and innovative ideas in response to Broad Agency Announcements and Small Business Innovation Research (SBIR) topics. In many cases, such ideas are actually "solicited" by technical personnel rather than by contracting personnel.

> Remember that only warranted contracting officers have the authority to contractually bind the government. Technical personnel who receive, handle, or evaluate unsolicited proposals are *not* authorized to commit the government.

Each federal agency uses different procedures for handling unsolicited proposals. To get information on an agency's submission procedures, contact the small business specialist at the agency of interest to you.

Note that federal agencies are not responsible for costs incurred in proposal preparation. It is always a good idea to consult with appropriate agency officials before starting on an unsolicited proposal. A valid unsolicited proposal must:

- Be innovative and unique
- Be independently originated and developed by the contractor
- Be prepared without government supervision, endorsement, or direction, although detailed discussions with agency personnel about the need often encourage the contractor to prepare and submit the proposal
- Include sufficient detail to determine that government support could be worthwhile and the proposed work could benefit the agency
- Not be an advance proposal for a known federal agency requirement that can be acquired by competitive methods.

Advertising material, commercial-item offers, contributions, or routine correspondence on technical issues are not considered unsolicited proposals.

Unsolicited proposals should contain the following basic information to permit objective and timely consideration:

- The offeror's name, address, and organization type
- Names and phone numbers of technical and business personnel to be contacted for evaluation or negotiation purposes
- Identification of proprietary or confidential data to be used only for evaluation purposes (be sure to clearly mark any confidential information you wish to protect from possible release to others)
- Submission date and signature of a person authorized to represent and contractually obligate the contractor
- A title and an abstract of the proposed effort (the abstract should be approximately 200 to 300 words, stating the proposal's basic purpose and expected end result)
- A report that discusses the contracting activity's objectives, approach, and anticipated results
- Key personnel names and bios
- Type of support needed from the agency (such as facilities or equipment)
- Proposed price or total estimated cost
- Time period for which the proposal is valid (a six-month minimum is suggested)

- Preferred contract type
- Brief description of the organization and relevant experience.

Federal agencies have procedures and contact points for controlling the receipt, evaluation, and timely disposition of unsolicited proposals. If the agency determines that it doesn't need the services, it returns the unsolicited proposal to the offeror, citing the reasons.

Government personnel are prohibited from disclosing restrictively marked information included in an unsolicited proposal. Also, unless the contractor is notified of and agrees to the intended use, the government should not use any data, concept, idea, or other part of an unsolicited proposal as the basis for a solicitation or in negotiations with other firms.

CONTINGENT FEES

Contingent fee arrangements are a very complicated area of government contracting. Simply stated, a *contingent fee* means any commission, percentage, brokerage, or other fee that is contingent on the success that a person or concern has in securing a government contract award. For example, if a company hires a consultant to help prepare a proposal for a government contract and the agreement states that payment is contingent upon the company's winning, the agreement would be considered a contingent fee arrangement.

Arrangements to pay contingent fees for soliciting or obtaining government contracts have long been considered contrary to public policy because they might lead to attempted or actual exercise of improper influence. In every negotiated contract, the government requires the contractor to provide a certification that it has not paid contingent fees to secure the contract. If the contractor fails to provide this documentation, the government may annul the contract without liability or deduct from the contract price the full amount of the contingent fee.

There is, however, an exception to this certification requirement. Contingent fee arrangements are permitted if they are made between contractors and "bona fide employees." A bona fide employee is a person employed by a contractor who is subject to the contractor's supervision and control with respect to time, place, and manner of performance. Therefore, this person neither exerts improper influence to obtain government contracts nor holds himself or herself out as being able to obtain them through improper influence.

Federal regulations allow this same type of bona fide employee relationship on a part-time basis for small businesses because they typically do not have the resources to employ salespeople full time. If a small business hires a consultant to help prepare price proposals, the consultant would be considered a bona fide employee if he or she is supervised by the company's president and performs the company's services two days a week throughout the year. A bona fide employee may represent more than one firm but should not bid or propose for more than one firm in the same line of work.

Contingent fee arrangements are complex. Be sure to obtain legal advice if you have questions or concerns about any of your contractual arrangements.

■ ■ ■

In the world of government contracting, proposals represent the point of sale for companies looking to do business with the federal government. Effective and efficient proposal development, preparation, management, and design are essential to your company's success. If any part of the solicitation is unclear, you're far better off asking the contracting officer to clarify than taking a guess and hoping for the best.

■ ■ ■

Contract Types and Administrative Requirements

Isn't having a smoking section in a restaurant sort of like having a peeing section in a pool?

—*George Carlin*

There is a perception in federal contracting that the lowest bidder always wins the contract. Sealed bidding procedures, for example, enable the bidder with the lowest-priced bid to win the contract. Low bids, however, do not apply to federal supply schedule orders, best-value procurements, or sole-source acquisitions. How comfortable would you be riding on the "space taxi" if you knew it was built by the contractor with the lowest-priced proposal?

The federal government contracts for products and services at fair and reasonable prices, but no set of standard rules defines a "fair and reasonable price." Eventually, no matter how the acquisition method is approached, the decision comes down to a matter of good personal judgment.

The contracting officer chooses a procurement method that best fits the contract's requirements (see Part IV). To purchase an item that can be clearly and accurately described, such as office furniture, the government would probably use sealed bidding procedures. If the contracting officer is unsure of a contractor's ability to provide acceptable items, negotiated procedures might be a better alternative. No matter which solicitation method is used, price must always be part of the evaluation criteria.

The selection of a contract type requires negotiation and the exercise of good judgment. A contracting officer usually considers several factors, including:

- Contract's expected length (or period of performance)
- Price competition
- Contract's technical complexity
- Urgency of the need
- Dollar value of the contract
- Contract's performance risks
- Market conditions
- Contractor's motivation to perform the contract.

The contractor may also propose an alternative contract type.

The federal government uses two basic types of contracts: fixed-price and cost-reimbursement. The primary differences between the contract types are the amount of responsibility placed on the contractor and the amount of profit incentive offered to the contractor for achieving or exceeding specified standards or goals.

With fixed-price contracts, the contractor assumes the risk of contract performance (or cost risk), and its performance determines its profit. Cost-reimbursement contracts, on the other hand, place the risk of contract performance on the government because this type reimburses the contractor for the expenses incurred during the contract's performance.

The other contract types available (discussed in Chapter 16) are variations of fixed-price or cost-reimbursement contracts:

- Indefinite-delivery contracts
- Time-and-materials
- Labor-hour contracts
- Letter contracts.

The solicitation document always indicates the contract type.

CHAPTER 14

Fixed-Price Contracts

Berry's World
"Remember, money can't buy happiness, but in Washington it CAN BUY access, jobs and influence."
11-5-96

What's in this chapter?

- Firm fixed-price contracts
- Fixed-price contracts with economic price adjustment
- Fixed-price incentive contracts
- Fixed-price contracts with prospective price redetermination
- Fixed-ceiling-price contracts with retroactive price redetermination

Under a fixed-price contract, the government agrees to pay a specific price (which includes the contractor's profit) for completed work and delivered products. Fixed-price contracts are used primarily to acquire commercial items but are increasingly being used for acquiring services. When a contract is fixed-price, acceptable performance by the contractor is the basic criterion for payment. (A contractor's bill under a fixed-price contract is called an *invoice*.)

The government generally prefers fixed-price contracts because the contract price is not subject to adjustment on the basis of the contractor's cost experience in performing it. If a contractor wins a fixed-price government contract, it must perform the contract at the award price, even if its actual costs of performance exceed the award price.

Fixed-price contracts place the cost risk on the contractor. However, there is no statutory limit on the profits that can be earned under fixed-price contracts. Maximum profit can be earned by managing fixed-price contracts aggressively and identifying, understanding, and controlling risk. Fixed-price contracts are typically used when:

- Price competition is adequate
- Reasonable price comparisons with past purchases of the same or similar products or services made on a competitive basis are available
- Available cost or pricing information permits realistic estimates of the probable performance costs
- Performance uncertainties can be identified, and reasonable estimates of their cost impact can be made.

The government uses fixed-price contracts in simplified acquisition and sealed bidding procedures. They are used in 80 percent of negotiated procurements as well.

FIRM FIXED-PRICE CONTRACTS

In a firm fixed-price (FFP) contract, the government agrees to pay a specific amount (or price) when a contractor's performance has been completed and accepted. The contract price does not change, regardless of the contractor's actual cost experience. A contractor accepts full cost responsibility when agreeing to this type of contract. FFP contracts are typically used when:

- The statement of work can be clearly and accurately described (FFP contracts are generally used for purchasing commercial items and standard services)
- A fair, accurate, and reasonable contract price can be established before contract award.

The government prefers this contract type because the contractor bears all the risk and the government's administrative burden is minimal. If the contracting officer determines that the agreed-upon prices are based on adequate price competition, FFP contracts require no cost or pricing data. (See the discussion of the Truth in Negotiations Act in Chapter 2.)

The government establishes the "firm" contract price and performance requirements during the pre-award negotiation phase. Suppose three contractors were awarded contracts to supply office furniture.

	RJC Furniture	**Joe's Office Supplies**	**All Office, Inc.**
	100 executive chairs	**5 conference tables**	**20 office desks**
Contract value	$75,000	$150,000	$200,000
Actual costs	$50,000	$185,000	$200,000
Profit (or loss)	$25,000	($35,000)	$0

In this example, RJC Furniture made a profit of $25,000, which the government will pay once the chairs are delivered and accepted. Joe's Office Supplies incurred unexpected costs during contract performance and lost $35,000. It must fulfill the contract requirements in spite of its loss. All Office, Inc., broke even.

Most FFP solicitations over $150,000 include FAR provision 52.203-2, Certificate of Independent Price Determination. This provision requires contractors to certify that they have not prepared their price proposals in collusion with another person or firm. A contractor's failure to submit a certificate (or submission of a false certificate) may be grounds for rejection of its proposal.

FFP Advantages for Contractors

- You can obtain a higher profit under an FFP contract if you control your costs.
- Because the government awards most FFP contracts under adequate price competition, your reporting requirements are minimal.
- FFP contracts require less administration for both the government and the contractor.

FFP Disadvantages for Contractors

- FFP contracts offer little flexibility. (Price cannot be adjusted.)
- If you do not control your costs, you can lose money.

FIXED-PRICE CONTRACTS WITH ECONOMIC PRICE ADJUSTMENT

Suppose the U.S. Treasury Department awarded a contract to Coppermine, Inc., to supply copper for minting pennies for two years. Because the price of copper tends to fluctuate over time, the contracting officer makes its price subject to an economic price adjustment. The price index for metals is used to reflect market changes to copper. Coppermine, Inc., delivers 5,000 pounds of copper each year:

	Year 1	Year 2
5,000 pounds of copper	$250,000	$275,000*
Labor costs	$50,000	$50,000
Shipping costs	$75,000	$75,000
Profit	$25,000	$25,000
Total contract value	$400,000	$425,000

*Per examination of the price index for metals, the price of 5,000 pounds of copper went up $25,000 in Year 2. This contract has a 10 percent ceiling, so the fluctuation could not exceed $40,000 (400,000 × 10% = $40,000).

In this contract, the price of copper is isolated to provide for a foreseeable economic price adjustment, but the other requirements remain the same. Labor, shipping, and profit are handled as an FFP contract. Allowance for increased profit never justifies an economic price adjustment.

A fixed-price contract with economic price adjustment (FP/EPA) is designed to protect against the contingencies that threaten multiyear contracts. It is basically an FFP contract with a clause that allows the contract price to be revised (either upward or downward) in case of economic uncertainties. Usually a ceiling on upward adjustments is set at 10 percent of the unit price. There is never a floor on downward adjustments.

The contracting officer chooses an FP/EPA contract that meets the government's requirements for the supply or service being purchased, including elements subject to cost fluctuations. The government generally allows for three types of economic price adjustments:

- ***Adjustments based on established prices.*** Price adjustments are based on increases or decreases of an agreed-upon published or otherwise established price.
- ***Adjustments based on actual costs of labor or material.*** Price adjustments are based on increases or decreases in specified costs of labor or material that the contractor actually experiences during contract performance.
- ***Adjustments based on cost indexes of labor or material.*** Price adjustments are based on increases or decreases in labor or material cost indexes that the contract specifically identifies. The indexes are largely dependent on two series of publications put out by the Department of Labor: (1) the Producer Price Index for industrial commodities and (2) the Wage and Income Series by North American Industry Classification System.

Economic price adjustments usually are restricted to industry-wide contingencies. If the price adjustment is based on labor and material costs, it should be limited to contingencies beyond the contractor's control.

The price that may be adjusted is typically determined as follows:

1. The contracting officer identifies the items subject to adjustment before contract performance. A ceiling is set for contingencies, and the ground rules for adjustments are made.
2. The contracting officer revises the prices up or down during the contract's performance as defined by market conditions. Support must be provided for these adjustments.

As with an FFP contract, FP/EPA contracts must include FAR provision 52.203-2.

FP/EPA Advantages for Contractors

- The contract price can be revised to reflect the effects of economic aberrations or changes in the marketplace.
- FP/EPA contracts offer many of the same benefits as FFP contracts.

FP/EPA Disadvantages for Contractors

- Price adjustments are limited to contingencies beyond the contractor's control.
- There is usually a ceiling on upward adjustments but no floor for downward adjustments.

FIXED-PRICE INCENTIVE CONTRACTS

Fixed-price contracts may contain incentives that increase or decrease a contractor's profit or fee on the basis of performance. A fixed-price incentive (FPI) contract, for example, might reward contractors for improving technical performance or making prompt deliveries.

In recent years, there has been an emphasis within the government on FPI contracts and other non-cost incentives, such as performance and schedule. By offering a chance of increased profits (kind of like a tip), the theory goes, contractors will be more motivated to enhance their performance.

A fixed-price incentive contract is also used when cost uncertainty still exists, but not to a sufficient degree to warrant the use of a cost-reimbursement contract (see Chapter 15). One example would be the latter stages of the development for a weapons system.

FPI contracts are appropriate when:

- The government and the contractor can negotiate at the outset (1) a firm target cost, target profit, and profit adjustment formula that offer a fair and reasonable incentive and (2) a ceiling to ensure that the contractor assumes an appropriate share of the risk.
- The contractor assumes a major share of the cost responsibility under the adjustment formula, which is reflected in the target profit.

The contracting officer calculates the final contract price (with the profit or loss) by applying a formula based on the relationship of total actual cost of performance to total target cost. To understand this formula, you need to be familiar with the following terms:

- ***Target cost*** is the estimated cost to complete the contract. Both parties agree to the target cost after analysis and negotiation. A contractor usually has an equal chance of overrunning or underrunning the total estimated cost.
- ***Target profit*** is the profit a contractor would earn if its costs equaled the target costs. The profit must be fair and reasonable.
- ***Target price*** is the sum of the target cost and the target profit.
- ***Ceiling price*** is the maximum amount the government will pay for the contract. When the contract costs reach this point, the contractor's profit is zero and it assumes responsibility for any additional costs.
- ***Sharing formula*** apportions the cost overruns or underruns between the government and the contractor. There may be two separate formulas—one for the overrun and one for the underrun—or the same formula may be used for both expressions. The share ratio is typically between 50/50 and 75/25.

Let's assume a contractor had an overrun of $50,000 and the sharing formula was 75/25:

The government's portion:

Overrun	($50,000)
Sharing formula	× 75%
	($37,500)

The contractor's portion:

Overrun	($50,000)
Sharing formula	× 25%
	($12,500)

Here's an illustration of how the FPI contract works: Suppose the Department of Defense awarded Scud, Inc., a contract to finish the development of a new long-range ballistic missile. Scud, Inc., negotiated the following contract cost projections:

Target cost	$12,000,000
Target profit	$500,000
Target price	$12,500,000
Ceiling price	$12,750,000
Sharing formula	60/40

The contracting officer used a sharing formula of 60/40 to strongly encourage Scud, Inc., to perform the contract for less than the cost projections. Therefore, if Scud, Inc., incurred $11,750,000 in contract costs, it would make the profit shown below on the contract:

Actual cost	$11,750,000
Less target cost	–($12,000,000)
Contract underrun	$250,000
Contractor sharing %	×40%
Total underrun profit	$100,000
Add target profit	+$500,000
Total profit	**$600,000**
Add actual cost	$11,750,000
Total contract value	**$ 12,350,000**

If Scud, Inc., had incurred $12,800,000 in contract costs, its profit on the contract would be as follows:

Actual cost	$12,800,000
Less target cost	–($12,000,000)
Contract overrun	($800,000)

Contractor sharing %	×40%
Total overrun profit	($320,000)
Add target profit	+$500,000
Total profit	**$180,000**
Add actual cost	+$12,800,000
Total contract value	**$12,980,000**

In this second example, Scud, Inc., exceeded the projected target cost, so its total profit was reduced. However, it also exceeded the contract ceiling price of $12,750,000. The sharing formula changes from 60/40 to 0/100 once Scud, Inc., reaches the ceiling price. Scud, Inc., must absorb the portion of the contract cost that exceeded the ceiling price:

Total contract value	$12,980,000
Ceiling price	–($12,750,000)
Additional loss to contractor	($230,000)

There are two types of FPI contracts, firm target and successive target. This chapter discusses only the FPI firm target contract. Successive target contracts are used only when available cost or pricing data are not sufficient to permit the negotiation of a realistic firm target cost and profit before award. Because of the uncertainties involved with successive target contracts, they are rarely used. (See FAR 16.403-2 for information on successive target contracts.)

FPI Advantages for Contractors

- FPI contracts combine the sharing incentive feature and the fixed-price feature into one contract type.
- The government shares in any cost overrun (up to the ceiling price).

FPI Disadvantages for Contractors

- The contractor is responsible for all costs beyond the ceiling price.
- The government shares in cost savings.

FIXED-PRICE CONTRACTS WITH PROSPECTIVE PRICE REDETERMINATION

Suppose the Department of Justice awarded Make It Shine, Inc., a five-year contract to provide janitorial services. This contract originally was awarded at $100,000 a year, starting on January 1, 2016, and it has a redetermination date of January 1, 2019:

Contract Year	Contract Amount
2016	$100,000
2017	$100,000
2018	$100,000
2019	$125,000
2020	$125,000
Total contract value	**$550,000**

On January 1, 2019, the contracting officer approved a price redetermination of $125,000 a year for this contract. In this example, the annual contract amount was increased; in many cases, however, the contract amount is lowered on the redetermination date.

A fixed-price contract with prospective price redetermination provides for a firm fixed price for the initial period of contract performance and a redetermination of the contract price (either up or down) at a stated date during performance. The initial period should be the longest period for which it is possible to negotiate a fair and reasonable firm fixed price. Each subsequent pricing period should be at least 12 months.

This contract type is used when:

- Negotiations have established that neither an FFP contract nor an FPI contract is appropriate.
- The contracting officer can provide reasonable assurance that price redetermination actions will take place promptly at the specified times.

The contract may establish a ceiling price based on uncertainties involved in the contract's performance and their possible cost impact. This ceiling price helps ensure a reasonable amount of risk is given to the contractor.

Prospective Price Redetermination Advantages for Contractors

- This contract type allows for a price redetermination during contract performance.

Prospective Price Redetermination Disadvantages for Contractors

- This contract type is typically used for multiple-year contracts only.
- Price redetermination periods should be at least 12 months apart.

FIXED-CEILING-PRICE CONTRACTS WITH RETRO-ACTIVE PRICE REDETERMINATION

The Environmental Protection Agency (EPA) awarded Virus Tech, Inc., a six-month contract to develop software to protect against computer viruses. The contracting officer determined the contract's estimated cost of $120,000, with a ceiling of $150,000, to be fair and reasonable.

On July 20, 2018, the contracting officer redetermined the total contract value, reducing it to $115,000:

Contract Period	Contract Amount
Jan. 1, 2018, through June 30, 2018	$120,000
Redetermination on July 20, 2018	–($5,000)
Total contract value	$115,000

A fixed-ceiling-price contract with retroactive price redetermination allows for a price redetermination (either up or down) after the contract is completed. The negotiated ceiling price ensures that the contractor assumes a reasonable amount of risk. This contract type is used only when:

- The contract is for research and development (R&D) and the estimated cost is $150,000 or less. The contract period of performance should be no longer than 12 months.

- The contracting officer can provide reasonable assurance that the price redetermination will take place promptly at the specified time.
- The head of the contracting activity approves the use of this contract type in writing.

The contracting officer considers the contractor's management effectiveness and ingenuity when the contract price is redetermined retroactively.

Retroactive Price Redetermination Advantages for Contractors

- This contract type allows for a price redetermination once the contract is completed.

Retroactive Price Redetermination Disadvantages for Contractors

- Estimated contract costs must be $150,000 or less, and the contract must be for research and development.
- The contract period is typically less than 12 months.

■ ■ ■

The government uses fixed-price contracts for most of its purchases. They tend to be the simplest contract type to administer and evaluate. Fixed-price contracts place the maximum amount of cost risk on the contractor. Why should the government bear the risk if it can make *you* bear it? Once the government signs a fixed-price contract, it must pay the full amount, even if it subsequently determines the price to be too high.

■ ■ ■

Cost-Reimbursement Contracts

"Paying close attention to every detail. That's the key to my success, Bob!"

What's in this chapter?

- Determining your contract cost
- Calculating contract cost
- Understanding rates
- Fee/profit
- Types of cost-reimbursement contracts

For many government projects it is almost impossible to estimate the costs to actually perform and complete the job. Goal-directed research and development (R&D) work, such as finding a cure for AIDS, is such an example. In these cases, the government prefers to enter into cost-reimbursement contracts.

With cost-reimbursement contracts, the government reimburses the contractor for the reasonable, allocable, and allowable costs it incurs under the terms and conditions of the contract. The government essentially carries all the risk. Because there is little incentive for contractors to control costs, contracting officers are hesitant to use this type of contract.

If a contracting officer insists on using a fixed-price contract for a job that would be better suited to a cost-reimbursement contract, the contractor has to inflate the proposed contract price to protect itself from the uncertainties involved in performing the contract. Any time a cost-reimbursement contract is used, it must be solicited using negotiated procedures (see Chapter 12).

A cost-reimbursement contract establishes a total cost estimate for the purpose of obligating funds and establishing a ceiling that the contractor may not exceed (except at its own risk). The contractor agrees to put forth its best effort to get the job done within a mutually agreed-upon cost estimate. The contracting officer closely monitors the contractor's performance to ensure that it performs the contract effectively and efficiently.

The contractor must notify the contracting officer when its expenditure rate reaches a specified percentage of the agreed-upon cost estimate. If the estimated cost to complete becomes greater than the originally agreed-upon cost estimate, the contractor is required to submit a revised cost estimate. The contract is then modified to reflect the revised estimate or brought to an end.

If the contractor completes the job for less than the estimated cost, the excess funds can be used for other projects. A contractor's bill under a cost-reimbursement contract is called a public voucher.

DETERMINING YOUR CONTRACT COST

Before the government issues a cost-reimbursement contract, it must determine whether the contractor's accounting system has the ability to accumulate costs by contract (commonly referred to as a *job cost accounting system*). A chart of accounts is used to segregate direct costs from indirect costs.

Direct costs are costs that can be specifically identified with a particular contract, such as labor costs incurred to build a warehouse for a construction contract.

Indirect costs are expenses incurred by a contractor that cannot be attributed to any one particular contract. Heat or air conditioning in a manufacturing area that houses the work of several contracts would be considered an indirect cost because it benefits all the contracts. Indirect costs are allocated to a contract during the period in which they are incurred.

Indirect costs are further classified as either overhead (O/H) expenses or general and administrative (G&A) expenses.

O/H expenses are general in nature, such as indirect labor, rent, supplies, insurance, and depreciation. O/H expenses are distinct from the costs necessary for overall business operation. By charging each customer for part of these O/H expenses, the contractor recoups enough money to meet its total O/H expenses. This is sometimes called *burden* or *loading*.

G&A expenses are any organizational, financial, or other expenses incurred by a company for the general management and administration of the business as a whole. The salary of a company's president is generally considered a G&A expense. A contractor recovers these expenses by including a portion of them in the charges made to each customer.

The total operating cost of a company for a period, such as a year, is the sum of all the direct and indirect costs the company incurs. In ascertaining what constitutes a cost, the contractor may use any generally accepted method of determining or estimating costs that is equitable and consistently applied. Costs applied to a cost-reimbursement contract must therefore be reasonable, allocable, and allowable.

Don't let all of this "accountant-speak" scare you. This chapter has several easy-to-follow examples that will help clarify how this works.

Reasonable Costs

A cost is accepted as reasonable if, by its nature and amount, it does not exceed that which would be incurred by a prudent person in the conduct of a competitive business. Determining cost reasonableness is mostly a matter of common sense. When a contractor's business is in a highly competitive industry, its costs are probably reasonable because the business must keep its costs competitive.

If the government contracts for specially designed products or services in a business market that is not highly competitive, it needs to ensure that the proposed costs are reasonable. If a specific cost is challenged, the contractor bears the burden of proving its reasonableness.

Allocable Costs

Contractors accumulate indirect expenses into logical cost groupings to permit the distribution of expenses in relation to benefits received by the contracts (or cost objectives). An indirect cost is allocable to a government contract if:

- It is incurred specifically for the contract
- It benefits the contract and can be distributed in reasonable proportion to the benefits received
- It is necessary to the overall operation of the business, although a direct relationship to any particular cost objective cannot be shown.

Each contractor must allocate its indirect costs to contracts in an equitable, logical, and consistent way. The FAR does not suggest or require the use of any particular cost distribution base. Instead, it allows for the use of alternative distribution bases that will bring about a substantial matching of the indirect costs with the appropriate cost objectives. See Calculating Contract Cost later in this chapter for an illustration of using direct labor to allocate O/H expenses.

Determining what is equitable should be objective, but often it is not. If a contractor hires a security guard for a specific contract but the guard's services are allocated to all contracts, the allocation probably wouldn't be considered equitable. On the other hand, if the security guard provides services for the entire company, this could be considered a benefit to each contract, in which case allocating such costs to all contracts would be appropriate if done in an equitable manner.

Allowable Costs

An allowable cost meets the tests of reasonableness and allocability, is in agreement with generally accepted accounting principles, and otherwise conforms to specific limitations or exclusions set forth in the FAR (Part 31). If the government determines a cost to be unallowable, the law prohibits its payment. This is a very hard concept for many contractors to understand because many of these unallowable costs are legitimate business expenses in the eyes of the Internal Revenue Service.

Bad debt expenses are not allocable to government contracts because the government always pays its debts. The reason for the apparent inconsistency of these unallowable costs is that the government pays the contractor for only those costs from which the government benefits. The decision for determining the allowability of a particular cost ultimately rests with the contracting officer.

Common unallowable costs include:

- ***Public relations and advertising costs.*** Public relations includes all functions and activities dedicated to maintaining, protecting, and enhancing the image of a company or its products. Advertising, the most common means for promoting public relations, includes conventions, exhibits, samples, magazines, direct mail, displays, radio, and television.

  The only allowable advertising costs are those that the contract specifically requires or that arise from government contract requirements and are exclusively for (1) recruiting personnel required for performing contractual obligations, (2) acquiring scarce items for contract performance, and (3) disposing of surplus materials acquired for contract performance.

  Allowable public relations costs include costs specifically required by contract and costs of (1) responding to inquiries on company policies and activities; (2) communicating with the public, press, stockholders, creditors, and customers; (3) conducting general liaison with news media and government public relations officers; (4) participating in community service, such as blood bank drives, charity drives, and disaster assistance; and (5) conducting plant tours and holding open houses.

All other advertising and public relations costs are unallowable.

- ***Bad debts.*** Bad debts, including actual or estimated losses arising from uncollectible accounts receivable due from customers and any directly associated costs, such as collection and legal costs, are unallowable.
- ***Contributions or donations.*** Gifts made to charities, including cash, property, and services are unallowable.
- ***Entertainment costs.*** Costs of amusement, such as tickets to shows or sporting events, meals, lodging, transportation, and gratuities, are unallowable. Membership costs to country clubs are also unallowable, regardless of whether the cost is reported as taxable income for employees. Moreover, the government expressly prohibits its employees from accepting contractor-provided gratuities or entertainment. The rationale behind this provision is that entertaining with government-provided funds is against public policy.
- ***Fines and penalties.*** Costs of fines and penalties resulting from a contractor's violations of or failure to comply with federal, state, local, or foreign laws and regulations are unallowable. The only exception is when the penalty is incurred as a result of compliance with specific terms and conditions of the contract or written instructions from the contracting officer.
- ***Interest and other financial costs.*** Interest on borrowings, bond discounts, costs of financing and refinancing capital, legal and professional fees paid in connection with preparing a prospectus, costs of issuing stock rights, and directly associated costs are unallowable. However, interest assessed by state or local taxing authorities is allowable.
- ***Organization costs.*** Unallowable organizational costs include (1) costs for planning or executing the organization or reorganization of the business's corporate structure (including mergers and acquisitions); (2) costs associated with raising capital; and (3) incorporation fees and the costs of attorneys, accountants, brokers, promoters, management consultants, and investment counselors (regardless of whether they are company employees).

- ***Alcoholic beverages.*** Don't even think about it!

The above list does not cover all unallowable costs, just those most common to commercial contractors. See Part 31 of the FAR for a complete listing of unallowable costs.

A cost-reimbursement contract itself also contains a variety of terms and conditions that will affect cost allowability. It cites the requirements and deliverables, which will define the scope of work to be performed. Other contract clauses will address cost-associated matters.

You will find, for example, clauses dealing with such topics as reimbursement for travel and other advance agreements peculiar to that specific contract. Such items are often referred to as *other direct charges* (ODCs), and it is not uncommon for the government to specify that these charges are reimbursable on a cost basis only, meaning that no fee is applied.

As a contractor, you are responsible for appropriately accounting for your business costs and maintaining proper records. This includes supporting documentation adequate to demonstrate that costs claimed have been incurred, are allocable to the contract, and comply with applicable cost principles.

Government auditors (the Defense Contract Audit Agency) will seek to identify unallowable costs, including directly associated costs incurred in the contract performance. This requirement enables the government to identify and eliminate unallowable costs from your billing, claim, or proposal.

CALCULATING CONTRACT COST

The following is an example of how to calculate the total contract cost for each cost-reimbursement contract owned by a company. I've used a chart of accounts or general ledger (G/L) structure similar to the one below for numerous government contracting firms over the years.

Suppose Microhard, Inc., a small business engineering services firm, had an accounting system that properly accumulates costs/expenses for the year ending December 31, 2016. Its chart of accounts segregates direct and indirect costs/expenses, as you can see below:

Chart of Accounts

Direct Costs

Direct labor	$700,000
Direct materials	$650,000

Indirect Costs

Overhead (O/H)		**General and Administrative (G&A)**	
O/H labor	$110,000	G&A labor	$126,000
O/H vacation expense	50,000	Marketing labor	5,000
O/H sick leave	21,000	G&A vacation expense	28,000
Holidays	24,000	G&A sick leave	18,000
FICA expense	18,000	Holidays	14,000
Unemployment taxes	1,200	FICA expense	9,000
Workers compensation	700	Unemployment taxes	1,000
Disability insurance	1,500	Workers comp.	800
Group health insurance	16,000	Disability insurance	1,500
Conferences & seminars	500	Group health insurance	11,500
Consultants	850	Bank service charges	8,000
Depreciation	20,000	Conferences & seminars	3,000
Dues & subscriptions	700	Consultants	8,000
Copy charges	5,450	Postage & shipping	750
Equipment rentals	2,000	Depreciation	3,500
Recruiting	400	Dues & subscriptions	2,000
Repairs & maintenance	700	Copy charges	2,800
Postage & shipping	200	Equipment rental	850
Rent	20,000	Legal costs	6,500
O/H office supplies	5,500	Recruiting	1,500
Travel costs	520	G&A office supplies	3,600
Misc. expenses	2,780	Rent	15,000
		Repairs & maintenance	3,500
		Taxes	1,000
		Travel	2,400
		Misc. expenses	2,800
Total O/H claimed	**$302,000**	**Total G&A expenses**	**$280,000**

These accumulated costs are referred to as *pools*. Microhard, Inc., has an overhead pool and a G&A pool. (If applicable, bid and proposal [B&P] and other business development costs are included in the G&A pool.)

The first step in determining your total cost for a cost-reimbursement contract is to calculate your O/H and G&A rates. An O/H rate is typically determined by dividing your indirect O/H expenses by your total direct labor.

> Any allocation base (or denominator) can be used if you can establish and defend a cause/benefit relationship, such as labor hours, square footage, or units of production.

Microhard, Inc., had the following rates:

Indirect O/H costs	$302,000	= **43%**
Total direct labor	$700,000*	

*Microhard, Inc., uses direct labor dollars for its allocation base.

In this example, Microhard, Inc.'s total cost input consisted of:

Direct labor	$700,000
Direct materials	$650,000
O/H costs	$302,000
Total cost input	$1,652,000

Microhard, Inc. calculates its G&A rate by dividing its G&A expenses by all other costs (total cost input):

Indirect G&A costs	$280,000	= **17%**
Total cost input	$1,652,000	

Now that Microhard, Inc., has determined its rates, the next step is to apply them to its various contracts:

Microhard, Inc. Analysis of Incurred Costs for the Year Ending 12/31/16						
Contract No.	**Direct Labor**	**O/H Rate (43%)**	**Direct Materials**	**Subtotal**	**G&A Rate (17%)**	**Total Contract Cost**
Cost-Reimbursement Contracts						
6000	150,000	64,710	125,000	339,710	57,580	397,290
6001	200,000	86,300	175,000	461,300	78,185	539,485
Time-and-Materials Contracts (see Chapter 16)						
6200	100,000	43,140	50,000	193,140	32,735	225,875
Fixed-Price Contracts (see Chapter 14)						
6300	150,000	64,710	150,000	364,710	61,815	426,525
Commercial Fixed-Price Contracts						
6301	100,000	43,140	150,000	293,140	49,685	342,825
Totals	**700,000**	**302,000**	**650,000**	**1,652,000***	**280,000**	**1,932,000** ↙

*This subtotal balance ties to Microhard's G&A base (total cost input).

This schedule details the allocation of the O/H rate and the G&A rate to Microhard's various contracts (both government and commercial).

Now, let's do a quick test check to ensure the above schedule captured all our general ledger (G/L) costs/expenses:

Direct labor	$700,000
Direct materials	$650,000
O/H costs	$302,000
G&A costs	$280,000
Total G/L costs	$1,932,000 ↙

Which of course, it did (see pointers). Who says accounting has to be hard?

UNDERSTANDING RATES

Rates are typically calculated yearly because O/H and G&A costs tend to fluctuate from month to month. For example, rent might be paid quarterly. Most businesses establish temporary or proposed rates, commonly referred to as *billing* or *provisional* rates, at the beginning of each business year. The government compares proposed rates with the actual rates incurred in previous years to determine their reasonableness.

By establishing provisional rates at the beginning of each business year, a contractor can seek government reimbursement using these rates at interim dates. The government and the contractor establish final indirect cost rates after the contractor's business year closes. The provisional rates are then adjusted as necessary by the contractor.

Settlement of final indirect cost rates is a lengthy process. The contractor submits a proposed set of final indirect cost rates for the year. In many cases, the approval process will require an audit from the Defense Contract Audit Agency (DCAA). Once these final indirect cost rates are approved, they are not subject to change. The contractor needs to prepare a schedule to recognize any differences between the final indirect cost rates and the provisional rates.

Suppose Pro-ZacCo, a pharmaceutical company, determined its provisional (or billing) rates as follows:

Provisional (or Billing) Rates:

O/H rate	**44%**
G&A rate	**18%**

The government approved these rates for the business year beginning January 1, 2016. On September 30, 2017, Pro-ZacCo completed an audit with DCAA and determined the final indirect cost rates to be:

Final Indirect Cost Rates:

O/H rate	**43%**
G&A rate	**17%**

As a result, Pro-ZacCo had to reimburse the government for the rate difference. This difference was calculated as follows.

		Provisional Rates		Final Indirect Rates	Difference
Direct labor		$200,000		$200,000	—
O/H	44%	$88,000	43%	$86,300	$1,700
Direct materials		$175,000		$175,000	—
Subtotal		$463,000		$461,000	$1,700
G&A	18%	$83,340	17%	$78,185	$5,155
Total billed		$546,340		$539,485	$6,855

Pro-ZacCo owes the government $6,855 for this contract. If Pro-ZacCo's final indirect cost rates had exceeded its provisional rates, it would be entitled to reimbursement for the difference (up to any ceiling rates stated in the contract).

Cost Calculation Recap

The FAR contains no specific requirements for the allocation of indirect costs. It merely dictates that indirect costs be allocated to provide for logical cost groupings that permit the costs to be distributed to the cost objectives receiving the corresponding benefits. The FAR does indicate, however, that manufacturing overhead costs, selling costs, and G&A costs are usually accounted for separately.

Most small- to medium-sized contractors use two cost pools: one for O/H and one for G&A. The use of a fringe benefits pool is becoming increasingly popular, probably because it creates the appearance of lower O/H rates. Fringe benefit costs typically include vacation, health insurance, bonuses, retirement plans, and payroll taxes.

If a contractor performs work at more than one location, including government sites, it might be advisable to use multiple O/H pools. These additional O/H pools enable the contractor to better associate its O/H costs with the specific activities receiving the corresponding benefits.

Contractors are always concerned about their rates because they express a percentage relationship between their indirect costs and their direct (base) costs. Having consistently low rates tends to enhance a contractor's competitiveness. The problem with examining a contractor's rates for competitiveness is that the rates themselves do not show the whole picture.

A manufacturing company that uses old, fully depreciated equipment might have a low O/H rate but be very inefficient, while a company that uses modern equipment might have a high O/H rate but be very efficient at manufacturing products at a low overall cost.

A contracting officer must look at the total cost of a proposal, as well as the individual cost elements, to make an accurate evaluation. An O/H rate is simply a device for allocating indirect costs. A rate by itself is meaningless!

FEE/PROFIT

The government defines *profit* as that element of the total remuneration that contractors may receive for contract performance over and above allowable costs. In laymen's terms, profit is whatever monies are left after all costs are paid. When talking about a particular contract, profit is the amount a contractor receives above its out-of-pocket costs. It is the reward for undertaking the contract in the first place. All contractors, except the narrow category of not-for-profit institutions, are primarily interested in profit.

Although the government wants to see businesses make a profit, that margin of profit is carefully examined to verify the contract's fairness. The government looks at various factors to justify the profit percentages, including risk, the economy, the time involved in the project, previous R&D expenditures, and the contractor's professional expertise.

The government puts statutory limitations on the amount of profit that may be earned on cost-reimbursement contracts. Profit on a cost-reimbursement contract is termed *fee*. The profit is a percentage of the total estimated (not actual) cost.

Cost-plus R&D contract profits may not exceed 15 percent of the agreed-to cost estimate. Most cost-plus-fixed-fee contracts have a profit ceiling of 10 percent. Federal law always limits the fee to some dollar amount on cost-reimbursement contracts. There is no limit on the profit you may include in your price on fixed-price contracts, but it must be reasonable. Many government procurements are so competitive that contractors will apply a low profit margin to reduce the overall proposal cost in an attempt to win the contract.

Federal law also prohibits the use of cost-plus-a-percentage-of-cost contracting. This contracting method encourages contractors to spend, not to manage costs, because profit is tied to increased expenditures and not to cost control or reduction. The more a contractor spends, the greater the profit it receives. The government also requires all prime contracts (other than firm fixed-price contracts) to prohibit cost-plus-a-percentage-of-cost subcontracts.

TYPES OF COST-REIMBURSEMENT CONTRACTS

The following are some common cost-reimbursement contract types.

Cost Contract

A cost contract is a cost-reimbursement contract in which the government reimburses the contractor for all allowable costs incurred during the contract's performance. The contractor receives no profit. This contract type is typically used for R&D, particularly with nonprofit organizations.

Cost-Sharing Contract

When the government agrees to reimburse a contractor for a predetermined portion of the allowable and allocable costs of contract performance, it uses a cost-sharing contract. With this contract type, the contractor agrees to absorb a portion of the contract costs, in expectation of substantial compensating benefits.

Normally used in a research and development setting, the benefits of this type of contract might include enhancing the contractor's operational capabilities and expertise or enhancing its position for follow-on work. A contractor would be in an ideal position for obtaining additional work on a development contract if the jobs are awarded in stages or phases. The contractor receives no profit/fee for its efforts.

Example Cost-Sharing Contract

Rockwell Collins, Inc., Cedar Rapids, Iowa, was awarded a $7.5 million cost-sharing contract ($4 million, government portion; $3.5 million, contractor portion) to provide for R&D to produce the next-generation security cards for programs employing GPS technology.

Nine firms were solicited and eight proposals were received. The expected contract completion date is December 31, 2016. The solicitation issue date was April 10, 2015, and the negotiation completion date was June 16, 2015. The Space and Missile Systems Center, California, is the contracting activity.

Cost-Plus-Fixed-Fee Contract

The cost-plus-fixed-fee (CPFF) contract is the most commonly used cost-reimbursement contract. Under this contract type, the government pays all of the contractor's allowable costs, in addition to a fixed fee (or profit). The fixed fee does not vary with the costs of performing the contract. The terms of the contract determine the allowability of costs.

A CPFF takes two basic forms, the completion form and the term form (see examples on the next page). The completion form describes the scope of work by stating a definite goal or target and specifying an end product. It normally requires the contractor to complete and deliver the specified end product, such as a final report.

The term form describes the scope of work in general terms and obligates the contractor to devote a specified level of effort for a stated time. Under this form, if the government considers the contractor's performance satisfactory, it pays the fixed fee at the expiration of the agreed-upon period. This form may be used only if the contractor is obligated by the contract to provide a specific level of effort within a definite time period.

Both completion and term types are used primarily when the contract price is significant, the work specifications cannot be precisely defined, and the uncertainties involved in performing the contract are significant. Normally, the government prefers the completion form over the term form because of the differences in obligation assumed by the contractor.

Example Completion Form

Suppose the government awarded First Aid, Inc., a CPFF contract to perform a study on AIDS. The contract requires First Aid to submit a report detailing its findings when the study is complete. The contract has an estimated cost of $500,000 and a fixed fee of $50,000. Assuming that First Aid had the following actual costs, it would be paid the following:

	Scenario 1	Scenario 2	Scenario 3
Actual costs	$450,000	$500,000	$550,000*
Fixed fee	$50,000	$50,000	$50,000
Total paid	$500,000	$550,000	$600,000

*This example assumes that the contracting officer gave the contractor permission to exceed the estimated contract value/cost.

Notice that the fixed fee is not affected by the actual costs of contract performance.

Example Term Form

The government awarded Joe's Security a CPFF contract for guard services. The contract is in the term form and requires Joe's Security to provide 10,000 staff hours at an estimated cost of $200,000. The contract has a fixed fee of $20,000.

Period of Performance	Level of Effort	Guard Rate	Actual Costs	
01/01-12/31/14	10,000 staff hours	$20.00/hr.	$200,000	
			+$20,000	Fixed fee
			$220,000	Total paid

In this example, the contractor certified that the level-of-effort hours (10,000 hours) specified in the contract were expended in performing the work.

If a contractor is in jeopardy of exceeding the level-of-effort hours during contract performance, the contracting officer may amend the contract or issue a new procurement for the remaining work. More than likely, the contracting officer will amend the contract before its expiration to avoid having to issue a new procurement, which tends to be time-consuming and costly.

The problem with CPFF contracts is that they give the contractor little incentive to control costs because the fee remains the same regardless of the actual costs. The government assumes all the cost risk. However, a contractor's costs may not exceed the contract's estimated cost unless the contracting officer approves the overrun beforehand.

CPFF Advantages for Contractors

- CPFF contracts offer little risk to the contractor.
- Fee/profit is fixed, despite actual performance costs.
- All allowable performance costs are reimbursed.

CPFF Disadvantages for Contractors

- Amount of profit or fee is limited to 15 percent if the contract is for experimental, developmental, or research work; otherwise, it's 10 percent.
- CPFF contracts give the contractor little incentive to control costs.
- CPFF contracts are costly for the government to administer.

Cost-Plus-Incentive-Fee Contract

A cost-plus-incentive-fee (CPIF) contract (see the example on the next page) is a cost-reimbursement contract that allows for an initially negotiated fee that is adjusted by a formula based on the relationship of total allowable costs to total target costs. It specifies a target cost, a target fee, minimum and maximum fees, and a fee adjustment formula. After contract performance, the fee payable to the contractor is determined in accordance with the formula.

This contract type has the basic incentive-sharing features of an FPI contract in terms of an expressed sharing formula. A CPIF contract does not, however, contain a total price ceiling. Instead, it contains a provision for a minimum/maximum fee. At predetermined points above and below the target cost (the point of maximum or minimum fee), the contract converts into a CPFF contract.

This means that a contractor is eligible for a minimum fee, no matter what its actual contract costs turn out to be. The maximum fee is usually limited to 15 percent of the target cost. A CPIF contract is typically used when realistic incentives can be negotiated and the government can establish reasonable performance objectives.

Example CPIF Contract

Suppose the Department of Agriculture awarded Bad Bug, Inc., a contract to develop a pesticide for cornfields. It negotiated the following contract cost projections:

Target cost	$6,000,000
Target fee	$500,000
Maximum fee	$600,000
Minimum fee	$400,000

Sharing formula 70/30 (government/contractor)

The contracting officer used a sharing formula of 70/30 to ensure that Bad Bug, Inc., is not unfairly penalized for contract overruns. If Bad Bug, Inc., actually incurred $6,250,000 in contract costs, it would make the following profit:

Actual cost	$6,250,000*
Less target cost	–($6,000,000)
Contract overrun	($250,000)
Contractor sharing %	×30%
Total overrun profit	($75,000)
Add target profit	+$500,000
Total profit	**$425,000**
Add actual cost	$6,250,000
Total contract value	**$6,675,000**

*This example assumes the contracting officer gave Bad Bug, Inc., permission to exceed the target cost.

If Bad Bug, Inc., had actually incurred $5,500,000 in contract costs, its profit would be:

Actual cost	$5,500,000
Less target cost	–($6,000,000)
Contract underrun	$500,000
Contractor sharing %	×30%
Total underrun profit	$100,000*
Add target profit	+$500,000
Total profit	**$600,000**
Add actual cost	$5,500,000
Total contract value	**$6,100,000**

*Bad Bug, Inc., is not entitled to the complete contract underrun ($500,000 x 30% = $150,000) because the maximum fee is limited to $600,000.

CPIF contracts are more likely to be used in situations where the cost reduction can be identified (e.g., energy contracts) and where the government and the contractor share in the reduction.

CPIF Advantages for Contractors

- If the contractor performs the job at less than the target cost, it accrues additional fee or profit (rewards for good management).
- All allowable costs of performance are reimbursed.

CPIF Disadvantages for Contractors

- CPIF contracts are costly for the government to administer.
- The amount of profit or fee is limited (usually to 15 percent).

Cost-Plus-Award-Fee Contract

A cost-plus-award-fee (CPAF) contract (see the example on the next page) is an incentive contract that provides for a base fee at inception and an award amount that the contractor earns in whole or in part upon completion. This award fee provision is commonly used when subjective criteria are required to measure contract performance.

The contractor receives the base fee provided it satisfactorily completes the contract. It is paid in the same manner as the fixed fee in a CPFF contract—independent of the award criteria. Not all CPAF contracts, however, have a base fee. Some firms forgo a base fee as a demonstration of their commitment to lower costs and their confidence that they will succeed and make it up in the award fee. (In DoD contracts, the base fee cannot exceed 3 percent of the total contract cost.)

The award fee preference should motivate the contractor to achieve excellence in such areas as quality, timeliness, technical ingenuity, and cost-effective management. The amount of the award fee to be paid is determined by the contracting officer's evaluation of the contractor's performance in terms of the criteria specifically stated in the contract.

Example CPAF Contract

Suppose Harvey's Moving Company was awarded a contract to move office furniture from the General Services Administration office in Washington, D.C., to the GSA office in Kansas City, Missouri. The contract states that the award fee paid to Harvey's Moving Company will be based on the following items:

- Estimated cost—the job should be completed at or below the estimated cost.
- Deadline—the job should be completed within two weeks.
- Packaging requirements—the furniture should be properly packaged.
- Proper distribution—the furniture should be delivered to the proper office locations in the new building.

This contract has the following features:

Estimated cost	$1,500,000
Base fee	$45,000
Award fee	$50,000

Let's assume that Harvey's Moving Company met most of these requirements, except that some furniture was delivered to the wrong office locations. It was paid the following:

Estimated cost	$1,475,000
Base fee	$45,000*
Award fee	$40,000
Total paid	$1,560,000

*The base fee is not affected by the actual contract performance costs.

Evaluation summaries are typically given to the contractor to allow for comments and observations on the government's findings. This practice gives the contractor an opportunity to appeal the award fee recommendation. The contractor must qualify or justify actions taken during contract performance.

After considering the contractor's comments, the contracting officer (or the fee-determining official) makes a unilateral award fee decision. That decision is not subject to further discussions, and the contractor may not appeal.

CPAF Advantages for Contractors

- The fee is made up of a fixed portion and an award fee portion. The fixed fee is guaranteed; the award fee is based on performance.
- All allowable performance costs are reimbursed.

CPAF Disadvantages for Contractors

- The base fee is typically small (usually around 3 percent of the target cost).
- The evaluation process can be very cumbersome and time-consuming.

■ ■ ■

Cost-reimbursement contracts are the government's least favorite contracting method because they place all, or essentially all, of the cost risk on the government. The government is prohibited from using cost-reimbursement contracts for acquiring commercial items. Once a cost-reimbursement contract is signed, the government must closely monitor the work to ensure that it is done in an effective and efficient manner.

■ ■ ■

CHAPTER 16

Other Contract Types

What's in this chapter?

- Indefinite-delivery contracts
- Time-and-materials contracts
- Labor-hour contracts
- Letter contracts
- Basic ordering agreements
- Performance-based contracting
- Multiyear contracts
- Options
- Life-cycle costing

Contracts come in all shapes and sizes. This chapter highlights many of the other contract types you are likely to run into. Don't be intimidated by these "other contract types." If you look closely, you'll notice they are all special modifications or variations of fixed-price or cost-reimbursement contracts. They are used to provide the government with greater flexibility in a number of different contracting situations.

INDEFINITE-DELIVERY CONTRACTS

Frequently, a buying office can specify accurately what it intends to purchase but cannot define the exact delivery dates and/or quantity that will be required. In that case, it uses indefinite-delivery contracts to procure such items.

The actual delivery of these commonly used supplies and services is made when the contracting officer places an order. One of the primary advantages of this contract type is that it permits contractors to maintain in storage depots a limited stock of the supplies that are being purchased. It also permits direct shipment by the contractor to federal agencies.

Two of the more common indefinite-delivery contracts are requirements contracts and indefinite-delivery/indefinite-quantity (ID/IQ) contracts.

Requirements Contracts

This contract type typically is used for acquiring supplies or services when the government anticipates recurring requirements but cannot specify the precise quantities it will need during the specified contract period. The delivery or performance is scheduled when orders are placed with the contractor. These are also known as *call contracts*.

The contracting officer determines a realistic estimate of the total quantity required in the solicitation and the resulting contract. Records of previous requirements and consumption are used to develop the estimate. This estimate is not, however, a representation to the contractor that the estimated quantity will be required or ordered.

The contract also may place limits on the contractor's obligation to deliver and the government's obligation to order. In fact, most requirements contracts do not guarantee that a contractor will receive any orders. Stated another way, the government promises to buy all of its requirements from one vendor, but it just doesn't know up front how much it will need of the items or services, or when it will need them, during the contract term.

Indefinite-Delivery/Indefinite-Quantity (ID/IQ) Contracts

Years ago, indefinite-delivery/indefinite-quantity (ID/IQ) contracts were most often associated with supplies as opposed to services. Concurrently, the government could award a single contract, whether for supplies or services, with one firm based on competitive procedures and then negotiate orders, for services especially, on an individual order basis, which meant each order effectively was sole source. Yet if a contracting officer wanted to be innovative and award multiple contracts to effectively compete the orders to obtain better prices, he or she could not do so because the orders were not considered subject to "full and open competition."

Fortunately, acquisition reform resolved this dilemma. The laws were changed to permit agencies to award indefinite-delivery, indefinite-quantity contracts. These contracts provide for an indefinite quantity, within stated limits, of supplies or services to be furnished during a fixed period.

Nowadays, the government encourages buying offices to make multiple awards of this contract type when a recurring need is anticipated for similar supplies or services. In fact, contracting activities are racing to ID/IQs as a way to deal with understaffing and to expedite purchasing. ID/IQ contracts are now done for a broad range of services. Current projections indicate that almost 80 percent of the federal IT budget will go through ID/IQ contracts by 2017.

Indefinite-delivery/indefinite-quantity contracts are also known as *delivery order contracts* and *task order contracts*, depending on whether supplies or services are being ordered, respectively. A delivery order contract is used to issue orders for the delivery of products or supplies, such as furniture and equipment. Firm quantities, other than a minimum or maximum quantity, are not specified in the delivery order during the contract period.

A task order contract, on the other hand, is used for services performed during the contract period, such as repairs and maintenance. Scientific, engineering, and technical assistance services also are commonly acquired under task order contracts.

ID/IQ contracts can be made for up to a five-year period, and orders thereunder can run for up to five years, so these contracts can become ten-year contracts. Delivery or performance is scheduled when the orders are placed with the contractor.

Rules are in place to ensure that contractors are given a "fair opportunity" to compete or be considered for most orders, although some may be set aside for various small business concerns. Each federal agency designates an ombudsman, who reviews contractor complaints and helps ensure that all contractors are considered for orders consistent with the contract. The ombudsman must be a senior agency official who is independent of the contracting officer and may be the agency's competition advocate.

> The Small Business Jobs Act of 2010 officially authorizes federal agencies to set aside or reserve task or delivery order contracts for small businesses. FAR 16.5 was amended to acknowledge that set-asides may be used in connection with the placement of orders under multiple-award contracts, notwithstanding the requirement to provide each contract holder a fair opportunity to be considered.
>
> This interim rule therefore gives agencies another tool to increase opportunities for small businesses to complete in the federal marketplace.

TIME-AND-MATERIALS CONTRACTS

Time-and-materials (T&M) contracts (see facing page) tend to be used for specialized or high-tech services, such as engineering and accounting. Basically, a T&M contract combines the features of a cost-reimbursement contract and a fixed-price contract. T&M contracts are typically used when estimating the costs or extent of the work is almost impossible at the time of contract award.

Direct labor is provided at specified fixed hourly rates that include wages, O/H expenses, G&A expenses, and profit. This combined direct labor rate is referred to as a loaded labor rate or a fully burdened labor rate. The contractor provides materials, at cost, including, if appropriate, material-handling costs.

Because T&M contracts give contractors an incentive to increase costs to increase profit, they are closely monitored by government officials. All T&M contract have a ceiling price that the contractor may not exceed, except at its own risk.

Example T&M Contract

Let's assume Bill Jobs, a senior systems engineer, receives a T&M contract to provide technical assistance to the Department of the Navy. Bill's annual salary is $83,200; therefore, he has the following base hourly rate:

Annual wage: $83,200/2,080 hours = $40.00

(52 weeks x 40 hours/week = 2,080 hours*)

*The government often requires the contractor to use a figure much lower than 2,080 hours/year to break out holidays, vacation, and sick leave. The remaining hours are referred to as *productive hours*. Productive hours are often figured at 1,920 hours/year.

Base Hourly Rate	O/H Rate (40%)	G&A Total Subtotal	Fee/Rate (22%)	Total Total Cost	Profit (10%)	Bill Rate/ Hour
$40.00	$16.00	$56.00	$12.32	$68.32	$6.84	$75.16*

*This balance represents the "fully burdened" or "fully loaded" labor rate.

Bill's next step is to determine his total billing. If this job took 200 hours to complete and required the purchase of a high-tech scanner, the total bill would be calculated as follows:

	Total Hours	Fully Loaded Labor Rate	Amount Billed
Senior systems engineer	200	$75.16	$15,032.00
Total labor			$15,032.00
Materials: scanner			$5,500.00*
Total billing			$20,532.00

*The scanner was billed at actual cost.

LABOR-HOUR CONTRACTS

A labor-hour contract is simply a variation of the T&M contract. The only difference is that the contractor does not supply materials.

LETTER CONTRACTS

If there is a national emergency, such as an earthquake or a hurricane (like Katrina), the government issues letter contracts to contractors to help provide immediate relief. A letter contract (or a letter-of-intent contract) is a written preliminary contractual instrument that authorizes a contractor to begin manufacturing products or performing services immediately. Depending on the circumstances, the letter contract should be as complete and definite as possible.

For its convenience, the government issues letter contracts without a firm contract price, but they do contain standard contract clauses and a limitation on the government's liability. Each letter contract must contain a negotiated definitization schedule that includes:

- Dates for submission of the contractor's price proposal, required cost or pricing data, and, if required, subcontracting plans
- Start date for negotiations
- Agreement between the government and the contractor on the date by which definitization is expected to be completed.

> *Definitization* means the agreement on, or determination of, contract terms, specifications, and price, which converts the letter contract into a definitive/standard contract.

The target date for definitization should be within 180 days of the date the letter contract is issued or before completion of 40 percent of the work, whichever occurs first. The contracting officer may, in extreme cases and according to agency procedures, authorize an additional period. Contractors are reimbursed for only 80 percent of expenditures and receive no fee while under a letter contract, which gives them a great incentive to get the contract definitized.

If, after exhausting all reasonable efforts, the parties fail to reach an agreement on price and fee, the contracting officer may unilaterally establish a reasonable price and fee. The contractor may appeal this determination in accordance with the disputes clause (see Chapter 17). Because of the uncertainties involved with letter contracts, they may be used only after the contracting officer determines in writing that no other contract is suitable and the determination is approved at a higher level.

BASIC ORDERING AGREEMENTS

A basic ordering agreement (BOA) is not a contract; it is a written instrument of understanding, negotiated between the government and a contractor. BOAs allow the government to expedite the procurement of products or services when specific items, quantities, and prices are unknown at the time of the agreement. If the government purchases a high-resolution printer, for example, it may establish a BOA for future toner purchases.

BOAs typically are used when past experience or future plans indicate the need for a contractor's particular products or services during the forthcoming year. They may be issued with fixed-price or cost-reimbursement contracts, but the contracting officer must still use competitive solicitations whenever possible. The BOA also lists the buying offices that are authorized to place orders under the agreement.

At a minimum, a BOA must contain:

- Terms and clauses applying to future contracts (orders) that might be awarded to the contractor
- Description of products or services
- Methods for pricing, issuing, and delivering future orders.

Each BOA specifies the point at which an order becomes a binding contract. The agreement, for example, may state that the issuance of an order gives rise to an immediate contract.

PERFORMANCE-BASED CONTRACTING

Performance-based contracting methods attempt to base the total amount paid to a contractor on the level of performance quality achieved and contract standards met. In other words, they are intended to motivate the contractor to perform at its best. A performance-based contract should:

- Describe the work in terms of what is to be the required output, rather than how the work is to be accomplished
- Use measurable performance standards, such as terms of quality, timeliness, and quantity
- Specify procedures for reductions of fee or for reductions to the price of a fixed-price contract when services are not performed or do not meet contract requirements
- Include performance incentives (where appropriate).

Contracting activities should also develop quality assurance surveillance plans when acquiring services. These plans should recognize the responsibility of the contractor to carry out its quality control obligations, and they should contain measurable inspection and acceptance criteria.

The contract type most likely to motivate the contractor to perform at an optimal level should be chosen. Fixed-price contracts are generally appropriate for services that can be objectively defined and for which the risk of performance is manageable.

MULTIYEAR CONTRACTS

In 1972 the Commission on Government Procurement recommended that Congress authorize all federal agencies to enter into multiyear contracts that are based on clearly specified requirements. A multiyear contract is for the purchase of products and services for more than one year, but not more than five years. This recommendation was based on the commission's findings that the use of multiyear contracts would result in significant savings to the government because they enable contractors to offer better overall prices while maintaining a steady workload.

Congress was reluctant to approve multiyear contracts because it has no authority to approve programs that future Congresses must fund. It was also reluctant to approve contracting arrangements that are difficult to change in subsequent years. Congress did, however, recognize that one- or two-year planning and funding horizons are generally too short for many of the government's larger procurements.

The FAR encourages the use of multiyear contracts to achieve:

- Lower costs and reduced administrative burdens
- Continuity of production and thus avoidance of annual start-up costs
- Stabilization of the contractor workforce
- A broader competitive base, resulting from greater opportunity for participation by firms that might not otherwise be willing or able to compete for lesser quantities—particularly for contracts involving high start-up costs
- Greater incentive for contractors to improve productivity through investment in capital facilities, equipment, and advanced technology.

Federal agencies that propose to use multiyear contracts must seek advance approval during the budget process.

Multiyear-Basis Contracts

If the government awards the contract on a multiyear basis, it obligates only the contract funds for the first-year requirement, with succeeding years' requirements funded annually. If the funds do not become available to support the succeeding years' requirements, the federal agency must cancel the contract, including the total requirements of all remaining program years.

Because of this cancellation risk, a multiyear contract often contains a contract provision that allows for reimbursement of unrecovered nonrecurring costs. These costs might include special tooling and test equipment; preproduction engineering; and costs incurred for the assembly, training, and transportation of a specialized workforce.

For each program year subject to cancellation, the contracting officer establishes a cancellation ceiling price by estimating the nonrecurring costs. The cancellation ceiling price is reduced each program year in direct proportion to the remaining requirements subject to cancellation.

> The big issue here is that Congress doesn't want to be committed to outyears (years in which funding for a requirement isn't available). (Remember Congress funds most everything on an annual basis.) Also, it doesn't care to have current-year appropriations set aside to pay outyear cancellation charges, which is why there are limits on the amount of cancellation charges that multiyear contracts can specify.

Suppose a contracting officer in the General Services Administration awarded a multiyear contract to Lock 'N' Chase, Inc., to install a new security system in its Washington, D.C., office. The contract is for three years, and the estimated cancellation ceiling price is 10 percent of the total multiyear contract price.

Total multiyear contract price	$5,000,000
	×10%
Cancellation ceiling price	$500,000

The cancellation ceiling price is then reduced by the contracting officer over the three-year contract period.

Cancellation ceiling price	$500,000
Year 1: 30% x $500,000	($150,000)
	$350,000
Year 2: 30% x $500,000	($150,000)
	$200,000
Year 3: 40% x $500,000	($200,000)
	0

The contracting officer also establishes cancellation dates for each program year's requirements.

Although multiyear-basis contract requirements are budgeted and financed for only the first program year, the government solicits prices for both the current-year program requirement alone and the total multiyear requirements. By obtaining dual proposals, the contracting officer is better able to establish the total job requirements and the contracting period. A 10 percent savings in favor of multiyear contracting has typically been used as an evaluation benchmark.

Either sealed bidding or negotiated procedures may be used when soliciting for multiyear contracts. Multiyear contracts typically result in a fixed-price contract; they may not result in a cost-reimbursement contract.

OPTIONS

Let's assume iComputer Center was awarded a contract with options to provide computer training services to the Department of Commerce. The contract has a one-year base period and four option periods.

	Beginning Date	End Date	Maximum Labor Costs	Contract Exercised
Base year	01/01/11	12/31/11	$1,800,000	Yes
Option I	01/01/12	12/31/12	$1,900,000	Yes
Option II	01/01/13	12/31/13	$2,000,000	Yes
Option III	01/01/14	12/31/14	$2,000,000	Yes
Option IV	01/01/15	12/31/15	$2,100,000	Pending
		Total contract value	$9,800,000	

An option gives the government a unilateral right to purchase additional products or services called for by the contract. Contracts containing options are not the same as multiyear contracts, which require the government to purchase the entire multiyear procurement (unless the requirement is canceled or the funds are made unavailable). To exercise an option, a contracting officer must determine that funds are available and the need for the option exists.

The presence of an option is no guarantee that the government will exercise the option and purchase additional items. The contracting officer considers price and other related factors when determining whether to exercise the option. If a new solicitation fails to produce a better price or more advantageous offer than that provided by the option, the government generally exercises an option.

The solicitation states the basis on which the options will be evaluated. To exercise an option, the contracting officer must provide a written notice to the contractor within the period specified in the contract. The contract is then modified to incorporate the option, citing the appropriate contract clause as the authority.

When soliciting for contracts containing options, the contracting officer may use sealed bidding or negotiated procedures.

LIFE-CYCLE COSTING

While life-cycle costing is not exactly a contract type per se, it is a method sometimes used in source selection as a part of cost analysis. It is also used for making program management choices and decisions.

Suppose the Department of Homeland Security is acquiring a satellite dish, the life of which is determined to be four years. Because satellite dishes tend to have high support costs, the contracting officer seeks information on costs that apply to the:

- Outright purchase of the satellite dish
- Total leased price/costs
- Total leased price/costs with an option to purchase.

Now let's assume that Satellites "R" Us submits the following prices/cost estimates to the government:

Total purchase price: $500,000

Estimated maintenance costs (by year):

2016	$15,000
2017	$18,000
2018	$21,000
2019	$24,000

Leased price/costs (by year):
2016 ($10,000 per month) $120,000
2017 ($12,000 per month) $144,000
2018 ($14,000 per month) $168,000
2019 ($16,000 per month) $192,000

Purchase option: The government has the option of purchasing the satellite dish for $375,000 at the beginning of 2018.

This satellite dish will also incur the following operating costs:
Electricity: $3,000 ($250 a month)
Rent: $12,000 ($1,000 a month)

The next step is to calculate the total cost of each purchase option:

1. **Outright purchase of the satellite dish:**

	2016	2017	2018	2019	Totals
Purchase price	$500,000	—	—	—	$500,000
Maintenance costs	$15,000	$18,000	$21,000	$24,000	$78,000
Electricity costs	$3,000	$3,000	$3,000	$3,000	$12,000
Rent	$12,000	$12,000	$12,000	$12,000	$48,000
Totals	**$530,000**	**$33,000**	**$36,000**	**$39,000**	**$638,000**

2. **Leased price/costs of the satellite dish:**

	2016	2017	2018	2019	Totals
Lease costs	$120,000	$144,000	$168,000	$192,000	$624,000
Maintenance costs	—	—	—	—	—
Electricity costs	$3,000	$3,000	$3,000	$3,000	$12,000
Rent	$12,000	$12,000	$12,000	$12,000	$48,000
Totals	**$135,000**	**$159,000**	**$183,000**	**$207,000**	**$684,000**

3. Total cost when the purchase option is exercised:

	2016	2017	2018	2019	Totals
Lease costs	$120,000	$144,000	—	—	$264,000
Purchase option	—	—	$375,000	—	$375,000
Maintenance costs	—	—	—	—	—
Electricity costs	$3,000	$3,000	$3,000	$3,000	$12,000
Rent	$12,000	$12,000	$12,000	$12,000	$48,000
Totals	**$135,000**	**$159,000**	**$390,000**	**$15,000**	**$699,000**

In this example, the contracting officer would purchase the satellite dish outright because that option offers the lowest overall cost to the government.

Life-cycle costing (LCC) is the estimation and analysis of the total cost of acquiring, developing, operating, supporting, and (if applicable) disposing of an item or system being acquired. Both direct and indirect costs make up the total LCC of the system. LCC enhances the decision-making process in system acquisitions and is used as a management tool throughout the process.

The government is concerned about a system's LCC because of the rapidly increasing cost of supporting the system once it is placed into operation. In fact, for many system acquisitions, the cost of operating and supporting the system over its useful life is greater than the acquisition cost. The LCC program is designed to reduce these operating and support costs by analyzing design alternatives.

When a federal agency determines that LCC could be an important aspect of a particular program, it decides on the degree and method of implementation. The solicitation states the requirements as they relate to the proposal and source-selection process.

An LCC model comprises one or more systematically arranged mathematical calculations that formulate a cost methodology to arrive at reliable cost estimates. The General Services Administration makes its LCC program, called BARS, available to agencies at no charge and to vendors for a nominal cost.

Various commercial packages also are in widespread government and commercial use.

To get more detailed information on LCC, contact:

National Technical Information Service (NTIS)
Technology Administration
U.S. Department of Commerce
(800) 553-6847
www.ntis.gov

■ ■ ■

Selection of a contract type should not be based on either the government's or the contractor's individual biases. Rather, the selection should be based on an objective analysis of all factors involved and of the contract type that fits the particular procurement.

■ ■ ■

CHAPTER 17

Contract Administration

© Randy Glasbergen.
GLASBERGEN
"Our billing system was perfect until the boss put in his two-cents worth. Now all of our figures are off by two cents."

What's in this chapter?

- Contract administration office
- Contract financing
- Getting paid
- Changes clause
- Contract modifications
- Constructive changes
- Government-furnished property
- Inspection and acceptance
- Contractor data rights
- Record retention
- Audits/examination of records
- Contract Disputes Act of 1978
- Alternative dispute resolution
- Termination for convenience
- Termination for default
- Contract closeout

You've followed many of the recommendations in this book, and the contracts are pouring in. Your company has achieved the ultimate status—being officially recognized as a federal insider. Champagne toasts all around!

But this now raises a question: what happens after the contract is awarded?

Simply put, a contractor must be prepared to deal with the responsibilities associated with contract performance. These include complying with applicable labor laws, preparing budgets and status reports, performing inspections, and preparing invoices, to name a few. All of the requirements are spelled out in the contract. This chapter highlights many of the administrative responsibilities your contract will require.

Both the government and the contractor are responsible for contract administration. The government acts through its agent, typically the administrative contracting officer (ACO), to perform or oversee contract-related functions. The ACO's degree of involvement depends on the type and nature of the contract.

CONTRACT ADMINISTRATION OFFICE

Many federal agencies use contract administration offices (CAOs), located throughout the country, to administer contract functions. Each CAO assists with tasks such as correcting administrative errors, explaining special clauses and requirements, ensuring on-time performance, inspecting and accepting final products, and ensuring payment. FAR 42.3 details the CAO's functions.

CONTRACT FINANCING

Government financing is available to contractors in certain circumstances. A contractor with a large fixed-price contract that has a long lead time would be a good candidate for contract financing. (Contracting officers may not treat the need for financing as a handicap during source selection.) The government typically uses three methods to finance a contract: progress payments, guaranteed loans, and advance payments.

Progress Payments

Construction contractors are often able to receive progress payments as work advances on a contract. Payments are typically based on the costs incurred by the contractor during contract performance. They do not relate to any contract milestones or completion stages.

Contracting activities customarily apply a standard progress payment rate to the contract performance costs. This standard rate ranges from 75 percent to 85 percent of the incurred costs for large businesses and 80 percent to 95 percent for small businesses. Progress payments are used only with fixed-price contracts.

Let's assume Street Works, Inc., received a firm fixed-price contract from the Department of Transportation to add some ramps to an existing highway on January 1, 2016. The contract's value is $4,000,000, and it is expected to be completed over a one-year period. The contracting officer determines that Street Works, Inc., is eligible for progress payments, which will be made quarterly:

Quarter	Costs Incurred QTD	Standard Rate	Payment
1st	$1,000,000	90%	$900,000
2nd	$900,000	90%	$810,000
3rd	$800,000	90%	$720,000
4th	$800,000	90%	$720,000
		Total payments	$3,150,000

Street Works, Inc., receives the remaining balance of $850,000 upon contract completion.

Before a contracting officer authorizes progress payments, he or she determines whether the contractor's accounting system can reliably segregate and accumulate contract costs and properly administer the progress payments.

Percentage-of-completion payments are usually treated as a method of payment, not as contract financing.

Guaranteed Loans

Guaranteed loans are essentially the same as conventional loans made by private financial institutions. The only difference is that the government shares in any losses up to its guaranteed percentage (usually 90 percent or less). The private lending institution handles all administrative aspects of the loan. The contractor makes the principal and interest payments to the lending institution and pays a fee to the government for the privilege of the guarantee.

Guarantees of loans by private financial institutions to borrowers performing contracts related to national defense may be made by the following federal agencies:

- Department of Defense
- Department of Energy
- Department of Commerce
- Department of the Interior
- Department of Agriculture
- General Services Administration
- National Aeronautics and Space Administration.

For more information on guaranteed loans, see FAR 32.3.

Advance Payments

Suppose the U.S. Department of Agriculture (USDA) awarded a firm fixed-price contract on July 1, 2016, to The Sky's the Limit, Inc., to design and build a satellite. The contract's total value is $12 million, and the estimated contract period is three years. Because of the satellite's high cost, the contracting officer agrees to advance the contractor $3 million each year of the contract.

Advance Payment	Amount
Year 1	3,000,000
Year 2	3,000,000
Year 3	3,000,000
Total advance payments	9,000,000

The Sky's the Limit, Inc., completes the satellite on August 15, 2019, at which time USDA pays the contract balance.

Advance Payment	Amount
Total advance payments	9,000,000
Total contract value	12,000,000
Final payment	3,000,000

For advance payments to be granted, the contracting officer must determine that doing so is in the government's best interests, and the contractor must post adequate security (bank accounts or other significant assets). These payments are then liquidated or applied against the contract amount owed the contractor upon the delivery of the contracted products or the performance of the contracted services.

Because advance payments are not based on or measured by contract performance, they differ from partial, progress, or other payment loan types. Prime contractors also may obtain advance payments to compensate subcontractors.

GETTING PAID

Now we turn our attention to every business owner's favorite subject: payment!

Each contract has specific instructions for preparing and submitting invoices. Information on where to send the invoice (or bill), the number of copies to send, and required government codes is generally included on the contract's cover page. More detailed instructions may be included in Section G, Contract Administration Data, of the contract schedule. If the instructions are incomplete or unclear, call the contracting officer immediately.

To be paid in a timely manner, you must prepare a "proper invoice" according to the contract's instructions. Each invoice submitted to the government must contain:

- Contractor's name and address
- Invoice date (as close as possible to the mailing date)

- Contract number (including order number and contract line item number)
- Price of supplies delivered or services performed
- Shipping and payment terms
- Name and address of the contractor official to whom payment is to be sent (must be the same as that in the contract)
- Name, title, phone number, and mailing address of the person to be notified in the event of a defective invoice
- Any other documentation required by the contract (such as evidence of shipment).

Contractors are strongly encouraged to assign an identification number to each invoice.

The contractor must support all of its invoices with an approved receiving report or any other government documentation authorizing payment. The Department of Defense uses DD Form 250, Material Inspection and Receiving Report (see example), to demonstrate government inspection and acceptance. Any receiving report authorizing payment must, at a minimum, include:

- Contract number for products delivered or services performed
- Description of products delivered or services performed
- Quantities of products received and accepted or services performed
- Date products were delivered or services performed
- Date products or services were accepted by the designated government official
- Signature or electronic equivalent (when permitted) and printed name, title, mailing address, and phone number of the designated government official responsible for acceptance or approval.

The agency receiving official should forward the receiving report to the designated payment office by the fifth working day after government acceptance or approval.

Payments will depend on the contract type, its terms and conditions, and the allowability of those costs. Under fixed-price contracts, final payment is typically due when the government accepts the completed contract. The

MATERIAL INSPECTION AND RECEIVING REPORT

Form Approved
OMB No. 0704-0248

The public reporting burden for this collection of information is estimated to average 30 minutes per response, including the time for reviewing instructions, searching existing data sources, gathering and maintaining the data needed, and completing and reviewing the collection of information. Send comments regarding this burden estimate or any other aspect of this collection of information, including suggestions for reducing the burden, to Department of Defense, Washington Headquarters Services, Directorate for Information Operations and Reports (0704-0248), 1215 Jefferson Davis Highway, Suite 1204, Arlington, VA 22202-4302. Respondents should be aware that notwithstanding any other provision of law, no person shall be subject to any penalty for failing to comply with a collection of information if it does not display a currently valid OMB control number.

PLEASE DO NOT RETURN YOUR COMPLETED FORM TO EITHER OF THESE ADDRESSES.
SEND THIS FORM IN ACCORDANCE WITH THE INSTRUCTIONS CONTAINED IN THE DFARS, APPENDIX F-401.

1. PROCUREMENT INSTRUMENT IDENTIFICATION (CONTRACT) NO. | ORDER NO.
6. INVOICE NO./DATE
7. PAGE | OF
8. ACCEPTANCE POINT
2. SHIPMENT NO.
3. DATE SHIPPED
4. B/L
TCN
5. DISCOUNT TERMS
9. PRIME CONTRACTOR CODE
10. ADMINISTERED BY CODE
11. SHIPPED FROM *(If other than 9)* CODE | FOB:
12. PAYMENT WILL BE MADE BY CODE
13. SHIPPED TO CODE
14. MARKED FOR CODE

15. ITEM NO.	16. STOCK/PART NO. DESCRIPTION *(Indicate number of shipping containers - type of container - container number.)*	17. QUANTITY SHIP/REC'D*	18. UNIT	19. UNIT PRICE	20. AMOUNT
					0
					0.00
					0.00
					0.00
					0.00
					0.00
					0.00
					0.00

21. CONTRACT QUALITY ASSURANCE

a. ORIGIN

☐ CQA ☐ ACCEPTANCE of listed items has been made by me or under my supervision and they conform to contract, except as noted herein or on supporting documents.

DATE — SIGNATURE OF AUTHORIZED GOVERNMENT REPRESENTATIVE
TYPED NAME:
TITLE:
MAILING ADDRESS:
COMMERCIAL TELEPHONE NUMBER:

b. DESTINATION

☐ CQA ☐ ACCEPTANCE of listed items has been made by me or under my supervision and they conform to contract, except as noted herein or on supporting documents.

DATE — SIGNATURE OF AUTHORIZED GOVERNMENT REPRESENTATIVE
TYPED NAME:
TITLE:
MAILING ADDRESS:
COMMERCIAL TELEPHONE NUMBER:

22. RECEIVER'S USE

Quantities shown in column 17 were received in apparent good condition except as noted.

DATE RECEIVED — SIGNATURE OF AUTHORIZED GOVERNMENT REPRESENTATIVE
TYPED NAME:
TITLE:
MAILING ADDRESS:
COMMERCIAL TELEPHONE NUMBER:

** If quantity received by the Government is the same as quantity shipped, indicate by (X) mark; if different, enter actual quantity received below quantity shipped and encircle.*

23. CONTRACTOR USE ONLY

DD FORM 250, AUG 2000 PREVIOUS EDITION IS OBSOLETE.

Example Material Inspection and Receiving Report (DD Form 250)

contractor obtains final payment by submitting a proper voucher or invoice with appropriate backup, such as DD Form 250.

For cost-reimbursement contracts, the normal payment procedure is to invoice the government for allowable costs and fees incurred as work progresses. Most contracting activities allow contractors to submit invoices monthly. Contractors typically use SF 1034, Public Voucher (see example), to bill the government. The voucher should be accompanied by appropriate backup documentation, such as the number of labor hours expended by labor category.

Prompt Payment Act

In 1982 Congress passed the Prompt Payment Act to require federal agencies to pay interest on contractor invoices that are not paid in a timely manner. The bill was enacted because contracting activities were chronically tardy in making payments, which caused many contractors to have cash flow problems, even putting some out of business.

If a contractor is not paid within 30 days of receipt of a properly prepared invoice, the paying office (or contracting activity) must pay interest on the overdue bills, at a rate periodically set by the Treasury Department. The interest penalty begins the day after the required payment date and ends on the date when payment is made. The temporary unavailability of funds needed to make timely payments does not excuse the buying agency from obligations to pay interest penalties.

The contracting activity must ask the contractor within seven days of receiving an erroneous invoice to explain any defects or improprieties.

This act also prohibits contracting activities from taking prompt payment discounts after the discount period has expired. The burden of completing formal acceptance and making payments on time to qualify for the discount falls on the government.

CHANGES CLAUSE

The changes clause allows the contracting officer to make unilateral changes to a contract in one or more of the following areas:

- The specifications (including drawings and designs)
- The method of work performance
- The government-furnished facilities, equipment, materials, services, or site
- Directing acceleration in the performance schedule.

Standard Form 1034

Standard Form 1034
Revised October 1987
Department of the Treasury
1 TFM 4-2000

PUBLIC VOUCHER FOR PURCHASES AND SERVICES OTHER THAN PERSONAL

VOUCHER NO.

U.S. DEPARTMENT, BUREAU, OR ESTABLISHMENT AND LOCATION

DATE VOUCHER PREPARED

SCHEDULE NO.

CONTRACT NUMBER AND DATE

PAID BY

REQUISITION NUMBER AND DATE

PAYEE'S NAME AND ADDRESS

DATE INVOICE RECEIVED

DISCOUNT TERMS

PAYEE'S ACCOUNT NUMBER

SHIPPED FROM | TO | WEIGHT

GOVERNMENT B/L NUMBER

NUMBER AND DATE OF ORDER	DATE OF DELIVERY OR SERVICE	ARTICLES OR SERVICES *(Enter description, item number of contract or Federal supply schedule, and other information deemed necessary)*	QUAN-TITY	UNIT PRICE COST	UNIT PRICE PER	AMOUNT (1)

(Use continuation sheet(s) if necessary)

(Payee must NOT use the space below) **TOTAL**

PAYMENT:
- PROVISIONAL
- COMPLETE
- PARTIAL
- FINAL
- PROGRESS
- ADVANCE

APPROVED FOR = $

EXCHANGE RATE = $1.00

DIFFERENCES

BY 2

TITLE

Amount verified; correct for

(Signature or initials)

Pursuant to authority vested in me, I certify that this voucher is correct and proper for payment.

(Date) *(Authorized Certifying Officer)* 2 *(Title)*

ACCOUNTING CLASSIFICATION

PAID BY

CHECK NUMBER | ON ACCOUNT OF U.S. TREASURY | CHECK NUMBER | ON *(Name of bank)*

CASH $ | DATE | PAYEE 3

PER

TITLE

1 When stated in foreign currency, insert name of currency.
2 If the ability to certify and authority to approve are combined in one person, one signature only is necessary; otherwise the approving officer will sign in the space provided, over his official title.
3 When a voucher is receipted in the name of a company or corporation, the name of the person writing the company or corporate name, as well as the capacity in which he signs, must appear. For example: "John Doe Company, per John

Previous edition usable.

NSN 7540-00-900-2234

PRIVACY ACT STATEMENT

The information requested on this form is required under the provisions of 31 U.S.C. 82b and 82c, for the purpose of disbursing Federal money. The information requested is to identify the particular creditor and the amounts to be paid. Failure to furnish this information will hinder discharge of the payment obligation.

Example Public Voucher (Standard Form 1034)

A unilateral change occurs when the government orders the contractor to change the performance requirements without prior contractor approval. The changes, however, must be within the scope of the original contract. The contracting officer, for example, cannot direct a construction contractor to perform R&D services. The changes clause depends on the contract type.

The contracting officer is the only person authorized to make these changes. For a change order, SF 30 (Amendment of Solicitation/Modification of Contract) is the document used to implement the change. If the change order requires the contractor to incur additional costs, the contracting officer must equitably adjust the contract to compensate the contractor.

CONTRACT MODIFICATIONS

Contract modifications (MODs) are written changes to an existing contract. These changes may be accomplished by unilateral action under a contract clause or by bilateral (or mutual) action of the contracting parties. MODs are typically used to:

- Make administrative changes
- Issue change orders
- Make changes authorized by a clause other than a change clause (such as property clause, options clause, or suspension of work clause)
- Issue termination notices
- Definitize letter contracts.

Bilateral changes, also called *supplemental agreements*, must be in writing and signed by both parties.

Only contracting officers, acting within the scope of their authority, may execute MODs on the government's behalf. As with change orders, SF 30 (Amendment of Solicitation/Modification of Contract) is used for making contract MODs.

Contract MODs, including those issued unilaterally, are priced before they are executed if the change can be done without adversely affecting the government's interest. If the modification could result in a significant cost increase, a new ceiling price is negotiated.

If the parties do not agree as to the cost and/or schedule impact of the MOD, the contracting officer makes a unilateral decision, which may be appealed by the contractor under the Contracts Disputes Act.

CONSTRUCTIVE CHANGES

Constructive changes, also known as *de facto* changes, are actions (or failures to act) by the government that cause the contractor to perform additional or different responsibilities from those expressed in the contract. These changes are not accompanied by a formal change order. The following constitute constructive changes:

- Defective specifications
- Requirements to adhere to delivery schedules when a contractor is entitled to an extension (e.g., weather-related delays)
- Excessive inspection requirements
- Unwarranted rejection of products following inspection
- Acceleration of the contract's performance requirements
- Interference with the contractor's performance by government personnel.

The contractor should notify the contracting officer in writing when a government action affects the contract terms and conditions. This notification or claim should be sent as soon as the change is identified. Upon claim receipt, the contracting officer investigates the circumstances of the alleged change.

If the contracting officer agrees with the claim, the alleged government action is confirmed as a legitimate change and appropriate written directions are issued. Contractors should be certain they receive written authorization before proceeding with a constructive change.

On the other hand, if the contracting officer feels the action is "within the scope of the contract," he or she may reject the claim. In that case, the contractor must file a claim under the disputes clause (see FAR 52.233-1).

GOVERNMENT-FURNISHED PROPERTY

For most government contracts, the contractor furnishes all property or equipment necessary to perform the requirements. However, the government allows contractors to use government property when its use results in significant savings, standardization, or expedited contract production. Common types of government-furnished property include facilities, materials, special tooling, and special test equipment.

Contractors must segregate the government-furnished property and equipment from their own. They must also maintain adequate control records, such as inventory documents and maintenance records. The government identifies all government-furnished property in the solicitation and resulting contract.

INSPECTION AND ACCEPTANCE

Inspection and acceptance requirements help protect the government's interests. For purchases at or below the simplified acquisition threshold ($150,000) and commercial purchases, the government typically relies on the contractor to test whether the items conform to the contract quality requirements. The contractor must keep complete records of its inspection work and make them available to the government.

For all other product purchases, the contractor has the following inspection requirements:

- The contractor must maintain an acceptable system for the inspection.
- The contractor must maintain records that completely document the inspections it conducts during contract performance.
- The government may inspect and test all products at any time prior to acceptance. It may also inspect subcontractors' plants.
- The government may require replacement or correction of products that fail to meet contract requirements. If the contractor fails to replace or fix rejected items, the government may have another contractor provide them and charge any additional costs to the defaulting contractor.

If the government fails to conduct inspections or tests, the contractor still must furnish the products specified by the contract.

Acceptance is the government's acknowledgment that the products meet the contractual requirements, as evidenced by the signature of the government's authorized representative (typically the contracting officer). Common inspection and receiving documents include:

- DD Form 250, Material Inspection and Receiving Report
- DD Form 1155, Order for Supplies and Services.

Each contract specifies the point of acceptance for the products. Title to the items passes to the government upon acceptance. This acceptance is final by the government except in the case of latent defects, fraud, and gross mistakes amounting to fraud.

First Article Approval

First article testing is a specialized type of government inspection required for some contracts. A first article is a preproduction sample of products prepared for the contract. This inspection procedure ensures that the contractor can furnish a product that conforms to the contract requirements. Commercial purchases and R&D contracts are usually not subject to first article testing.

First article testing may be appropriate when:

- The contractor has not previously furnished the product to the government
- The government requires assurance that the product is appropriate for its intended use
- An approved first article will serve as a manufacturing standard.

The contract may require the government, the contractor, or both to perform first article testing; upon successful completion, the contractor may begin production. Normally, the government does not authorize the acquisition of materials for production until the first article is approved.

A first article should not be confused with a bid sample. Bid samples are used by contractors to demonstrate their products' characteristics. First articles, in contrast, are actual samples of the items required by the contract.

CONTRACTOR DATA RIGHTS

One of the most complex and misunderstood areas in federal contracting is determining the owner of data produced or used under a contract. Do the data rights belong to the government or to the contractor? Both have valid and specific interest in data.

The government has extensive needs for technical data, such as research results, engineering drawings, and manuals. Therefore, in most contracts, the government exerts its authority to acquire data rights. Contractors, on the other hand, have an economic interest in the data components or processes that they have developed at their own expense. Public disclosure of these data could jeopardize their competitive advantage.

Each contract arrangement includes provisions to balance the government's need for data rights against the contractor's interest in protecting proprietary data. The government uses three types of data rights to protect its interests:

- ***Unlimited rights.*** The government's right to use, duplicate, or disclose data for any purpose (and to have or permit others to do so).
- ***Limited rights.*** Limited data rights may include restrictions on the data's being (1) released or disclosed outside the government, (2) used by the government for manufacture, or (3) in the case of computer software documentation, used for preparing the same or similar computer software.
- ***Government purpose license rights.*** Rights to use, duplicate, or disclose data, in whole or in part and in any manner, for government purposes only, or to permit others to do so for government purposes only (such as for competitive procurements).

The source of funds used in developing data dictates the type of data rights clause in a contract. If the data were developed at the government's expense (i.e., the government paid the contractor for developing the product), the government holds unlimited rights. When the contractor develops the data wholly at its private expense and the information has not been made available to the public without restrictions, the government holds limited rights.

The limited rights protection is effective only if the contractor suitably identifies and marks the data to which the government asserts limited rights. Government purpose license rights typically apply to partially funded contracts (or contracts for which the contractor has contributed more than 50 percent of the development costs).

Memo to all contractors: it's very important to recognize that the government wants your intellectual property. Be sure to address this issue *before* you sign a contract!

RECORD RETENTION

Contractors and subcontractors must retain and make available to the government certain books, records, documents, and other supporting evidence if the contract exceeds the simplified acquisition threshold. Generally, contractors must retain these records for three years after final contract payment.

Most accounting or financial records have a retention period of four years. The retention period is calculated from the end of the fiscal year during which the contractor entered a charge or allocated a cost to a government contract or subcontract. The contract itself may also specify a retention policy of its own.

Let's assume Urban Crisis, Inc., researched highway congestion in urban areas for the Department of Transportation and received the final contract payment on November 15, 2015. Urban Crisis, Inc., operates on a calendar-year basis (January 1 through December 31), and the contract requires a four-year retention period. In this case, the contractor must maintain the contract records until December 31, 2019.

Final payment date	November 15, 2015
Retention period	4 years
End of retention period	December 31, 2019

If the contractor operated on a fiscal-year basis (October 1 through September 30), the end of the retention period would be September 30, 2020.

Final payment date	November 15, 2015
Retention period	4 years
End of retention period	September 30, 2020

AUDITS/EXAMINATION OF RECORDS

Oh no, more audit stuff . . . where's Bob in accounting?

The government can examine and audit books, records, and other data relating to claimed performance costs; cost/pricing data used to support proposals; and any status reports required under the contract. This audit requirement applies to virtually all contracts. However, because audits require significant time and expense to perform, they are typically not used for proposals under the certified cost or pricing data threshold of $700,000 and almost never for proposals resulting from adequate price competition.

As discussed in Chapter 2, the Defense Contract Audit Agency performs the contract audit functions required by DoD and many civilian agencies. Auditors act as the contracting officer's principal financial advisors on matters relating to contract cost/price. They express opinions on the allowability, allocability, and reasonableness of contract costs claimed by contractors for reimbursement. Auditors use applicable public laws, procurement regulations (the FAR), and cost accounting standards to determine contractor compliance.

The government's right of examination also includes the right to inspect at all reasonable times a contractor's plants that are engaged in performing the contracts. This right begins at the start of the contract and continues until the retention period expires.

CONTRACT DISPUTES ACT OF 1978

For the majority of companies doing business with the federal government, contracts tend to run smoothly and are successfully completed. However, in the rare instances where contractual issues or problems arise that can't be resolved, more formal resolution procedures may be required.

The Contract Disputes Act of 1978 established procedures and requirements for asserting and resolving claims by (or against) contractors. This act allows contractors with a dispute to seek redress outside the judiciary system, thereby saving the government and the contractor time and money (it is hoped). The main provisions of this act include:

- Strengthening the authority and capabilities of the Board of Contract Appeals
- Giving contractors the option of direct appeal to the U.S. Court of Claims, bypassing the Board of Contract Appeals
- Providing contracting activities with more flexibility in negotiating and settling contract disputes

- Establishing new Board of Contract Appeals procedures for handling small claims
- Establishing a requirement for certification of contractor claims.

The disputes clause applies to all government contracts, either expressed or implied. This clause requires the contractor to pursue resolution of its claims through the administrative procedures delineated in the Contract Disputes Act. Contractors are required to continue contract performance pending resolution of a dispute, unless the dispute arises outside the contract or in breach of the contract.

Claims and Disputes

All disputes under federal contracts begin with a claim submitted by a contractor. A claim is a written demand by one of the contracting parties seeking, as a matter of right, an adjustment to the contract terms, payment, or other relief arising under the contract. If contractual issues or differences persist between a contractor and the government, a written claim should be submitted to the contracting officer.

For a claim to be valid, it must:

- Be in writing. A voucher, invoice, or other routine request for payment does not, in itself, constitute a claim.
- Seek the payment of a specific sum, adjustment of the contract terms, or other relief.
- Be certified by the contractor, if the claim seeks relief in excess of $100,000. A certification example:

  > I certify that the claim is made in good faith; that the supporting data are accurate and complete to the best of my knowledge and belief; that the amount requested accurately reflects the contract adjustment for which the contractor believes the government is liable; and that I am duly authorized to certify the claim on behalf of the contractor.

The government tries to resolve all claims by mutual agreement at the contracting officer's level and to avoid litigation if at all possible. Normally, the contracting officer reviews the pertinent facts of the claim and, after discussions with the contractor, reaches agreement and modifies the contract. Advice and assistance from legal and other advisors may be obtained, but ultimately the contracting officer is responsible for making the final decision.

The contracting officer is required to issue a decision on any claim of $100,000 or less within 60 days from receipt. If the claim exceeds $100,000, the contracting officer must either issue a decision or notify the contractor of when a decision will be issued within 60 days from receipt of a written request.

The final decision is furnished in writing. A decision statement, at a minimum, includes:

- Description of the claim or dispute
- References to pertinent contract provisions
- Statements of the factual areas of agreement/disagreement
- Statement of the contracting officer's decision, with supporting rationale.

If the contractor disagrees with the determination, it may appeal the decision to the Board of Contract Appeals within 90 days from receipt of the decision. The notice should indicate that an appeal is planned, reference the decision, and identify the contract by number.

Board of Contract Appeals

The appropriate Board of Contract Appeals hears and decides contract disputes. In performing its functions, the board may issue subpoenas that are enforceable by the U.S. District Courts. It can also seek related facts and data through the discovery process and take depositions, as necessary.

The Armed Services Board of Contract Appeals handles all DoD contract disputes. The Civilian Board of Contract Appeals covers all agencies other than DoD, NASA, the U.S. Postal Service, and the Tennessee Valley Authority (see www.cbca.gsa.gov).

For a claim of $50,000 or less, small claim or expedited procedures provide a decision within 120 days. Claims for $100,000 or less come under accelerated procedures, which require a decision within 180 days, whenever possible. If the claim is for more than $100,000, the board will conduct a formal hearing with no time limit on the decision.

Either the contractor or the government may appeal the board's decision within 120 days to the U.S. Court of Appeals. If either party disagrees with the Court of Appeals' decision, it must file an appeal with the Supreme Court within 60 days. Supreme Court decisions are final.

The Contract Disputes Act allows contractors to appeal a contracting officer's decision directly to the U.S. Court of Claims, bypassing the Board of Contract Appeals. If a contractor chooses this route, it must file the appeal within one year of the contracting officer's final decision. There are no time limits on the court to make a decision. Most contractors favor using the Board of Contract Appeals because doing so tends to be less costly and time-consuming.

The Equal Access to Justice Act permits small businesses and individuals to recover attorney or agent fees if they prevail in administrative or court actions brought against the government. The contractor has 30 days from the decision date to submit an application for reimbursement to the government (or the agency involved in the dispute).

ALTERNATIVE DISPUTE RESOLUTION

Let's face it. Federal courts are swamped with cases. The average dispute takes more than a year to resolve. If a contractor wants an accelerated decision, it might look at alternative dispute resolution (ADR). The Administrative Disputes Act of 1990 authorizes the use of ADR to settle disputes brought to the Board of Contract Appeals. Each ADR must have:

- An issue in controversy
- A voluntary election by both parties to participate in the ADR process
- An agreement on alternative procedures and terms to be used in lieu of formal litigation
- Process participation by officials of both parties who have the authority to resolve the issue.

Requests to use ADR must be made jointly by the government and the contractor to the board or court that is responsible for hearing the dispute. The board then examines the issues associated with the dispute and determines whether ADR would be appropriate. If a contracting officer rejects a contractor's request for ADR, the contractor must be given a written explanation citing the reasons. Contractors that reject an ADR request must inform the agency of their objections in writing.

Alternative dispute resolution procedures may include, but are not limited to, mediation, fact-finding, minitrials, arbitration, and use of ombudsmen. Federal agencies are encouraged to use ADR procedures to the maximum extent practicable. Oftentimes, the parties agree to split the cost of the mediator or arbitrator.

TERMINATION FOR CONVENIENCE

As with everything in life, circumstances that affect a federal contract occasionally arise. Each government contract contains a provision not found in commercial contracts—the ability to terminate the contract for any reason. This "termination for convenience" provision exists because of the government's need to end contracts when its requirements are eliminated, such as when a war ends or when Congress eliminates a program.

The government may terminate the entire contract or just part of it. Partial terminations can actually occur several times during the life of a contract. The contracting officer makes those decisions. With a complete termination, all the remaining work is terminated, even though work or deliveries may have already been accepted.

When a contracting officer terminates a contract for the government's convenience, he or she provides the contractor with a written notice of termination stating:

- That the contract is being terminated for the convenience of the government
- The effective date of termination
- The extent of termination
- Any special instructions
- The steps the contractor should take to minimize the impact of the termination on the company's personnel.

If the government terminates a contract for convenience, it must pay the costs incurred by the contractor up to the termination date, plus a reasonable profit, if applicable. The government uses different termination clauses depending on the type of contract.

> On a cost-reimbursement contract, settling a termination is usually easier than on a fixed-price contract because the contractor continues to "cost-out"—that is, bill the government for its costs—up to the point of termination. Typically, the fee the government owes the contractor is reduced proportionately.

TERMINATION FOR DEFAULT

Human nature being what it is, contracting officers try very hard not to let conditions deteriorate to the point where they must terminate a contract for default. First, doing so shows poor contract management. Second, it brands a contractor as a "nonperformer" and endangers its future business. Most contracting officers much prefer to terminate a contract using termination for convenience procedures, which enables them to negotiate the remaining contract requirements with another contractor.

The government may exercise its right to terminate a contract, in whole or in part, if a contractor fails to:

- Deliver products or perform services within the time specified in the contract
- Perform other contract provisions
- Make progress, endangering performance of the contract.

When a contract is terminated for default, the contracting officer provides the contractor with a written notice of termination. This written notice of termination for default must be unequivocally clear and state:

- The contract number and date
- The acts or omissions constituting the default
- That the contractor's right to proceed with further performance of the contract has been terminated

- That the products and services under the terminated contract are subject to reprocurement against the contractor's account and that the contractor is liable for any excess costs
- That the notice constitutes a decision of the contracting officer that the contractor is in default as specified, and the contractor may appeal according to the procedures stated in the disputes clause.

If the government terminates a contract for default, the contractor becomes liable for expenditures on undelivered work and must repay any advance payments. The contracting officer may direct the contractor to transfer title and deliver all completed or partially completed (but not yet accepted) products and materials to the government. The government then pays the contractor the contract price for any completed products and negotiates a value for the remaining materials.

Clearly, termination for default is serious business. Not only does a contractor lose its contract, but it must also pay the government for any excess reprocurement costs. The contractor is therefore responsible for the costs the government pays to an alternate source that exceed the price payable under the existing contract.

Suppose a contractor defaulted on its contract to build five computer network mainframes for $500,000. The contractor completed and installed two mainframes but was behind schedule on the others. A termination for default notice was issued.

5 computer mainframes	$500,000
Payment for 2 completed mainframes	–$200,000
Balance of contract	$300,000

Next, the government decided to purchase the remaining mainframes from an alternate source for $375,000. The defaulted contractor must pay the difference.

Alternate source price	$375,000
Original contract price (3 mainframes)	–$300,000
Balance owed by default contractor	$75,000

Terminations for default are not abrupt. Before termination, the contractor typically has the chance to improve performance or to explain why the contract should continue. If a contract was terminated for default and it is subsequently determined that the contractor's delay was excusable, the termination for default may be converted to a termination for convenience. Excusable circumstances include:

- Defective specifications
- Late or defective government-furnished property
- Suspensions of work and stop-work orders received
- Strikes
- Floods or fires
- Freight embargoes.

If the contractor believes that the termination for default was improper, it may file a claim under the disputes clause.

CONTRACT CLOSEOUT

Contract closeout, as you probably guessed, is the action that occurs when a contractor completes a contract. You're out of the woods, so to speak—at least for this job! The contract is considered fully completed when:

- The contractor has completed the required deliveries and the government has inspected and accepted the items.
- The contractor has performed all services and the government has accepted these services.
- All option provisions, if any, have expired.
- The government has given the contractor a notice of complete contract termination.

Proper contract closeout helps ensure that the contractor has complied with all the contractual requirements and that the government has fulfilled its obligations.

■ ■ ■

Contract performance is just the tip of the iceberg when it comes to fulfilling your contractual obligations. Contractors also must comply with applicable laws, prepare required reports, seek contract modifications, prepare invoices, retain contractual records, and carry out other administrative duties. All requirements that apply to your contract are spelled out in the contract document.

■ ■ ■

Closing Remarks

To quote a famous tennis maxim, the ball is now in your court. This book tells you what you need to know to break into and succeed in the vast federal government marketplace. If you learn the system and are patient and persistent, you can make good money, even big money, doing business with the federal government.

Acronyms

"I knew it was time to simplify our organization when we started creating acronyms for our acronyms."

Confused by all the government contracting acronyms? You're not alone! There are literally thousands of acronyms in the federal marketplace. The alphabet soup of acronyms starts at the agency level and trickles on down from there.

If you are looking to do business as a federal contractor, it's important to realize that the government has its own language and culture. The following commonly used acronyms should help get you started.

Executive Branch Cabinet-Level Departments (and the General Services Administration)

DHS	Department of Homeland Security
DOC	Department of Commerce
DOE	Department of Energy
DOI	Department of the Interior
DOJ	Department of Justice

DOL	Department of Labor
DOS	Department of State
DOT	Department of Transportation
DoD	Department of Defense
ED	Department of Education
GSA	General Services Administration
HHS	Department of Health and Human Services
HUD	Department of Housing and Urban Development
TREAS	Department of the Treasury
USDA	Department of Agriculture
VA	Department of Veterans Affairs

Other Acronyms

ACO	Administrative Contracting Officer
ADR	Alternative Dispute Resolution
B&P	Bid and Proposal
BAFO	Best and Final Offer
BOA	Basic Ordering Agreement
BPA	Blanket Purchase Agreement
CAGE	Commercial and Government Entity
CAO	Contract Administration Office
CAS	Cost Accounting Standards
CBD	*Commerce Business Daily*
CBO	Congressional Budget Office
CCR	Central Contractor Registration
CFR	Code of Federal Regulations
CICA	Competition in Contracting Act (1984)
CLIN	Contract Line Item Number
CO	Contracting Officer
COC	Certificate of Competency
COR	Contracting Officer's Representative
COTR	Contracting Officer's Technical Representative
CPAF	Cost Plus Award Fee
CPFF	Cost Plus Fixed Fee
CPIF	Cost Plus Incentive Fee
D&B	Dun & Bradstreet
DARPA	Defense Advanced Research Projects Agency

DCAA	Defense Contract Audit Agency
DCMA	Defense Contract Management Agency
DFARS	Department of Defense FAR Supplement
DFAS	Defense Finance and Accounting Service
DLIS	Defense Logistics Information Service
DUNS	Data Universal Numbering System
EDWOSB	Economically Disadvantaged Women-Owned Small Business
eSRS	Electronic Subcontracting Reporting System
FAC	Federal Acquisition Circular
FAR	Federal Acquisition Regulation
FARA	Federal Acquisition Reform Act (of 1996)
FAS	Federal Acquisition Service
FASA	Federal Acquisition Streamlining Act (of 1994)
FBO	FedBizOpps
FFP	Firm Fixed-Price
FOB	Free on Board
FOIA	Freedom of Information Act
FPDS	Federal Procurement Data System
FP/EPA	Fixed-Price with Economic Price Adjustment
FPI	Fixed-Price Incentive
FR	*Federal Register*
FSC	Federal Supply Classification
FSG	Federal Supply Group
FSS	Federal Supply Schedule
FY	Fiscal Year
G&A	General and Administrative
GAAP	Generally Accepted Accounting Principles
GAO	Government Accountability Office
GFP	Government-Furnished Property
GPO	Government Printing Office
GWAC	Government-Wide Acquisition Contract
HCA	Head of the Contracting Activity
HUBZone	Historically Underutilized Business Zone
ID/IQ	Indefinite Delivery/Indefinite Quantity
IFB	Invitation for Bid
IFSS	International Federal Supply Schedule
IR&D	Independent Research and Development
IT	Information Technology

LOE	Level-of-Effort
LH	Labor-Hour
MAS	Multiple Award Schedule
M&IE	Meals and Incidental Expenses
MODS	Modifications
NAICS	North American Industry Classification System
NCMA	National Contract Management Association
NIIS	New Item Introductory Schedule
NIST	National Institute of Standards and Technology
NOA	Notice of Award
NTIS	National Technical Information Service
ODC	Other Direct Cost(s)
OFPP	Office of Federal Procurement Policy
O/H	Overhead
OMB	Office of Management and Budget
ORCA	Online Representations & Certifications Application
OSBP	Office of Small Business Programs (DoD)
OSDBU	Office of Small and Disadvantaged Business Utilization
PCO	Principal Contracting Officer or Procuring Contracting Officer
PIIN	Procurement Instrument Identification Number
PM	Program Manager
PO	Purchase Order
POC	Point of Contact
POP	Period of Performance
PR	Purchase Request
PSA	Presolicitation Announcement
PSC	Product Service Code
PTAC	Procurement Technical Assistance Centers
R&D	Research and Development
RFI	Request for Information
RFP	Request for Proposal
RFQ	Request for Quotation
RFTP	Request for Technical Proposals
SADBUS	Small and Disadvantaged Business Utilization Specialist
SAM	System for Award Management
SAP	Simplified Acquisition Procedures
SAT	Simplified Acquisition Threshold
SBA	Small Business Administration

SBDC	Small Business Development Center
SBIR	Small Business Innovation Research
SCA	Service Contract Act
SCF	Simplified Contract Format
SCORE	Service Corps of Retired Executives
SDB	Small Disadvantaged Business
SDVOSB	Service-Disabled Veteran-Owned Small Business
SF	Standard Form
SIC	Standard Industrial Classification
SPECS	Specifications
SOW	Statement of Work
SSA	Source Selection Authority
STTR	Small Business Technology Transfer Research Program
T&M	Time-and-Materials
TCO	Termination Contracting Officer
TINA	Truth in Negotiations Act
UCF	Uniform Contract Format
USC	*United States Code*
VOSB	Veteran-Owned Small Business
VSC	Vendor Support Center
WBC	Women's Business Center
WOSB	Women-Owned Small Business

Federal Agencies and Departments

"I heard on TV that everyone is getting rich on the Internet. Is this little slot where the money comes out?"

The federal government is huge. There are so many federal agencies and departments that it would take more than 50 pages of this book to list them all. The best way to find information on them is to visit the federal agency directory at www.lib.lsu.edu/gov. This Web site provides a listing of most government agencies and departments (including links to their Web sites).

The United States Government Manual

The official handbook of the federal government is *The United States Government Manual*. It provides comprehensive information on the agencies of the legislative, judicial, and executive branches. A typical agency description includes a list of principal officials, programs, and activities, and a Source of Information section. The last section provides information on contracts and other areas of public interest. The *Manual* is updated annually and is available online at www.usgovernmentmanual.gov.

Glossary

Copyright 2001 by Randy Glasbergen. www.glasbergen.com
GLASBERGEN
"Yes, I have some management experience.
When I was ten, I ran a lemonade stand.
I had 40 lemons working for me."

The glossary terms enclosed in a box represent a little government contracting humor. (They may or may not be more accurate than the formal definitions).

Accumulating Costs
The collecting of cost data in an organized and consistent manner, such as through a chart of accounts or a general ledger.

Administrative Contracting Officer (ACO)
A contracting officer who is responsible for administrative functions after a contract is awarded.

Advance Payments
Advances of money by the government to a contractor prior to contract performance.

Affiliates
Business concerns, organizations, or individuals related, directly or indirectly, when (1) either one controls or has the power to control the other, or (2) a third party controls or has the power to control both.

Agency Supplements
Regulations issued by individual federal agencies for the purpose of supplementing the basic Federal Acquisition Regulation (FAR).

Allocable Cost
A cost that is assignable or chargeable to one or more cost objectives in accordance with the relative benefits received.

Allowable Cost
A cost that (1) meets the tests of reasonableness and allocability and (2) complies with generally accepted accounting principles and cost accounting standards, as well as specific exclusions set forth in FAR Part 31.

Amendment
A change (correction, deletion, or addition) to a solicitation *before* it is due. The amendment becomes part of the resulting contract.

Appropriation
Authority to obligate public funds that will result in immediate or future outlays.

AUDITORS—People who go in after the war is lost and bayonet the wounded.

Basic Ordering Agreement (BOA)
A written instrument of understanding negotiated between a contractor and a federal buying office that contains (1) terms and clauses applying to future contracts (orders) between the parties during its term; (2) a description of supplies or services to be provided; and (3) methods for pricing, issuing, and delivering future orders. It is not a contract.

Bid
An offer submitted in response to an invitation for bid (IFB).

BID—A wild guess carried out to two decimal places.

Bid and Proposal (B&P) Costs
Costs incurred in preparing, submitting, or supporting any bid or proposal, which are neither sponsored by a grant nor required in the performance of a contract.

BID OPENING—A poker game in which the losing hand wins.

Bidder
A contractor who submits a bid in response to an IFB.

Blanket Purchase Agreement (BPA)
A simplified method of filling anticipated repetitive needs for services and products. BPAs are "charge accounts" that ordering offices establish with GSA schedule contractors.

CAGE Code (Commercial and Government Entity Code)
A five-character ID number that identifies government contractors.

Capability Statement
A document that summarizes a company's background, including certifications, expertise, past performance, and pertinent codes, such as DUNS and CAGE.

Central Contractor Registration (CCR)
The primary government repository for contractor information required for the conduct of business with the federal government (see www.sam.gov).

Certificate of Competency (COC)
A certificate issued by the Small Business Administration stating that the holder is responsible (with respect to elements of responsibility, including capacity, credit, and integrity) for the purpose of receiving and performing a specific government contract.

Certified 8(a) Firm
A firm that is owned and operated by socially and economically disadvantaged individuals and eligible to receive federal contracts under the Small Business Administration's 8(a) Business Development Program.

Closeout
The process for closing out a contract file following contract completion.

Commercial Items
Products that are sold competitively to the general public.

Competitive Range
All proposals that the contracting officer determines to have a reasonable chance of being selected for award based on cost/price data and other factors stated in the solicitation.

COMPLETION DATE—The point at which liquidated damages begin.

Contract
A mutually binding legal relationship obligating the seller to furnish supplies or services and the buyer to pay for them.

Contracting Officer (CO)
A government agent with the authority to enter into, administer, or terminate contracts and make related determinations and findings.

Contracting Officer's Technical Representative (COTR)
A federal employee to whom a contracting officer has delegated limited authority (in writing) to make specific contract-related decisions.

CONTRACTOR—A gambler who never gets to shuffle, cut, or deal.

Cost Accounting Standards (CAS)
Standards designed to achieve uniformity and consistency in the cost accounting principles followed by government contractors and subcontractors on selected large-dollar-value contracts (see FAR Part 30).

Cost-Reimbursement Contracts

Contracts that provide for payment of allowable incurred costs to the extent prescribed in the contract. These contracts establish an estimate of total cost for the purpose of obligating funds and establishing a ceiling that the contractor may not exceed, except at its own risk.

COST-PLUS-NO-INCENTIVE-TO-COMPLETE (CPNITC) CONTRACT—Begin with a cost-plus-fixed-fee contract; continue funding indefinitely!

Debriefing

Informing unsuccessful offerors of the basis for the selection decision and contract award. This information includes the government's evaluation of the significant weak or deficient factors in the offeror's proposal.

DELAYED PAYMENT—A tourniquet applied at the pockets.

Delivery Order

A written order for supplies under an indefinite-delivery contract.

Direct Costs

Any allowable cost that is directly attributable to or specifically identified as part of a contract or project, such as equipment and salaries.

DUNS (Data Universal Numbering System)

Nine-digit number issued by Dun & Bradstreet that the federal government uses to identify a contractor and list its address, number of employees, and other information.

Emerging Small Business

A firm that is no larger than 50 percent of the applicable small business size standard.

ENGINEER'S ESTIMATE—The cost of construction in heaven.

FedBizOpps

The single government point of entry on the Internet for federal procurement opportunities over $25,000 (see www.fbo.gov).

Federal Acquisition Regulation (FAR)
The body of regulations that is the primary source of authority over the government procurement process.

Federal Register
A daily publication that informs the public of proposed rules and other legal notices issued by federal agencies.

Federal Specifications (Specs)
Specifications and standards that have been implemented for use by all federal agencies.

Fee (or Profit)
Money paid to a contractor over and above total reimbursements for allowable costs.

Fixed-Price (FP) Contract
A contract type that establishes a firm price regardless of the actual cost of contract performance.

> **FIRM FIXED-PRICE NO-DELIVERABLE ITEMS (FFPNDI) CONTRACT**—Common contract form used for low-bid awards, inadequately funded projects, and awards to nonresponsible vendors.

Government Accountability Office (GAO)
The audit agency of the U.S. Congress. GAO has broad authority to conduct investigations on behalf of Congress and to review certain contract decisions, including contract award protests.

Government-Furnished Property
Property in the possession of, or directly acquired by, the government and subsequently made available to the contractor.

Government-Wide Acquisition Contracts (GWACs)
GWACs are task orders or delivery order contracts for information technology (IT) established by a federal agency for government-wide use.

GSA Schedule (or Federal Supply Schedule)
A "fishing license" to go after federal contracts. Get one! (See Chapter 7 for details.)

Historically Underutilized Business Zone (HUBZone)
The HUBZone Empowerment Contracting program provides federal contracting opportunities for qualified small businesses located in distressed areas.

Indefinite-Delivery Contract
A type of contract used when the exact times or quantities of future deliveries or both are unknown at the time of contract award. There are three variations of indefinite-delivery contracts: definite-quantity, requirements, and indefinite-quantity.

Independent Research and Development (IR&D) Cost
The cost effort that is neither sponsored by a grant nor required in performing a contract that falls within any of four areas: (1) basic research, (2) applied research, (3) development, and (4) systems and other concept formulation studies.

Invitation for Bid (IFB)
The solicitation document used in sealed bidding.

LAWYERS—People who go in after the auditors and strip the bodies.

Letter Contract
A written preliminary contractual instrument that authorizes the contractor to begin manufacturing products or performing services immediately.

Level of Effort (LOE)
A contract term used in program management to define the amount of work needed to complete a specific task within a specified time frame. It is usually measured in hours.

LIQUIDATED DAMAGES—A penalty for failing to achieve the impossible.

LOW BIDDERS—Contractors who are wondering what they left out of their bids.

Micropurchases
Purchases for $3,000 or less.

Modifications (MODs)
Written changes to an *existing* contract, such as changes to the specifications, delivery schedule, contract period, price, quantity, or other contract provisions.

Online Representations & Certifications Application (ORCA)
The primary government database for contractor-submitted representations and certifications required for the conduct of business with the federal government (see https://orca.bpn.gov).

Option
The unilateral right in a contract by which, for a specified time, the government may elect to purchase additional supplies or services called for by the contract, extend the term, or both.

Order of Precedence
A provision that establishes priority among various parts of a solicitation.

Pre-Award Survey
An evaluation by the government of a prospective contractor's capability to perform a proposed contract.

Pre-Bid/Pre-Proposal Conference
A meeting held with prospective offerors before bid opening or before the closing date for proposal submission. The purpose of this conference is to brief the offerors and explain complicated specifications and requirements.

Prime Contract
A contract awarded directly by the federal government.

Progress Payments
Payments made under a fixed-price contract on the basis of costs incurred by the contractor as work progresses under the contract.

> **PROJECT MANAGER**—The conductor of an orchestra in which every musician is in a different union.

Protest
A written objection by an interested party to a solicitation, proposed award, or contract award.

Request for Proposal (RFP)
The solicitation document used in negotiated procurement procedures.

Request for Quotation (RFQ)
A document used in soliciting quotations. RFQs are used when the government does not intend to award a contract on the basis of the solicitation but wishes to obtain price, delivery, or other market information for planning purposes.

Sealed Bidding
Method of procurement (prescribed in FAR Part 14) in which the government publicly opens bids and awards the contract to the lowest responsive, responsible bidder.

Set-Aside
An acquisition reserved exclusively for offerors that fit into a specified category. Set-asides are commonly established for small businesses and businesses in labor surplus areas.

Simplified Acquisition Procedures (SAP)
Procurement procedures used for obtaining supplies and services that are no more than $150,000.

Simplified Acquisition Threshold (SAT)
The $150,000 ceiling (or limit) on purchases of supplies and services using simplified acquisition procedures.

Size Standards
Measures established by the Small Business Administration to determine whether a business qualifies as a small business for purposes of implementing the socioeconomic programs enumerated in FAR Part 19.

Small Business Concern
A concern (including its affiliates) that is independently owned and operated, is not dominant in the field in which it bids or proposes on government contracts, and qualifies as a small business under the size standards in 13 CFR Part 121.

Small Disadvantaged Business
A small business that is at least 51 percent owned and operated by one or more persons who are both socially and economically disadvantaged.

Sole-Source Acquisition
A contract for the purchase of products and services that is entered into by a federal agency after soliciting and negotiating with only one source.

Source Selection
The process of soliciting and evaluating offers for award.

Specification
A document prepared by the government that describes the technical requirements of the products and services being acquired, including the criteria for determining whether these requirements are met.

Statement of Work (SOW)
A detailed statement describing the government buyer's requirements, including, if necessary, what products, services, and methods will be used to fulfill the need.

Statute
A law enacted by the legislative branch of the government and signed by the president.

Subcontractor
Any supplier, distributor, vendor, or firm that furnishes supplies or services to or for a prime contractor as part of an overall contract.

System for Award Management (SAM)
SAM has replaced GSA's outmoded Integrated Acquisition Environment as its one-stop repository and application service. CCR, Online Representations and Certifications Application (ORCA), and the Excluded Parties Listing System (EPLS) have been migrated to SAM. More acquisition systems—including FedBizOpps, the Past Performance Information Retrieval System (PPIRS), and the electronic subcontracting reporting system (eSRS)—are expected to migrate to SAM in coming years.

Task Order
A written order for services under an indefinite-delivery contract.

Time-and-Materials (T&M) Contract
A type of contract that provides for acquiring services and materials on the basis of (1) direct labor hours at specified fixed hourly rates that include wages, overhead, general and administrative expenses, and profits, and (2) material handling costs as part of material costs.

DOUBLE TIME-AND-MATERIALS (DT&DM) CONTRACT—T&M contract type that accurately reflects the real time and cost figures.

Unallowable Costs
Any cost that, under the provisions of any pertinent federal law, regulation, or contract, may not be included in prices, cost reimbursements, or other settlements under a government contract.

Uniform Contract Format (UCF)
The solicitation/contract format used in most invitations for bids and requests for proposals.

Unsolicited Proposal
A written proposal for a new and innovative idea that is submitted to an agency on the offeror's initiative for the purpose of obtaining a government contract. It is not submitted in response to a formal or informal request.

Index

S

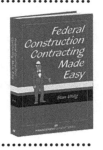